# Enhanced Interrogation

# Enhanced Interrogation

Inside the Minds and Motives of the
Islamic Terrorists Trying to Destroy America

JAMES E. MITCHELL, PhD
with Bill Harlow

CROWN
FORUM
NEW YORK

This does not constitute an official release of CIA information. All statements of fact, opinion, or analysis expressed are those of the author and do not reflect the official positions or views of the Central Intelligence Agency (CIA) or any other U.S. government agency. Nothing in the contents should be construed as asserting or implying U.S. government authentication of information or CIA endorsement of the author's views. This material has been reviewed solely for classification.

Copyright © 2016 by Dr. James Elmer Mitchell

Published in the United States by Crown Forum, an imprint of the
Crown Publishing Group, a division of Penguin Random House LLC, New York.
crownpublishing.com

Crown Forum and colophon is a registered trademark of
Penguin Random House LLC.

Library of Congress Cataloging-in-Publication Data is available upon request.

ISBN 978-1-101-90684-2
eBook ISBN 978-1-101-90685-9

Printed in the United States of America

Book design by Ellen Cipriano
Jacket design by Tal Goretsky
Jacket photograph by Ryan McVay/Getty Images
Pages ii–iii photograph by © Can Stock Photo Inc./albund

10 9 8 7 6 5 4 3 2 1

First Edition

*For my wife, Kathy, and in memory of her father, Leon, a Marine who survived being blown up on day five of the battle for the island of Iwo Jima during World War II. He embodied the values and sacrifices that made this country great.*

# Contents

The authors are donating a portion of their proceeds from this book to the CIA Officers Memorial Foundation, a charitable organization dedicated to supporting the children and spouses of CIA officers who fall in the line of duty. More information about this organization can be found at https://ciamemorialfoundation.org/.

# Preface

"You need to leave your home immediately." It was the chief of security for the CIA on the phone. "We have a credible death threat by ISIS against your life, and we want you to evacuate until we determine how viable it is." ISIS had tweeted a request that a jihadist cut my head off, and according to the CIA, someone had just volunteered to do the job. The agency's security officer said it was possible the person was already en route. It was December 2014.

Minutes later the FBI was in my driveway. Later, the local sheriff's department's SWAT team commanders were in my living room and wandering around my yard, determining likely avenues of assault and deciding where to position men for the best shot. As it started getting dark, retired SEAL team members and special operators from various shadowy counterterrorist units who had gotten wind of the threat called, offering to bring their long guns to watch our backs while my wife and I slept. My bedroom smelled of gun oil. My house felt like a kill zone for anyone stupid enough to try to breach its security.

A target had been placed on my back and was endangering my family. Sadly, the notion that my family and I might be targets was not new. I had interrogated the worst terrorists in the world for the CIA—the al-Qa'ida operatives who had sucker-punched the United States in the September 11, 2001, terror attacks that had killed approximately three thousand innocent Americans—and although the CIA had tried to keep my identity secret, lawyers for the terrorists made sure the killers, and thus anyone those killers could smuggle messages out to, knew who I was.

My thoughts flashed back to July 2009, when officers from the CIA's counterintelligence unit sat on a rumpled bed in a small, nondescript motel off the interstate. An aging air conditioner rattled and clanked. The noise was like sitting next to a running bus; that was good because it masked the sound of our conversation. The air smelled of dank mold and burned coffee.

"Do you recognize any of these people?" one officer asked me.

"Well, this one is me, obviously, and I know three or four of these other guys," I said, leafing through the stack of photos he had handed me a few minutes before. Several were obviously surveillance photos surreptitiously taken outside homes and office buildings. The one of me was a driver's license photo.

All the photos had been found recently in the cell of Mustafa Ahmed al-Hawsawi, an al-Qa'ida planner and financier now in Guantanamo Bay, during a routine search for contraband. The photos had been obtained surreptitiously by private investigators hired by the lawyers defending the terrorists who attacked the United States. The attorneys smuggled the photos into the cells of terrorists held there, including Khalid Sheikh Mohammed, the mastermind of the 9/11 attacks, to reveal the true names of CIA interrogators who had questioned them. I was told by the counterintelligence agents that I needed to "watch my back." My life and the lives of my family might be in danger because it was possible that my true name, home address, and image also had been passed to terrorists still at large.

Since items going in and out of detainee lockup at Gitmo are supposed to be searched for contraband, you might ask yourself how those photos got past the guards. The lawyers did it by hiding them among documents that could not be searched because of attorney-client privilege.

Later, when the incident was being investigated by a reluctant Department of Justice, the lawyers who were responsible claimed that sneaking around taking surreptitious photos of CIA officers (many of whom were undercover) and contractors was a legitimate enterprise motivated by a deep concern for providing the best defense for the terrorists they were representing.

I was concerned when those lawyers gave my true name and location to the terrorists they were defending, but those terrorists were locked up, and the threat was hypothetical. That concern was nothing compared with the way I felt after the phone call from CIA security in December 2014 alerting me that a terrorist might actually be coming to harm me and my family. I was frightened for my wife, ramped up and angry. Not at ISIS but at those who had put a target on my back. Here is how that happened.

In December 2014 Senator Dianne Feinstein and her Democratic colleagues on the Senate Select Committee on Intelligence (SSCI) released a report on the CIA's Rendition, Detention, and Interrogation program, claiming it was the program's definitive history.

But it wasn't. Feinstein and her colleagues had ransacked through millions of CIA documents, selecting those which supported her claims and ignoring the ones that didn't. They refused to interview any of the CIA officers or contractors who actually had been involved in the program, including me. After five years and $40 million they released a one-sided report that claimed the CIA's interrogation program tortured detainees; was run by lying, incompetent, and corrupt senior CIA officers; and produced not one detail of intelligence value: zero, nothing, nada, zilch, diddly-squat—a ridiculous and categorically untrue claim.

The CIA and the minority Republican members of the committee tried to push back, describing Feinstein's report as deeply flawed and riddled with factual errors. The information used to produce the report was cherry-picked, taken out of context, and framed to produce a misleading narrative of what had happened. The CIA released a previously classified rebuttal, and the Republican SSCI members debunked Feinstein's ludicrous claim that the CIA's interrogation program had produced nothing with intelligence value. Most of the media ignored the contrarian views.

When Feinstein released her report, she left my true name out of it. Instead, I was assigned a pseudonym to hide my identity. However, reporters immediately came to me looking for my reaction. Several told me that Feinstein's staffers had told them on "deep background" which pseudonym referred to me. Feinstein's report claimed that I lacked the background and experience to do what the CIA had asked of me and that I tortured detainees, and it clearly implied that I bamboozled the taxpayers out of $81 million for my personal gain. The committee never gave me the opportunity to answer a single question. Instead, Feinstein's inaccurate report stirred up the crazies and jihadists, essentially issuing a fatwa against me and everyone past or present working to protect Americans from jihadist terror attacks.

Some people who have not followed the issue closely might wonder why I would write this book. "That chapter of our history is over," they might say. "Just let it go. Bringing it up again only reopens old wounds." But that's not true. It isn't over. Hardly a week goes by without lurid new articles falsely attributing horrendous acts to me and those with whom I worked. The larger issue, however, is that the American public has a right to know what was—and wasn't—done in their names. Within sensible national security bounds, the few of us who were present cannot let others distort history.

Feinstein's report was not the first media leak about my involvement with the CIA's interrogation program. For over a decade I had been the target of rumor and innuendo. But my nondisclosure agreement with the U.S. government prevented me from discussing my role. I was not allowed to defend myself or the program. I was told by the government that its promise of indemnification could be taken away if I told Americans my side of the story. The only good thing that has come out of the Feinstein report is that now—finally—the government is allowing me to defend myself.

The truth matters. It matters to the American people. Senator Feinstein and her colleagues tried to rewrite history. It is important for people to know what really happened and why.

Al-Qa'ida tried to decapitate the United States on 9/11 by simultaneously attacking our most important financial center and our senior military leadership. It would have taken out our center of government, the Capitol Building, if it hadn't been for the brave passengers of United Flight 93 sacrificing themselves to save others. In the turmoil and confusion after the attacks of 9/11 and under the threat of new ones, possibly involving a nuclear device, the CIA followed the president's orders and took forward-leaning action that kept Americans safe. Those actions were cleared by the Department of Justice, approved by the president, and reported to the congressional leadership.

I believe it is time for Americans to hear the facts from the person who helped develop the high-level terrorist interrogation program. Someone who was there, on the ground, in the interrogation rooms, doing the work. These ground-level facts are not in Feinstein's report. They are not even in the CIA rebuttal or the Senate minority response. None of those documents put you in the room with the action so that you can get a sense of what was actually going on and why. That's what I intend to do.

# CHAPTER 1

# Come Back Immediately

In a black site on the other side of the world, Khalid Sheikh Mohammed, the mastermind of the September 11, 2001, terror attacks, stood naked, hands and feet shackled, glaring at me. His unruly mop of hair and full dark beard had been shorn. With his short stature and his fat belly, KSM, as he had come to be known, looked more like an angry, defiant Buddha than the world's most wanted terrorist. It was March 2003.

"Call me Mukhtar," KSM demanded in perfect, easily understood English and with a hint of pride in his voice. Then, in a lecturing tone, he added, "Mukhtar means 'the Brain.' I was the amir of the 9/11 attacks." *Amir* means "commander" in Arabic.

I told him that I wasn't there for a confession and that although we were interested in what he had to say about the attacks on 9/11, someone else would go over that with him later. "I'm here," I said, "to see if you are willing to talk to us about the other attacks you have planned, the ones that haven't occurred yet."

KSM smirked and then said, "I'll think about talking when I

get to New York, meet the cowboy, President Bush, and talk to my lawyer."

It was my turn to smile. "That's not going to happen," I said, slowly shaking my head. "You see, you've disappeared. As far as anyone knows, you no longer exist. But it doesn't have to be that way.

"We caught you," I explained. "You know the brothers are going to find out and adjust themselves," I continued, using the wording that another top terrorist, Abu Zubaydah, had used about seven months earlier, when he finally started cooperating.

"All we want is information to stop operations," I said in a neutral tone of voice. "If you talk to us, if you answer our questions, then we will improve your conditions and nothing bad will happen to you. No one will harm you. But if you play games with us, if you jerk us around, then you will make yourself suffer needlessly."

I paused and said nothing for a minute or so to see if KSM would respond. He did not.

I went on. "No one here wants to hurt you, but we're not going away and we're not going to stand by and let more innocent people die. We know you have information we can use to stop operations, and we're here to get it out of you."

KSM got a small twinkle in his eyes, nonchalantly picked at hairs on the back of his shackled hands, and stared back at me.

I leaned forward, placed my mouth next to his ear, and said in a low, serious voice, "This is your one opportunity to forever change what happens to you, now and in the future. The offer is on the table until I walk out of this room. After that, you won't like what happens next." Then I told him, "We want information to stop operations inside the United States. We want to know who. We want to know where. We want to know when. We know you have people inside the United States. Let's start there. Who are they and where are they?"

KSM looked up at me defiantly and half smiled. "Soon you will know," he said, taunting me. "The Brain always has something to think about, but I have nothing for you."

I looked away, glancing up at the camera through which I knew the others were watching. Then I looked back to him and said, "The next time somebody talks to you, he is going to ask you for information to stop operations inside the United States. He's going to ask you about the people you have there. How you answer that question is going to determine what happens next."

I turned and walked out of the room. Our effort to avoid using harsh interrogation methods on KSM, methods the CIA had dubbed "enhanced interrogation techniques," was abandoned. An hour later he again refused to answer, and things got much worse in KSM's world.

Thus began my involvement in the interrogation of KSM, the man behind the 9/11 attacks on the World Trade Center and the Pentagon and the crash of United Flight 93. But my story doesn't start here. It begins about a year earlier.

In early April 2002, I was driving on I-95 just outside of Philadelphia, weaving in and out of heavy afternoon traffic and fussing with a malfunctioning GPS, when my cell phone rang. It was the chief of the department that housed the CIA's operational psychologists.

"Come back immediately," he said. He sounded excited. I had been at Langley earlier that day for a meeting.

"I can't," I said, trying to sort out what was going on and still stay in my own lane in the heavy traffic. "Why?" At first I thought it might have something to do with the professional services arrangement I had to consult with the CIA. They had put me under contract in August 2001 to help develop new strategies for making assessments of foreign CIA operatives (known as "assets") in high-risk situations. But by reading between the lines of what the department head was saying, I realized it couldn't have anything to do with that. He was too excited.

I pressed him, but he wouldn't give me any more details. He said he couldn't. He stressed that it was critical that I be back at CIA headquarters early the next afternoon for briefings and planning sessions. "You should be ready to leave the country immediately after the meetings," he said with an unmistakable undertone of urgency and importance.

This seemed very odd. I had not signed up to be a clandestine operative whose job it was to fly off in the middle of the night. It wasn't in my contract. I had been hired to be a consultant for the CIA, leveraging my PhD in psychology and my research skills, not my crisis intervention skills or my background as a bomb tech. I thought I'd put unexpected calls to report immediately behind me when I retired from the military eight months previously.

In the car with me were Dr. John Bruce Jessen—a former air force colleague of mine—and the CIA operational psychologist who handled my contract. We were on our way to Philadelphia to ask Dr. Martin Seligman, a renowned psychologist, if he would be a guest speaker at a U.S. Air Force–sponsored conference in San Diego that summer. The conference was for operational psychologists who worked with U.S. and allied military services providing Survival, Evasion, Resistance, and Escape (SERE) training for members at high risk of capture. SERE's focus was to develop strategies that fighting men and women could use to survive the stress and shock of being held as hostages or POWs, keep their honor intact, and emotionally adjust once they were freed and returned home.

We spent that night in Philadelphia, excited about the prospect of asking Dr. Seligman if he would volunteer to give a talk on "learned optimism" to the hundred or so psychologists and survival trainers slated to gather in San Diego that summer. All thoughts about the call earlier in the day were put aside. Bruce and I discussed the logistics of the summer conference that he had organized and at which we were both scheduled to do presentations. I broached the idea of Bruce leaving the Department of Defense (DOD) and joining me as an independent contractor, an issue I had first raised during a Canadian ice-climbing trip we took the previous December. But Bruce remained noncommittal. He was a senior DOD employee and was hesitant to walk away from the time he had invested toward retirement.

The next morning, we asked Dr. Seligman about addressing our conference and he was gracious enough to accept. By early afternoon my companions and I were back at CIA headquarters in Langley. On arrival Bruce and I immediately were escorted by the department head who had called me the day before into a briefing in the agency's Counterterrorism Center.

I didn't know it at the time, but we had been asked to attend because a few months earlier Bruce and I had written a paper describing the resistance to interrogation techniques that terrorists familiar with the "Manchester Manual" were likely to use. The Manchester Manual is a set of how-to instructions for resisting interrogation. It was created from resistance-to-interrogation course materials stolen from U.S. Army Special Forces at Fort Bragg, North Carolina, by Ali Mohammed, a former Egyptian military officer who had immigrated to the United States and enlisted in the U.S. Army Special Forces. It turned out Mohammed was a valuable al-Qa'ida asset, and the information he stole from the U.S. military ended up being widely circulated in multiple languages among Islamic jihadists.

The windowless conference room in the CIA Counterterrorism Center (CTC) was crowded with analysts, operations officers, case officers, physicians, an agency operational psychologist assigned to CTC, and senior CTC personnel. Also present were a group of targeting analysts: people whose specialty was pinpointing the location of terrorists. The place was packed. Some CIA officers sat at the main table, and many more sat or stood crammed against the walls. All were talking, waiting for the meeting to start. I knew few of the people in the room; to me it was a buzzing sea of unfamiliar faces. The room crackled with excitement. I could tell something big had happened.

**THE DEPUTY CHIEF** of the CTC, Jose Rodriguez, arrived to chair the meeting. A Puerto Rico–born career member of the clandestine service, Jose was all business. He quickly asked a female officer, who I would later learn worked in CTC's bin Ladin targeting group, Alec Station, to lay out some ground rules for the meeting. She said the information about to be discussed was highly compartmentalized and could not be released to any organization outside the CIA, including the Department of Defense. Bruce Jessen raised his hand and said that he was a DOD civilian employee. He was politely asked to leave. "No harm, no foul," he said to me as he got up to go, meaning he wasn't offended. We had both worked with "need to know" secrets before and were familiar with the routine.

Great start, I thought to myself. Someone in the CIA had invited Bruce to the meeting, and now someone else was inviting him to leave. I had a sinking feeling that I was going to be on my own, without his help. At that point I had known Bruce for fourteen years. We had worked on a lot of top secret projects together. But I was new to the CIA. I was only four months into my contract, and although I had consulted with them in the past, I wasn't part of their culture.

One or two others left as well: CIA employees, I guessed, who apparently did not have the right security clearance or were not necessary for the meeting. Later, I found out that some left to complete arrangements for the interrogation team's departure.

Everyone looked at his or her shoes for a bit as Bruce and the others gathered their things and departed. Once the door shut behind them, we were told that a prominent al-Qa'ida operative called Abu Zubaydah had just been captured in a raid in Pakistan. He had been severely wounded, and we were told he might not survive. Another CIA officer quickly walked us through a remarkable sequence of events that had culminated in Abu Zubaydah's capture. The briefer explained that to date Abu Zubaydah was the highest-ranking operative working with al-Qa'ida ever taken into U.S. custody. She said that it was believed that he would personally know many Al-Qa'ida members because of his role in training jihadists, forging identity documents, and arranging clandestine travel. As a result, it was widely believed that Abu Zubaydah might also be aware of al-Qa'ida's plans for follow-on attacks on the United States. Because he ran training camps for Islamic jihadists, someone said, there was a good possibility that he had been trained to resist interrogation. Months later Abu Zubaydah would tell me that he not only had *studied* resistance to interrogation, he had *taught* it in his training camp.

A physician briefed us on Abu Zubaydah's medical condition. CIA lawyers briefed us about a "presidential finding" that authorized the CIA to capture, detain, and interrogate people like Abu Zubaydah. During this meeting, I heard for the first of many times that "the gloves are off" and that the CIA had to do everything that was legally possible to prevent another catastrophic terror attack. Both the fear of a second wave of attacks and the pressure from the president and Congress to stop them were palpable in the room.

It was obvious that several planning meetings had taken place since Abu Zubaydah's capture. The CTC's leaders were in the finishing stages of putting together an interrogation team that would be dispatched later that night. To my surprise, I was asked to deploy with that team. I was told that my role was to observe Abu Zubaydah's interrogations and identify resistance techniques he might be using to prevent interrogators from obtaining actionable intelligence that might prevent the next attack. I also was asked to help the team brainstorm possible countermeasures if that became necessary, using my resistance-to-interrogation background to get him to cooperate. I was told to "think outside the box."

Although such a mission wasn't part of my contract, this didn't seem like an odd request to me. They were asking me to do something I had done many times before. I had spent thousands of hours in resistance-to-interrogation training laboratories monitoring warfighters as they attempted to protect secrets both before and after training in specialized techniques to thwart interrogations. I had received basic and advanced resistance-to-interrogation training myself. And I had worked to identify resistance techniques employed by nuclear bomber aircrews and counterterrorist units in readiness exercises that realistically tested their ability to protect secrets.

Nor was I a stranger to real-world psychological profiling. Among other things, I had worked as a psychologist on a hostage negotiation team, with real-world experience profiling and predicting the behavior of armed barricaded subjects and suicidal individuals. Also, my background on the bomb squad had taught me to get inside the minds of those planting improvised explosive devices to get a better feel for their goals in using the devices and likely triggering mechanisms. Both provide invaluable insight into the way the device is likely to function. I'd helped the Joint Special Operations Command (JSOC) chief psychologist develop strategies for the psychological profiling of war criminals and terrorists and developed techniques for profiling and predicting the behavior during rescue of hostages wired into improvised explosive devices.

Being asked to tell CIA interrogators which resistance-to-interrogation techniques Abu Zubaydah was using didn't seem like an unusual request. My career had been full of unusual requests.

It was made clear to me that decisions regarding what would be done during interrogations were the responsibility of the senior CIA officer serving as chief of base (COB) at a secret location that they referred to as "the black site." It was during this meeting that I also heard that CIA intended to videotape the Abu Zubaydah interrogations. Their rationale at the time was that he was critically wounded, weak, and hard to understand. They were concerned that he might die before the team could figure out what he was trying to say. If he died, they wanted to be able to show that the agency didn't cause his demise. No one there could have imagined how much controversy the decision to videotape would cause.

After the meeting broke up, I received a more in-depth briefing on Abu Zubaydah from Jennifer Matthews, the primary CIA officer who had been targeting and tracking him. She was joined by several of her coworkers. They took me into a smaller conference room and showed me colorful link charts and graphs while going into detail about what was known about Abu Zubaydah's background, jihadist activities, and known associates. It was a massive data dump, like being fed from a fire hose. Jennifer was excited and talked fast. She said that at that point, a little more than six months after the attacks of 9/11, very little was known about al-Qa'ida. Her eyes flashed when she stressed that Abu Zubaydah represented the intelligence community's first solid chance to gain insight into the inner workings of al-Qa'ida's hierarchy and operational plans. She said that obtaining actionable intelligence from him was critical to preventing the follow-up terrorist attacks that were expected to occur on U.S. soil at any time. She said there were indications that the next attack might involve chemical, biological, or nuclear devices, resulting in catastrophic loss of innocent life. (Tragically, Jennifer and eight others would be killed by an al-Qa'ida suicide bomber in Khost, Afghanistan, in December 2009.)

The afternoon progressed, evening arrived, and the time to leave for the black site was getting close. I was in a bind. Although the decision to ask me to be part of the interrogation team had been debated and resolved before I arrived at CIA headquarters that afternoon, it was new information to me. I had left my home outside Fort Bragg, North Carolina, a couple of days before, expecting to be gone overnight. The only clothing I had with me was the suit I was wearing and the jeans and polo shirt I had worn driving up. Now I was being asked to leave the country for who knows where or how long with a crumpled suit, one change of clothes, and a pair of operationally worthless dress shoes. To complicate matters, my contract with the CIA did not cover what they were asking me to do. Both had to be remedied that night before departure.

The early evening was spent negotiating a new contract. Because of time constraints, it was written in ballpoint ink on the front side of a single sheet of yellow legal paper. After some back-and-forth with the contracting office to iron out details, we agreed on terms and I was finally free to scramble hurriedly through a nearby shopping center in Tyson's Corner to buy a suitcase, work shoes, and a few clothes for the trip.

The expectation was that I would be gone for two weeks. I called my wife and told her I was going on an unexpected trip. My wife was used to my leaving on a moment's notice at all hours of the day and night for unpredictable amounts of time. She took it in stride. At that time, we had been married thirty-two years. Over the course of that time, I had been on a bomb squad and often had been called away to work on emergencies involving explosive devices or dropped into aircraft crashes to disarm dangerous missiles and bombs in the remote Alaskan wilderness. I had been on a hostage negotiation team and had been called out to work on barricaded gunmen and attempted suicides. As a psychologist, I had worked in acute psychiatric emergencies, with sudden calls to deal with everything from mass shootings to homicidal psychiatric patients. And in the last phase of my air force career, I had been an operational psychologist, part of an air force special operations unit.

I couldn't tell Kathy where I was going, but she was used to that as well. And I couldn't tell her how I was traveling or when I would be able to contact her again. I told her I would be home in a couple of weeks and would call if I could. But I never did call during that deployment. I couldn't. I wasn't allowed to contact her. Every few weeks a CIA officer from agency headquarters would ring to let her know I was still alive and healthy. I did not see home again for several months.

I WASN'T TOLD where we were going until we were in the air. There was lots of time to sit and think. I thought about 9/11 and how I got involved with the CIA. Between 1998 and early 2000, I'd done several briefings for the agency's operational psychologists and officers on a variety of topics, but I had never expressed any interest in working for the agency.

Then, in May 2001, I was mowing the side yard of the house my wife and I were renting in a lakeside community near Fort Bragg. My wife stuck her head out the front door and shouted at me. I couldn't hear her over the noise of the mower, and so I shut it down.

"There is a guy on the phone from the CIA. He wants to talk to you about your job interview."

I walked over, brushing the dirt and grass clippings off my pants. "What job interview? I don't have an application in with the CIA," I said.

She looked at me and shrugged, then passed me the cordless phone.

Curious, I answered. "Hi, it's Jim."

"Dr. Mitchell," said the man on the other end of the line. "I'm calling to set up the travel arrangements for your job interview. Do you prefer to fly or drive?"

"I'm a little confused. I didn't apply for a job at CIA."

"I have a request to make travel arrangements for your job interview. Are you saying you don't want to come?"

"No, no," I said. "Let's make the arrangements."

We did. On the day before my appointment, I drove up to the DC area and stayed overnight in the hotel he booked for me. The next day I found my way through security and into a remote parking lot. I was parked about as far from the building as you could be and remain inside the fence. It was raining hard, and I didn't have an umbrella. When I got inside the main building I was a wet mess. I wandered around until I found the room designated on my paperwork. Since I had not expected to hike a half mile in the rain and then wander around in a maze with confusing room numbers to get to where I needed to be, I was about fifteen minutes late.

When I entered the room, there was a panel of five or six people sitting at a long table facing a single chair. I introduced myself and sat down, apologizing for being late. They said it was understandable given the weather, and we made a little small talk about my drive up. Eventually the man in the center of the group asked me, "What made you apply for a job at the CIA?"

"I didn't apply for a job."

"You don't want to work for the CIA? You didn't put in a job application?"

"No. I never approached you guys. I'm going to get out of the air force in a few months and I want to do some contracting, but I want to start my own business."

"Then why did you come?"

"Good question," I said. "You guys called me, and I was curious about why you did that."

The guy in the middle looked at me, seemingly confused, and then slowly turned his head to look at a surprisingly tall dark-haired man sitting to his right. "This is your doing," he said. It was a declaration, not a question.

There's a little nod of the head from the tall man. The man in the middle stands, looks at a woman to his left, and says, "We're not needed here." All but two of the people at the table gather their pens and legal pads and leave.

"Let's go down to the cafeteria and get a cup of coffee," the big guy says, "and we'll tell you why you're here."

He wanted to offer me a job as chief of a research branch in the department that housed the operational psychologists. He told me a little about it. I said the job sounded interesting but I didn't want to be a government employee. I couldn't imagine living in the DC area, and I really wanted to start my own business. He was gracious about it. We talked for a while longer, and he told me one of his best officers had recommended that he offer me the job because we had known each other for almost two decades. "Look," he said, "call me when you are out of the air force. We're going to bring *somebody* in for that job you just turned down. I'll hook you up with him. We will need subcontractors."

In late August 2001, I returned to the CIA, met with the man who took the job originally offered to me, and agreed to do some subcontracting for them completely unrelated to SERE training. My intention was to have a small personal services contract with the CIA and pick and choose among interesting projects. Little did I realize how the decision to take that contract would derail my life.

On the morning of 9/11 I was home working on a report for a different client. My neighbor, a retired Green Beret sergeant major, called: "A plane just hit the World Trade Center. There's a big fire. It's on TV right now."

I hung up, switched on the set in the living room, and watched. American Airlines Flight 11 had already crashed into the North Tower, and flames were boiling out of the windows and out of the gaping hole the plane had torn in the side of the building. I thought there was no way a plane could get that far off course by accident.

Within moments of that thought, the second passenger jet, United Airlines Flight 175, slammed into the South Tower. My heart sank. I felt a tremendous sadness for the loss of life. I watched people jump to their death rather than burn alive. I heard comments about the number of people falling out of the sky. I watched as the building collapsed and people fled the dust cloud, covered with ash. News broke that a third plane, American Airlines Flight 77, had slammed into the Pentagon and a fourth, United Flight 93, had crashed into a field near Shanksville, Pennsylvania. It felt like we were in a running street battle, blindsided by an enemy trying to destroy our way of life. I thought, What's next?

I sat for a while on the floor in my living room, staring blankly at the TV as images of death and destruction and chaos flitted across the screen. I vacillated between profound sadness for the suffering of the victims of the attacks and a blood fever that made me want to get up right then, find the cowards who had ordered this, and fix it so that they could never do it again. I thought about driving to ground zero to volunteer. I thought about asking the air force to take me out of inactive reserves.

Instead, I called my contact at the CIA. As soon as he picked up his phone I said, "I want to be part of the solution." No small talk. No salutations. No greeting.

"You will be," he said. "We'll all have to be part of it. It's the only way our nation will survive this."

Now, six months later, sitting on a private chartered jet speeding along at forty-five thousand feet toward the black site, I thought this might be the way I could help. I had not asked to be here, but now that I was, I was all in.

I sat next to the Counterterrorism Center operational psychologist. Big guy. Ruddy-faced. He told me he was against my coming along as part of the team, but one of the CTC lawyers had recommended to Alec Station, the CTC unit responsible for targeting al-Qa'ida, that I be included and his objection had been brushed aside. He made it clear that he would be making all the decisions and that any recommendations concerning the psychological aspects of the interrogation would be coming from him. I'd learned a long time earlier not to be offended by this sort of posturing. It frequently went away when you got on the ground and started working.

The operational psychologist told me that our task on the way over was to rough out a design for the cell where Abu Zubaydah was to be held. We were told that because of his importance as a potential source of intelligence and the severity of his injury, the cell had to be lit twenty-four hours a day. Closed circuit TV cameras were also required. We wanted Abu Zubaydah to be focused on the interrogators and the cell not to be a source of distracting stimulation, and so we recommended that they paint it white. Speakers were needed so that music could be played, mostly as sound masking for security reasons because the guards were situated just outside the door, but also, if ordered, as an irritant to wear on him if he chose not to cooperate. The finished product looked like a jail cell in an American cowboy movie, a big white jail cell with black steel bars and a steel bar door across the front.

## The First Few Weeks

Shortly after arriving at the black site on the other side of the world, we met with CIA officers who had been dealing with Abu Zubaydah since he had arrived there from Pakistan and two FBI special agents. One FBI agent was an Arabic-speaking Shia Muslim named Ali Soufan; the other was a fit, red-haired, more senior special agent who spoke with a New England accent. I name Soufan here only because in the ensuing dozen years he has spoken frequently and publicly about the several months he spent there.

By the time we got to the black site, Abu Zubaydah's identity had been confirmed definitively. Abu Zubaydah had almost died after being shot in an exchange of automatic-weapons fire on the roof of the building where he was captured. A doctor from Johns Hopkins who flew over with us saved his life and stabilized his condition.

For the first couple of weeks Abu Zubaydah was in the hospital, drifting in and out of consciousness. To convince his captors that he was worth saving, he gave up one or two tidbits that turned out to be valuable. He told me years later that he thought the American government knew or eventually would find out what he told the CIA and FBI interrogators while he was in the hospital. His gambit paid off.

While Abu Zubaydah was hospitalized, my day consisted of morning meetings with the rest of the team to discuss the intelligence requirements: the questions the CIA wanted answered. The CIA and FBI interrogators would lay out their game plan for the day, outlining which topics they were going to try to cover and how they were going to approach doing it. In the beginning, Abu Zubaydah was responsive for only a few minutes every now and then throughout the day, and the interrogators spent most of the day in his hospital room waiting for the opportunity to talk with him.

Once our morning meeting broke up, the operational psychologist and I would return to the black site and check on the progress of building the cell where he would be moved if and when his health permitted. Then we would come back, watch videotapes of Abu Zubaydah being questioned, and participate in what the military calls a "hot wash" of how the interrogations went that day. After that we would discuss what information, if any, had been obtained. Finally, we reviewed any new messages that had come in from headquarters during the day. In the beginning twelve-hour days were common, stretching out to sixteen- to eighteen-hour days after Abu Zubaydah was moved from the hospital to the black site.

I didn't mind the long hours. I really didn't like where the operational psychologist and I were assigned to stay during the initial two weeks and tried to avoid being in my room. That room was large, made of stone, with almost no furniture except a sad bed and a shabby dresser that wobbled and lurched whenever I tried to pull out a broken drawer. My bathroom, also all stone, was outfitted with leaky mismatched fixtures from another century. There was no shower, and the bottom of the giant stone tub was V-shaped, making it impossible for me to stand up. Being in my room was like camping out in a mausoleum. There was actually an echo. I could hear it when I kicked off my shoes. Other than that it was okay.

Abu Zubaydah said he was grateful that the CIA saved his life and then progressively became less responsive to questions. He played the FBI and CIA interrogators off one another. He said, "I'll tell you anything," and then told them almost nothing of consequence, just enough to keep them expecting the mother lode at any moment.

When Abu Zubaydah was medically stable, he was moved to the black site. While working long shifts there, I sometimes slept on one of the two cots where the security guards had their monitors stationed just outside his cell. The interrogation team had moved our billets to be closer to the black site. My new room was an oasis compared with the last place, but I spent only a few hours there. It was very primitive, with no electronics, but was pleasant and restful. Best of all, it had a working shower.

I can't tell you how many people there were at the black site. The CIA is funny about numbers, but as has been partially reported elsewhere, there were two FBI special agents and more than a handful of CIA officers. (One of the CIA officers was the chief of base. He also interrogated Abu Zubaydah. The second CIA officer who interrogated Abu Zubaydah was an expert in the Reid technique of law enforcement interrogations.) There were also computer and communications geeks, analysts, targeters, subject matter experts, many, many agency police officers to act as security guards, two psychologists (counting me), nurses, and a physician.

After Abu Zubaydah was transferred to his cell, the typical day went something like this. We would meet in the morning to review intelligence requirements and go over e-mail and cable traffic from headquarters. The interrogators would review the plans for their sessions, the physician would go over Abu Zubaydah's medical condition, and then the COB would go around the room and anyone who had any issues to bring up could discuss them. Interrogations sometimes ran around the clock, with interrogators being switched while Abu Zubaydah remained awake. Care was taken to make sure he didn't get so sleepy that his ability to attend to and understand questions was thrown off. Everyone knew that anyone could stop an interrogation at any time for safety reasons.

After an interrogation was over, the interrogator would debrief those of us who were around, and I would give my observations about resistance strategies I observed Abu Zubaydah using and provide an estimate of how successful he had been in that endeavor. The physicians would talk about how the session affected Abu Zubaydah's medical condition, and the analysts and targeters would give a rough estimate of how useful or actionable the information obtained from him in that session was. Abu Zubaydah's medical care took precedence over other activities, and the physician and nurses carefully monitored his condition. The CIA and FBI sometimes interrogated together and sometimes worked separately. How many interrogations there were a day depended on the medical care Abu Zubaydah required and how the interrogators were working that day.

Early on during Abu Zubaydah's detention at the first black site, while his leg wound was still healing, his physicians wanted him to sit most of the day to keep the weight off it. We provided him with one of the dozen or so identical heavy plastic patio chairs we used for seating at the black site. At some point, out of meanness, boredom, or contempt, he began breaking them.

The first time Abu Zubaydah broke a chair, we were willing to write it off as a defect in the product. The chair's legs were splayed, and the plastic was so weakened where the legs attached to the seat bottom that it would no longer support its own weight. But the guards were suspicious; they said they had seen him bouncing up and down just before the chair collapsed.

The chair was replaced with an identical one, and Abu Zubaydah broke it within a day. It took several hours, but he put the time and effort into it, and this time he didn't try to hide what he was doing. He bounced up and down until the legs splayed and the chair collapsed and he fell out onto the floor. The COB asked him not to do that anymore.

The guards replaced the second broken chair with a third, and it met the same fate. The guards replaced it with a fourth, and he started bouncing up and down on that one. Abu Zubaydah seemed intent on breaking every chair the guards put in his cell.

My job at the time was to consult on the psychological aspects of

Abu Zubaydah's detention and interrogation, and so the COB asked me to come up with something that would stop him from breaking the chairs. He was concerned that Abu Zubaydah might hurt himself on the concrete floor when one of the chairs collapsed and he went sprawling.

Because Abu Zubaydah seemed intent on making a contest out of breaking the chairs, I knew asking him to stop would be more of a reward than a deterrent. Instead, I recommended using what in psychology is called a paradoxical intervention. The idea, based on the notion that people do things for a reason, is to prescribe more of the behavior you are trying to eliminate. It's sometimes called reverse psychology.

I reasoned that for the intervention to work, we needed Abu Zubaydah to believe that we had so many plastic patio chairs that we weren't bothered when he broke them. I had the guards collect all the identical patio chairs we had on-site, but that wasn't enough, and so we had fifteen chairs identical to ours brought to the black site. When we added the new ones to the ones we already had, we ended up with two stacks of identical chairs, both reaching from the floor to the high ceiling.

The guards waited until the next time Abu Zubaydah started bouncing up and down in his chair. They then wordlessly carried in the two huge stacks of chairs and placed them within his sight line just outside his cell door, prepositioning the chairs so that they would be handy the next time a broken one needed to be replaced. The guards turned and left without even looking in Abu Zubaydah's direction. He stopped bouncing up and down in his chair. His eyes traveled up the two stacks of chairs from floor to ceiling and back down again. He covered his mouth with his hands and shook his head. The chair breaking stopped and never started again.

. . .

**TWO WEEKS AFTER** Abu Zubaydah was moved to the black site, the operational psychologist left and was replaced by another who stayed with the team throughout.

A rift between the CIA interrogators and Soufan started to form early on. The more senior red-haired FBI agent was well liked and worked well with the CIA team, but Soufan did not. The CIA officers and FBI agents at the black site seemed to have different agendas. The CIA officers were focused exclusively on obtaining actionable information to stop potential upcoming terror attacks. In contrast, the FBI, especially Soufan, seemed interested in obtaining a confession of wrongdoing and building a criminal case. Soufan seemed more interested in following his own line of questioning than on focusing on intelligence requirements coming from CIA headquarters.

Shortly after I initially arrived, one of the CIA officers who had been there all along took me aside and told me about a puzzling interaction he had witnessed involving Ali Soufan. He told me that Soufan walked over to where Abu Zubaydah lay drifting in and out of consciousness in the back of a vehicle, briefly looked at the detainee, and then told those present, "This man is not Abu Zubaydah. I am an expert on Abu Zubaydah. I have studied Abu Zubaydah. I know Abu Zubaydah, and this man is not him." The CIA officer said that shortly after that Abu Zubaydah identified himself to the FBI agents and Soufan acted as if he thought all along it was him. Soufan's confusion can be explained by the fact that, as we later learned, Abu Zubaydah had recently undergone plastic surgery to conceal his identity. This became significant later on.

One of the many misleading impressions that have been left with the public is that in the early days of Abu Zubaydah's detention, he gave up treasure troves of information solely as the result of bonding with the FBI team and establishing rapport with them. But he didn't. Otherwise the CIA never would have changed tactics. Abu Zubaydah made it clear that he was unwilling to cooperate in any significant manner in the hospital. After transfer to the black site he was subjected to sleep deprivation, nudity, loud noise, and dietary manipulation, which, though approved by CIA headquarters and not as harsh as the techniques that would be authorized later by the Department of Justice, were rougher than traditional law enforcement interrogation methods. Abu Zubaydah's early disclosures to CIA and FBI interrogators of threats against the United States occurred during exposure to the harsher tactics.

A good illustration of the early combined use of rapport plus harsh tactics such as sleep deprivation was Abu Zubaydah's identification of an al-Qa'ida operative who wanted to set off a "dirty bomb"—an improvised explosive device laced with radiological material—in a major U.S. city. Abu Zubaydah sent the operative, who turned out to be José Padilla, to KSM to "join others on the ground" inside the United States. The so-called dirty bomber was captured in May 2002 entering the United States with $5,000 in cash and instructions from KSM to blow up apartment buildings in Chicago's financial district during rush hour. The idea was to rent an apartment, seal the air leaks, fill it with natural gas, and then remotely detonate it, raining fire and falling debris on innocent people trying to get to work. Here is the real story of how José Padilla was identified.

After he was moved from the hospital, Abu Zubaydah realized that he wasn't going to die. Watching the interrogations, I could see the change in his resistance posture. His initial willingness to provide answers, even vague ones consisting of one or two words, began to fade, and he started using a variety of resistance techniques to protect information.

After consultation with CIA headquarters, the team started depriving Abu Zubaydah of sleep to weaken his resistance and resolve. We questioned him around the clock with both FBI and CIA interrogators working in tag teams. This went on for about three days.

**BY THEN ABU** Zubaydah was nodding off and slurring his words. We wanted him tired but not incapacitated, and so he was allowed to sleep for three hours. That way he could focus better on questions and his answers wouldn't be compromised. After that, except for catnaps that were too short for quality sleep, he was kept awake and questioned for two more days.

Late at night on the fourth or fifth day of Abu Zubaydah's disrupted sleep, the redheaded FBI agent was questioning him again about potential attacks in the United States. I was monitoring that interrogation, and it seemed possible to me that Abu Zubaydah was approaching some kind of tipping point, a time when his sleepiness would shift his priority from protecting information to obtaining rest. He was mumbling about fragments of dreams concerning people who wanted to attack America. He said they were intruding, flitting in and out of his waking thoughts, but he was too tired to make sense of it. From the bits and pieces of what he said, he seemed to be struggling, searching for some way to reconcile his overwhelming need for sleep with his desire to keep faith with what he believed Allah and his radical Islamist ideology demanded of him.

The FBI agent noticed it too and stepped out of the cell to consult with me. We focused on figuring out a way for Abu Zubaydah to reconcile the conflict he was experiencing between his obligation to protect jihadi brothers still on the loose and his urge to give up some information because of his biological need for sleep.

As a psychologist, I knew that when asked a question we focus our attention on those things we know that would answer that question. We can't help it. Even if we choose not to say it out loud, the answer flits through our minds and is reflected in our physiological responses. The FBI agent had been asking Abu Zubaydah about potential attacks in the United States, and so I knew Abu Zubaydah's attention had been channeled to the things that he believed were a real threat to American lives. I thought perhaps it was this threat information that was flitting in and out of his thoughts, leaking out as dream fragments during bursts of microsleep and maybe causing him to try on the idea of talking about what he had on his mind in order to get some rest.

The FBI agent and I figured that if we could find a way to get Abu Zubaydah to think it was okay to tell us about those intrusive thoughts and dream fragments, there was a good possibility he would reveal some threat information.

Fortunately, in earlier interrogations, the FBI agent had been trying to establish rapport with Abu Zubaydah by saying he was thinking of marrying a Muslim girl and converting to Islam. We reasoned that we could use this as a way forward. Abu Zubaydah was comfortable discussing Islamic beliefs with the agent. He was also tired and extremely suggestible. We wanted to use that suggestibility but not plant false information, and so we had to be careful about our next steps. We had to get him to tell us what was on his mind without asking leading questions that could plant false memories.

Together, we hit on the idea of Abu Zubaydah praying the *Istikharah*, an Islamic prayer asking Allah for guidance when a person is confused or unable to choose between conflicting alternatives. Traditionally it is believed that Allah answers this prayer and provides correct guidance through a dream or an idea that comes to the person immediately upon waking.

Therefore, we decided to try to reframe Abu Zubaydah's intrusive dream fragments as a sign that Allah might be trying to communicate with him through dreams and images as he nodded off during questioning. We didn't care whether he believed this or simply used it as a face-saving device that would allow him to give us information and get some sleep.

The FBI special agent did an amazing job. He went back into the cell and, playing off something Abu Zubaydah said, brought up the idea of the *Istikharah* as if it were a spontaneous part of the conversation. The FBI agent asked Abu Zubaydah what he thought about the possibility that Allah might be trying to provide guidance to him by way of the dream fragments that kept intruding into his sleepy thoughts.

Abu Zubaydah seized on the idea and said that he had been seeing a fleeting image of an American who wanted to do dirty bombs in the United States but was too tired to remember much about it. Abu Zubaydah said he needed several hours of sleep before he would be able to tell the FBI agent about this person. The FBI agent and I had discussed this before he went in. We knew that if our tactic worked, we were going to have to let Abu Zubaydah sleep, but we didn't want to let him sleep so long that the effects of sleep deprivation fully wore off.

I remembered the story of Ernest Shackleton, a British explorer who had saved his men after his ship, the *Endurance,* had been crushed in Antarctic pack ice. At one point while crossing the glaciered, avalanche-prone mountains of South Georgia Island his men became too exhausted to continue. He lied to them to save their lives. Shackleton ordered a brief rest, let them fall asleep for five minutes, and then woke them and told them they had slept a half hour. After that they climbed down the mountains to the Stromness whaling station and safety. I suggested that we use the same ruse on Abu Zubaydah. He had no way to tell time and could not know how long we let him sleep.

When Abu Zubaydah said he wanted to pray the *Istikharah*, the FBI agent got a commitment from him to discuss his dreams when he woke up and then told him we were going to let him sleep for four hours.

But we didn't. We woke him up after only two hours and gave him time to pray, eat, and complete a medical checkup. This was the routine when he had been allowed to sleep uninterruptedly, and we thought following it would help us pull off the deception.

FBI agents and CIA officers then questioned Abu Zubaydah. He started by telling us how he had prayed the *Istikharah* and had received guidance to tell us about two brothers he had sent to KSM. He then told us he had sent two operatives, Abu Ameriki and Abu Jamaki, to KSM to join the others KSM already had on the ground in the United States. Abu Zubaydah said he sent the brothers to KSM because they were "too hot" to attack America and were driving him crazy with talk about dirty bombs. He said the brothers were so insistent that he thought they might compromise his security and draw the attention of the Pakistani authorities.

He said that he didn't think Abu Ameriki could pull off a dirty bomb attack. It wasn't practical, he said; the radiological material would be too hard to find, and Abu Ameriki wasn't smart enough to build a dirty bomb. I got the impression that Abu Zubaydah thought Abu Ameriki was the brains of the outfit and the other one, Abu Jamaki, was his sidekick. Abu Zubaydah said he thought KSM probably would use them for some other kind of terror attack because he was always working on some way to attack America.

Abu Zubaydah claimed he didn't know Abu Ameriki and Abu Jamaki's real names, how they were traveling, or anything else that would help us capture them, something that turned out to be untrue. I recognized what he was doing at the time as an effort to "hide in the truth," a favorite technique employed by high-value detainees in which they give up vague, technically truthful information while trying to hold back details that would make what they told you actionable.

An intelligence report based on Abu Zubaydah's threat information was released almost immediately. Fortunately, a CIA officer in Pakistan recalled a report of a possible illegal traveler regarding a man who matched Abu Ameriki's description. Ten days earlier, two men, José Padilla and Binyan Muhammad, had been traveling together, trying to leave Pakistan. Muhammad's passport was fake, and he was detained by Pakistani authorities, but Padilla had a valid American passport and was allowed to leave.

The importance of the suspicious traveler alert was recognized by the CIA officer in Pakistan because of the intelligence report that came out of our black site. The suspicious traveler report contained Abu Ameriki's true name, José Padilla, and the intelligence report said Abu Zubaydah had sent someone matching his description to KSM to use for attacks in the United States. Clearly it was important to find Padilla and stop him. Neither report would have been sufficient alone. This example illustrates how analysts and targeters work together to put vague, seemingly unrelated information together and make it actionable, in this case resulting in the arrest of Padilla before he could kill innocent Americans.

FBI Agent Soufan has claimed multiple times in the press and before Congress that FBI agents acting alone using only rapport-building interrogation techniques obtained the information that led to the capture of José Padilla and derailed a potentially catastrophic terror attack on U.S. soil. But in truth it was a team effort. If I were passing out a most valuable player award, it wouldn't go to Soufan but to the red-haired FBI agent who initially made the breakthrough with Abu Zubaydah that night. At the same time, you can't discount the role of sleep deprivation in weakening Abu Zubaydah's resolve and shifting his priorities from protecting information to getting some rest. The initial breakthrough happened after 126 hours of sleep deprivation during around-the-clock interrogations conducted over a little more than five and a half days. That is hardly "rapport only" interrogation.

**AS THE MONTH** of June approached, Abu Zubaydah's health got better and his attitude got worse. He became less forthcoming and more arrogant, sometimes sullen and withdrawn and sometimes taunting.

Most of the time, Abu Zubaydah carried himself with the dignity and grace of a caged cat, similar to the way Star Wars fans might imagine a Jedi Knight would carry himself if held captive by his enemies. However, when the mood to be petulant struck, he would drop the noble-warrior facade and a crude thug would emerge. At times, Abu Zubaydah could be unbelievably contemptuous of his CIA and FBI interrogators. The two FBI agents were questioning him once about al-Qa'ida's efforts to acquire radioactive material to build an improvised nuclear bomb. Abu Zubaydah appeared disengaged from the conversation and looked lost in thought, waiting for them to shut up and go away. At one point, while they were pressing him to be more specific about past conversations with al-Qa'ida operatives seeking nuclear weapons, he leaned forward as if he were about to say something important. The FBI agents leaned in. Abu Zubaydah then let loose a long, noisy, wet-sounding fart while looking them straight in the eye. From the looks of disgust on the faces of the FBI agents as we watched them on closed circuit TV, it must have smelled exceptionally foul. As the sound of the fart faded, Abu Zubaydah said, "Now, *that's* nuclear," and laughed uproariously as the FBI agents awkwardly tried to go back to questioning him.

It was clear that our prospects of getting the actionable intelligence we needed were fading. Talk of using more coercive interrogation methods increased at CIA headquarters, as did talk of the FBI leaving the black site. Soufan said he was uncomfortable about some of the nontraditional interrogation techniques already in use. His superior, the redheaded FBI special agent, was less so, as he indicated to the FBI inspector general (IG) a couple years later when asked during the Justice Department IG investigation into FBI participation in detainee interrogations. The CIA made it clear that it was in charge and did not want to wait around to see if Abu Zubaydah would suddenly become talkative in response to FBI relationship-building efforts. After a while, the FBI decided to try some new tactics.

Two incidents happened involving the FBI that in my opinion shut down Abu Zubaydah completely and hastened the CIA's decision to use more coercive pressures on him. The first was when the FBI agents, frustrated with Abu Zubaydah's continued resistance, decided to go Sipowicz, as they referred to it. Andy Sipowicz was a character from *NYPD Blue,* a TV cop show, known for his angry and aggressive interrogation style. The FBI agents reasoned that they had built up enough rapport with Abu Zubaydah that if they suddenly displayed a lot of anger, Abu Zubaydah might fear the loss of their relationship and provide more information. Early in the session, one of the agents called Abu Zubaydah a "son of a bitch." The phrase was used the way we do in the West to refer to someone who makes us angry, but that was not how Abu Zubaydah took it. He translated it literally, thinking that the FBI agent had called his mother a dog. Dogs are considered vile and filthy in Arab culture. Abu Zubaydah had a close and loving relationship with his mother. When he heard the slur, he became angry, stopped talking, and refused to make eye contact. The FBI agents persisted at trying to get him to engage and eventually out of frustration called him a "motherfucker." There was dead silence for a dozen heartbeats. Then Abu Zubaydah shut down and completely disengaged. The session was a total failure.

The second incident occurred when, in a desperate attempt to repair the damage done during the Sipowicz debacle, the FBI agents tried to sell Abu Zubaydah on the idea of working for them. The notion of trying that tactic had been discussed before, but they had been told by the CIA personnel in charge not to do it. That didn't stop the FBI. Shortly after the FBI agents had been told not to "pitch" Abu Zubaydah (the term of art for trying to recruit someone to be a double agent), the CIA operational psychologist and I were watching the two FBI agents try to question an unresponsive Abu Zubaydah when, in a sort of tag-team approach, they began to offer him incentives for working with them. They started out by saying, "America remembers her friends," and went on to imply that in exchange for his cooperation, they could arrange for the U.S. government to take care of his mother and pay him. I say "imply" because they never stated this directly, though the meaning was clear. They even suggested they could bring him candy and Pepsi and improve his confinement conditions. Abu Zubaydah listened and then leaned back in his chair and said: "What makes you think I would abandon Allah for money or Pepsi?" He told them he was done with them and put his hand on his crotch and said they should "go home and have babies." After that he refused to answer questions from any of the interrogators.

The FBI agents made one last effort to get Abu Zubaydah to talk to them again. That session ended with one of the FBI agents lying on the floor outside of his cell, holding Abu Zubaydah's hand and pleading with him to talk to them, and the other inside trying to smooth things over. Abu Zubaydah was sitting in his chair, leaning back, his hand on his crotch, acting like an indifferent urban street thug, ignoring their pleas.

During this time, Soufan became more argumentative at meet-ings and was quick to show his anger. One day while a CIA opera-tional psychologist and I were watching Abu Zubaydah on closed circuit TV monitors between interrogations, Soufan came into the room where we were. We were sitting on cots with our backs against the wall. Soufan approached, screaming at me. He said he wanted to arrest me. It was apparent he blamed me for the increasing friction between him and CIA personnel at the black site. I have no idea what triggered the outburst. I sat there for a while listening, thinking he just needed to vent. He told me I was the source of all his problems because the CIA was listening to me, not to him.

To me this sounded ridiculous. The black site was run by a CIA officer called the chief of base (COB) who reported to the chief of the CIA's Counterterrorism Center, who in turn took orders from the senior leadership of the CIA. I had zero decision-making power. My activities were controlled by the COB.

I reminded Soufan that I was just a consultant and told him I wasn't the person making decisions. When I suggested that he talk to the COB about his complaints, Soufan loomed over where I was sitting and threatened to hit me. I stood up in case he tried. As I stood, our faces were inches apart and he started bouncing his chest off mine, yelling threats.

Although Soufan is about fifteen years younger than I am, I said: "Ali, you may be an FBI agent, but if you hit me I'm going to knock you on your ass."

It was then that the operational psychologist, still sitting, eyes the size of saucers, spoke up in a calm, commanding voice that didn't quite match the look of incredulity on his face. He told Soufan to calm down, insisted that I wasn't the source of his problems, and told me to disengage.

Maybe it was because he realized there was a witness to his out-

# CHAPTER 2

# Getting Rough

Abu Zubaydah simply wasn't talking. Before he shut down, he had at least engaged with the interrogators. True, he employed a variety of resistance techniques to protect the things he wanted to keep secret: he hedged, feigned forgetfulness, answered questions with questions, glossed over critical facts, and provided superficial details while trying to sidestep the specifics that would make the information actionable. But by engaging, Abu Zubaydah occasionally revealed a piece of information that CIA analysts and targeters could combine with other intelligence to make it actionable. But after the run-in with the FBI agents, he completely disengaged. The FBI's efforts to bribe him into cooperating made matters worse.

CIA targeters and analysts were sure he had information he was holding back that could save lives. I was asked by Jose Rodriguez, who by that time had been elevated to chief of the CIA Counterterrorism Center, to accompany other senior members of the interrogation team back to the United States to attend a meeting at Langley. The agenda was to discuss Abu Zubaydah's interrogation thus far and what could be done to get him not only talking again but providing fuller and more complete answers than he had provided before.

The meeting started with physicians providing a medical update. The discussion then went around the room as the senior operations officer who served as COB at the black site, analysts, targeters, and an agency criminal investigator all provided their assessments of the successes and failures of the first few months of Abu Zubaydah's interrogation. CIA analysts contrasted the information gotten from Abu Zubaydah with threat updates from elsewhere, emphasizing credible intelligence that suggested that another wave of catastrophic attacks was imminent.

It was clear to me from discussions I had been part of and from comments I'd overheard that CIA officers and agency lawyers had been thinking for some months about getting rough, if necessary, to stop future attacks. The lawyers said that the president, using his constitutional authority, had directed that al-Qa'ida operatives in CIA custody be treated as unlawful combatants rather than prisoners of war (POWs), a designation that at that time meant al-Qa'ida terrorists did not qualify for the protections of the Third Geneva Convention. I understood that because of this they were considering using coercive physical pressure on high-value detainees who were withholding information if they were convinced a detainee had information that could save lives. Officers were being asked to think outside the box. I had been asked to do that myself several times.

In the climate of fear after 9/11 and with near certainty among intelligence experts that follow-on terror attacks by radical jihadists were imminent, CIA officers were encouraged by political leaders to do everything and anything that was legal, to take it right up to the line of what was lawful if necessary to get actionable intelligence. I realized as I sat and listened that CIA officers were going to use physical coercion to interrogate Abu Zubaydah; it was just a question of which techniques they decided to use.

Eventually it was my turn to make comments and answer questions. Jose asked me to discuss some of the resistance-to-interrogation ploys I'd seen Abu Zubaydah use, such as hedging, distracting with less important or dead-end topics, glossing over critical facts, and providing vague, superficial details. I also emphasized his success at turning the interrogators against one another. It's called "splitting" in psychology and is similar to the way crafty teenagers play parents against each other.

Abu Zubaydah was manipulating each interrogator to believe that he had a special relationship with the terrorist and that he would finally deliver the mother lode if the interrogator could just cut the others out of the picture.

I believe his splitting technique was especially effective on Soufan, who made several pitches early on to be the primary interrogator of Abu Zubaydah. He told me and the operational psychologist who replaced the first one, "There is only one interrogator you need to question Abu Zubaydah. It is Ali Soufan, Ali Soufan, Ali Soufan." Meanwhile, Abu Zubaydah led him on with tidbits implying he was about to deliver the goods but instead provided information that was vague, superficial, and nonactionable.

I also outlined the way Abu Zubaydah would distract interrogators by providing hours of details on some terror operative who, when interrogators asked where Abu Zubaydah thought he might be, would turn out to be long dead, killed fighting during the jihad against the Soviets in Afghanistan decades before. He did the same thing with terror plots. He would spend hours going into detail, only to acknowledge that the plot in question was against the Soviets or other targets decades back. He also would willingly provide vague details of past successful plots against U.S. targets of interest and the jihadi brothers killed in them. These were not things that would allow CIA officers to stop upcoming attacks but things that suggested he might have been part of a conspiracy and could be useful during prosecution. This was something that would meet Soufan's goals but not the CIA's.

Since I was certain the CIA intended to use physical coercion, I suggested that if they were going to go down that path, they should consider using a clearly defined set of some of the harsh techniques employed by U.S. military SERE schools. I knew these techniques had been used for over five decades without significant injuries to train warfighters to protect secrets. I had been subjected to them myself, I had used them to train others, and I had researched the injury rates associated with them when I helped the Air Force Survival School revise its approach to resistance training after the first Gulf War.

As a psychologist with a strong background in emotionally demanding resistance to interrogation training, I knew things could escalate quickly and get out of hand if interrogators were allowed to make stuff up on the fly. In my opinion, the techniques the CIA used, whatever they were, needed to be carefully controlled and monitored to prevent "abusive drift," a term Bruce and I used to describe the tendency for the intensity of physical coercion to escalate in the absence of careful supervision by noninvolved observers. That was why I thought it important that whatever was done be clearly laid out and authorized.

I think in retrospect that the troublesome things done later on by the few officers who did go outside approved guidelines illustrates how bad it could have been throughout the CIA's interrogation program without a carefully crafted list of techniques approved by the Department of Justice and closely monitored during implementation.

In the highly volatile atmosphere in the months after 9/11, with the ongoing fear of another catastrophic attack looming and the clamor to do anything it took to prevent it, the decision to adopt specific procedures that became known as enhanced interrogation techniques (EITs) was the right one. Although they were unpleasant, their use protected detainees from being subjected to unproven and perhaps harsher techniques made up on the fly that could have been much worse.

One false claim subsequently made by my critics and critics of the CIA's interrogation program is that I somehow manipulated the CIA into adopting coercive techniques to the exclusion of other measures. The claim asserts that if it had not been for me, the CIA would have used traditional rapport-based law enforcement approaches to interrogate detainees rather than coercion.

That is simply not true. CIA officers had been using a rapport-based approach with Abu Zubaydah, and it clearly wasn't working. They had already decided to get rough. The question was how that would be achieved.

At the meeting, I described some of the SERE techniques that eventually were adopted.

Jose asked how long I thought it would take to know whether a detainee exposed to those techniques would be willing to cooperate or would "take his secrets to the grave." I told him thirty days. In my mind that was the upper limit. I fully expected that it would take a lot less time than that for hard-case high-value detainees initially intent on withholding information to begin engaging with interrogators and debriefers in ways that allowed a switch to non-EIT, social influence–based approaches. Social influence tactics are defined as noncoercive techniques, devices, procedures, and manipulations a person or a group can use to change the thoughts, feelings, and actions of another individual or group. That's an academic definition.

It may be simpler to think of social influence techniques as ways we can interact with others to influence what they think, feel, and do.

In that meeting I described some of the harsh techniques that were in use for SERE training, but the topic of waterboarding did not come up. In fact, I didn't think of waterboarding until later that night back in my hotel room. I was mulling over the different SERE techniques, making a short list of the ones I thought were most effective, when it dawned on me that I had left waterboarding, the most effective SERE technique I knew of, off the list I had discussed with Rodriguez earlier that day.

As senior SERE psychologists, Bruce Jessen and I had spent several years trying to get the Navy SERE School to abandon its use of waterboarding not because it didn't work but because we thought it was *too* effective. One hundred percent of the warfighters exposed to it in training capitulated even if it cost them their jobs. In my view, waterboarding students did the enemy's job for them. The point of resistance training is to teach students that they can protect secrets, but my personal experience interviewing POWs and warfighters who had been waterboarded at the Navy SERE School was that after waterboarding they didn't believe they could protect secrets anymore. I told Jose about waterboarding at a meeting the next day.

A day or so later Rodriguez asked me if I would help put together an interrogation program using EITs. I told him I would, thinking I would remain in the role I had occupied during the first few months, pointing out resistance techniques employed by the detainees and advising on the psychological aspects of interrogation. But that was not what he had in mind. Jose not only wanted me to help them craft the program, he wanted me to conduct the interrogations using EITs myself.

I was surprised. And reluctant. I knew that if I agreed, my life as I knew it would be over. I would never again be able to work as a psychologist. Hesitantly, I said, "I can help you find somebody—" But then one of Jose's colleagues cut me off, saying, "Knowing all you know about the threat, if you're not willing to help, how can we ask someone else?"

My mind flashed to the victims of 9/11, to the "falling man" who chose to dive headfirst off the Twin Towers rather than burn to death, and to the passengers of United Flight 93 who bravely sacrificed their lives to save the lives of other Americans. I thought, if they can sacrifice their lives, I can do this. I didn't want to, but I would.

Thus, I agreed. "But," I said, "I can't do it by myself. I need someone more familiar with the techniques than I am." Rodriguez said, "Who do you need?" I said, "Bruce Jessen." He was on board by the end of the next week.

Back in my room that night I had trouble sleeping. The magnitude of what I had agreed to do for Rodriguez was gnawing at me. In the stillness of my hotel room with nothing to distract me, two things were pulling at the edge of my thoughts, keeping me awake: Could I do it and should I do it?

Could I do it? I ran a mental checklist of experiences that prepared me to do what they were asking and concluded that I could, especially with Bruce's help.

Rodriguez wasn't asking me to do law enforcement interrogations. They had tried that already and it wasn't working, and I knew they were going to have a CIA law enforcement interrogation expert deployed with us. By this time, I'd watched him and the two FBI agents conduct hundreds of interrogations.

I also knew that they were going to get rough with Abu Zubaydah whether I helped or not.

No, my question concerned my qualifications to put together a psychologically based interrogation program that would condition

Abu Zubaydah to cooperate and my ability to interrogate him using it. I knew it would have to be based on what is called Pavlovian classical conditioning (more on this later), and I was very familiar with that because my early training was as a behavioral psychologist. I had used Pavlovian conditioning many, many times to help people overcome fear and anxiety. I thought about how to use it for what Rodriguez was asking me to do.

Then I ran through a mental checklist of other things that prepared me for this assignment. At that time, I had thirteen years of experience with resistance-to-interrogation training, but that wasn't all.

I had undergone both basic and advanced resistance-to-interrogation training myself. I had experienced all the enhanced measures I eventually recommended except for waterboarding. (I experienced that before we waterboarded Abu Zubaydah.) Also, I had been taught to use enhanced measures and had applied them in training situations.

In those thirteen years I spent over fourteen thousand hours monitoring the psychological reactions of warfighters attempting to withhold information during interrogation laboratory exercises that employed enhanced measures. The behavioral and emotional responses of both instructors and students during those exercises could be unpredictable.

I had observed hundreds of survival instructors and DOD interrogators apply enhanced measures. My job was to note what went wrong, what caused those problems, and what could be done to prevent similar outcomes in the future. A big component of that was to monitor and directly intervene to prevent escalating abusive drift in the brutality of enhanced measures that could lead to increased risk of lasting mental or physical harm among students.

I had watched thousands of trained and untrained people try to lie or use sophisticated resistance techniques to protect information under conditions that involved the use of the same coercive psychological and physical pressures I had proposed that the CIA consider. I had monitored people trying to be deceptive before they were trained to resist and then watched the same people apply what they had learned after resistance training.

I had observed a select set of the special-mission warfighters who were interrogated several times over a period of years. In this setting, part of my job was to help put together interrogation plans that were as realistic as possible and used enhanced measures to challenge the will to resist in people who were too cocky or strengthen the will to resist in those who were overwhelmed without producing lasting mental or physical harm.

I conducted in excess of 215 post–resistance-to-interrogation training psychological debriefs for groups ranging from ten to one hundred twenty people, discussing their psychological reactions to captivity and interrogation using enhanced measures.

I worked to develop strategies for resisting sexual exploitation and media exploitation as an interrogation tool. I developed resistance-to-interrogation strategies for women. I spearheaded a survival school program to increase the realism of training while reducing the risk of physical and mental harm.

I studied the types and rates of injuries associated with using enhanced measures, and in the course of that work I identified which measures had the desired effect while reducing the risk of lasting mental or physical harm.

I worked with a survival school commander who was an ex-POW to conduct interrogation and exploitation activities during an air force mission readiness test in which aircrews tasked with flying nuclear weapons were captured and interrogated in a nontraining environment to evaluate the effectiveness of their resistance training.

I had studied and written and lectured on the social influence and self-persuasion mechanisms that turn ordinary people into terrorists, on the psychological aspects of interrogation and resistance to interrogation, and on the use of coercive psychological and physical pressures during interrogations and resistance-to-interrogation training.

Equally important, as a psychologist with a PhD in clinical psychology and decades of experience dealing with people during my training and as a professional, I knew how to establish rapport and ask questions. That's what psychologists do. It is the core skill they acquire.

Moreover, I had extensive experience questioning hostile, deceptive subjects for suitability for continued duty assessments, security evaluations, psychological profiling, sanity evaluations, and forensic assessments for individuals who had committed a variety of criminal offenses, including murder, sexual assault, kidnapping, and child sexual assault. I had conducted psychological autopsies. All of which I was trained to do with the appropriate course work and supervision.

In addition, I was a trained and experienced bomb tech (explosive ordnance disposal technician) who learned investigative procedures in school and applied them in working incidents involving explosive devices.

Finally, I was a law enforcement–trained and experienced hostage/crisis negotiator who had handled barricaded gunmen and numerous suicidal individuals and de-escalated combative and delusional people.

I was not your typical mental health–focused psychologist. Some at the CIA knew this. In fact, the agency would later tell Congress in a classified report talking about me and Bruce, "We believe their expertise was so unique that we would have been derelict had we not sought them out when it became clear that CIA would be heading into the uncharted territory of the program."

Okay, I thought. I could do it. The next question was, *Should* I do it?

For some people, I know the answer would have been no. I respect that. But as I lay there that night and thought, I decided I had a duty to use what I knew to protect American citizens and our way of life. I was told that another deadly attack could occur at any moment, possibly involving a nuclear device or chemical or biological agents. I concluded that conducting coercive interrogations on a small number of Islamic terrorists who were actively withholding information that could disrupt a potentially catastrophic attack was justified as long as those methods were lawful, authorized, and carefully monitored. I dismissed the notion, later put forward by some, that it was somehow unfair or unethical to put the lives of thousands of innocent Americans ahead of the interests of a handful of Islamic terrorists who not only had made the personal decision to attack us and continued to try to mount terror attacks but also had continued deliberately to withhold information that could stop attacks and save lives. Instead, I concluded that it would be immoral and unethical to ignore my obligation to use what I knew to defend our citizens and our way of life against enemies who themselves had initiated the conflict and whose stated goal was to destroy us.

In the end I decided I should do it. This wouldn't be the last time I had to examine the ethics and morality of what I was being asked to do.


**LESS THAN A** week after the CTC had decided to move ahead with efforts to incorporate SERE interrogation techniques into the CIA's interrogation program, Jose asked me to accompany him to go see the CIA's director, George Tenet. That meeting took place in the early evening in Tenet's wood-paneled office on the seventh floor of agency headquarters. John Rizzo, the CIA's chief legal advisor, was also there. Rodriguez introduced me and said that I was the person who had agreed to help them put together the CIA's interrogation program. Tenet and Rizzo greeted me graciously, and we shook hands. Then we all sat down around a coffee table in the front section of the director's large private office. Floor-to-ceiling windows on one side looked out toward the Potomac River and beyond that to Washington, DC.

It was apparent that both Tenet and Rizzo already had been briefed about what CTC was about to propose. Rodriguez quickly laid out the idea of incorporating the SERE techniques to the director and his chief legal advisor. In his initial remarks, Jose made it clear that he wanted Tenet's approval before moving ahead, and he then asked me to walk them through a brief description of each technique.

I remember illustrating some of the techniques that were harder to visualize with hand gestures and occasionally getting out of my seat to demonstrate, because that sometimes seemed like the clearest way to get across what was being proposed. Tenet and Rizzo listened intently and asked lots of questions. They were particularly interested in the fact that all the techniques we were discussing had been used on thousands of U.S. military personnel at high risk of capture for fifty-plus years.

As the meeting wound down and it was obvious that Jose was waiting for Tenet to tell him if he should press forward, Tenet stood up from his chair at the coffee table. He made eye contact with Rizzo and motioned with his head for him to follow as he stepped behind a large desk deeper in the room. Tenet began rummaging around in a cigar case and then turned his head away from those of us sitting around the coffee table and in a low voice, probably so that he would not be overheard, told Rizzo, "Make sure this is legal before we do it." Tenet then stuck the unlit cigar in this mouth, turned toward us, and told Rodriguez to press forward but to be sure the Justice Department was fully on board and considered these steps legal before the techniques actually were employed.

Getting that clearance took a couple of months. What I didn't know at the time but subsequently learned was that Tenet, Rodriguez, Rizzo, and others also spent that time getting the approval of the White House lawyers; the national security advisor, Condoleezza Rice; and Vice President Cheney. Rice in turn had briefed the president. In his 2011 memoir, Bush wrote that he personally approved the use of the interrogation techniques.

LET ME STEP back. Before I recommended him for the CIA's interrogation program, Dr. John Bruce Jessen had been a SERE psychologist for eighteen years, first as the chief psychologist at the U.S. Air Force Survival School and then for a longer period as the senior Defense Department SERE psychologist. In those roles he had debriefed and helped repatriate numerous returning hostages and POWs, both civilian and military. He had spent thousands of hours working in the highly volatile resistance-training laboratories both at the basic school and at DOD-level advanced training courses. During that time he had observed literally thousands of people of varied ethnic backgrounds, intellect, and job assignments attempt to be deceptive and hold back intelligence information during the use of enhanced pressures. Not only had he worked as a psychologist monitoring instructors and students, after receiving extensive training he worked as a senior instructor *applying* the SERE interrogation techniques on which the CIA's program was to be based. He had attended several intelligence-gathering interrogation courses and was familiar with standard law enforcement interrogation techniques. Over the years, he had consulted with the military special operations, the CIA, and the FBI on a variety of topics. But more than this, he was and remains my friend. He was my climbing partner, and I trusted him with my life. For years not only had we worked together professionally, we had had each other's back on big scary ice climbs and dangerous mountaineering adventures. To me it was only natural to seek Bruce's help. He had the one-of-a-kind skills this mission required and was someone in whom I had complete confidence.

Shortly after Bruce was read into the program in June, the two of us were shown to a small cubicle at CIA headquarters and asked to provide a list and short descriptions of how the EITs would be applied. This is a list of the techniques that finally were approved:

- *Attention grasp.* Grasping the detainee with both hands, with one hand on each side of the collar opening, in a controlled and quick motion. In the same motion as the grasp, the detainee is drawn toward the interrogator.

- *Walling.* The detainee is pulled forward and then quickly and firmly pushed into a flexible false wall so that his shoulder blades hit the wall. His head and neck are supported with a rolled towel to prevent whiplash.

- *Facial hold.* The interrogator places an open palm on either side of the detainee's face with the interrogator's fingertips kept well way from the detainee's eyes.

- *Facial or insult slap.* The interrogator's fingers are slightly spread apart, and his hand makes contact with the area between the tip of the detainee's chin and the bottom of the corresponding earlobe.

- *Cramped confinement.* The detainee is placed in a confined space, typically a small or large box, which is usually dark. Confinement in the smaller space lasts no more than two hours, and in the larger space it lasts for up to eighteen hours.

- *Insects.* Harmless insects can be placed in the confinement box with the detainee.

- *Stress positions.* The detainee sits on the floor with his legs extended straight out in front of him and with his arms raised above his head, or kneels on the floor while leaning back at a 45-degree angle.

- *Wall standing.* The detainee may stand about four to five feet from a wall with his feet spread approximately to shoulder width. His arms are stretched out in front of him, and his fingers rest on the wall to support all of his body weight. The detainee is not allowed to reposition his hands or feet.

- *Sleep deprivation.* Not to exceed eleven days at a time.

- *Waterboard.* The detainee is bound to a bench with his feet elevated above his head. The detainee's head is immobilized, and an interrogator places a cloth over the detainee's mouth and nose while pouring water onto the cloth in a controlled manner. Airflow is restricted for twenty to forty seconds, and the technique produces the sensation of drowning and suffocation.

The list we provided the CIA was only a partial list of the co-ercive techniques used at that time in DOD SERE training. Two techniques that we recommended against using and that thus never made the list that the CIA sought approvals for were "manhandling" and "smoking." In manhandling, a towel is rolled up and placed like a cervical collar around the neck. The person then is pulled for-ward until he is on his tiptoes and violently shaken back and forth in a figure-eight pattern. A review of SERE-related injuries that I conducted when the U.S. Air Force was updating its resistance-to-interrogation training after the first Gulf War revealed that manhan-dling resulted in lower-back and whiplash injuries to the neck that could keep pilots from flying for weeks. As for smoking, the navy has two SERE schools and smoking was used by the one that didn't use waterboarding. It was used on students who were too cocky. The technique consisted of blowing smoke in a student's face until the student became nauseous, capitulated by providing information, and changed his attitude.

As we were drawing up the list, I spoke to CTC lawyers about the possibility of using a particular non–physically coercive tech-nique. It involved using a confederate to trick a detainee into be-lieving the confederate was being waterboarded because that person refused to answer, when in fact the confederate wasn't really being waterboarded. It just looked and sounded that way from the flail-ing legs and gurgling noises the collaborator was coached to make. This method has been used effectively in advanced resistance-to-interrogation training to get warfighters to give up protected in-formation even when doing so might cost them the jobs they are applying for. It required that no actual physical coercion be used, but the lawyers told me this probably would violate the torture conven-tions because the detainee being questioned was led to believe that a fellow Islamic terrorist was in danger of imminent harm.

I thought it odd at the time and even odder today. We were being told we might get permission to actually waterboard a detainee—to use physical coercion for refusal to answer questions—but we couldn't trick that detainee into answering questions by using only his sense of responsibility for another detainee's harsh treatment even though no harsh treatment was being used.

I think it would have worked. Here's why. Years later, I got Abu Zubaydah to act as a confederate to get another senior al-Qa'ida operative, Abd al-Rahim al-Nashiri, to clean his cell. In a fit of rage, al-Nashiri had trashed it with his own urine and fecal matter. Abu Zubaydah agreed to go in with me and pretend I was making him clean up al-Nashiri's mess. I sat al-Nashiri in a chair with a clear view of the mess he had made. I then told him that since he was too good to clean up his own mess, someone else would pay for his arrogance and he could just sit there and watch. I brought Abu Zubaydah in and put him to work with a mop and bucket. Up to that point al-Nashiri was unaware that he was being held at the same black site as Abu Zubaydah. Al-Nashiri immediately recognized Abu Zubaydah (that says something about how well known Abu Zubaydah was among al-Qa'ida operatives). Al-Nashiri leaped to his feet and frantically insisted that Abu Zubaydah was a very important man and that he couldn't stand the idea of such a high-ranking person being forced to clean up a mess for which he was not responsible. Al-Nashiri grabbed the cleaning tools from Abu Zubaydah and did the cleaning himself.

Fake waterboarding was not the only non–physically coercive technique ruled out by the lawyers because of concerns about what the detainees would think was going on even if what they believed was happening wasn't really happening at all. For example, we were told that we couldn't lead a detainee to believe that we were preparing to move him to a federal prison where he would be put in the general population with people who were likely to harm him even if it wasn't true. Again, it was the detainee's belief about being in danger of imminent harm that was the sticking point.

Bruce and I recommended the techniques we did because we were familiar with them and thought they would lend themselves to a Pavlovian process to condition compliance. We knew we needed a lot more experience with the waterboard. We decided to use the time waiting for DOJ approval to get familiar enough to use it safely or determine that we should recommend against its use. We knew we would have a physician on hand while we were getting familiar with waterboarding, the chance to work out emergency procedures, and the opportunity to practice the procedure before actually using it. We made up our minds that we were both going to experience it before we waterboarded Abu Zubaydah.

After we compiled the list, the CIA's operational psychologists were asked to perform due diligence, independent of us, to be sure the techniques were unlikely to result in severe or prolonged mental harm. I was told that they called the DOD agency that oversees all the military SERE schools and learned that the techniques being considered had indeed been used safely for more than fifty years.

One common misconception is that the descriptions of EITs we provided were intended to be exactly the same as those used in the basic resistance-to-interrogation training that took place in U.S. military SERE schools. That was not the case. Instead, we based our descriptions on how they were employed in the DOD-level advanced resistance-to-interrogation exercises used to train warfighters who already had been trained to protect secrets at the basic SERE schools. (We had been told that senior high-value al-Qa'ida detainees might have been trained to resist interrogation and thought that we would need to use advanced techniques to break through their defenses.) This advanced training still falls under the SERE umbrella but is far more realistic and in-depth than are the basic courses. It focuses more on protecting secrets than the basic courses do. It's like getting a master's degree in protecting secrets. It is often used as part of the selection process by military units with clandestine missions. Not passing the advanced course by failing to protect secrets often kept otherwise war-ready candidates with years of military experience who were on the short list for assignment from being selected for specialized units with top secret missions.

Shortly after handing in the list, Bruce and I were deployed to the black site to await further instructions. We used the time to practice and get ready in case approvals were granted. We received briefings from medical personnel about the kinds of medical emergencies that might occur during the use of EITs. We practiced emergency procedures until all the members of the team understood where they were supposed to be during an emergency and what they were supposed to do. We refreshed our familiarity with the techniques, especially waterboarding, and practiced, practiced, practiced. CIA operations officers and analysts would be upstairs while Bruce and I would be downstairs with the guards practicing each step in the process, from prisoner handling to what to do in case a detainee got violent, to the actual use of EITs. In this period we received in-depth briefings on Abu Zubaydah and al-Qa'ida from subject matter experts on scene. We also reviewed intelligence requirements. Targeters and analysts told us which threats we should focus on first and how they thought we could best fill in the blanks. In addition, our Arab linguist briefed us on important cultural and religious factors. Finally, the CIA criminal investigator who had been deployed to advise us on law enforcement interrogation techniques went over the various methods of employing them with us.

We also observed Abu Zubaydah every day. In recent years some people have alleged that we couldn't have been all that concerned about what information Abu Zubaydah had in his head since there was a gap in his interrogation. That is not true at all. But since he had shut down and because we were instructed by CIA headquarters to wait for legal and policy authorization, at the black site our hands were tied.

Meanwhile, psychologists back at headquarters had completed a psychological profile of our high-value detainee, and so we reviewed that. We read his very extensive diaries. We tried to find out as much as we could about Abu Zubaydah. Fortunately for us, we had the CIA's vast resources to draw on. We also had the tapes of the earlier interrogations conducted by the CIA and FBI. We reviewed the resistance techniques Abu Zubaydah used and identified his poker "tells," or body language that would tip us off to when he was telling the truth and when he was being deceitful. We saw how the wording of different questions aroused his suspicions or put him at ease. I had observed most, if not all, of the interrogations of Abu Zubaydah in real time, but it was helpful to review some of the more important ones with Bruce. Counting all the previous interrogations by the FBI and CIA, I had observed and participated in the debriefing of hundreds of Abu Zubaydah's interrogations. I had observed the CIA's direct questioning approach, the FBI's rapport-building approach, the CIA law enforcement expert's use of the nine-step Reid technique of interrogation, and a combination of these approaches used with the coercive pressures that were authorized at the time.

IN EARLY AUGUST 2002, once the Department of Justice and the White House had approved the use of EITs, the enhanced interrogation of Abu Zubaydah began. The FBI had left the black site by then. The team on-site consisted of the chief of base; a handful of operations officers; several analysts and targeters; a reports officer; medical personnel, including a physician; an operational psychologist (with a PhD in clinical psychology who was charged with monitoring the mental health of both Abu Zubaydah *and* the interrogators); an Arab translator (at least two people on-site spoke Arabic, but Abu Zubaydah had lived in the United States and spoke excellent English); a lot of guards; and a subject matter expert on law enforcement interrogations. And, of course, me and Bruce.

The COB informed us that the Justice Department had reviewed the proposed list of EITs and determined that the CIA could lawfully apply ten of them in Abu Zubaydah's interrogations. The COB reviewed a cable summarizing the legal approvals. The cable from CIA headquarters gave explicit guidance on the use of the EITs on Abu Zubaydah and then the go-ahead to start.

The whole team discussed how the interrogation would unfold, including when and if EITs would be introduced. We were all still hoping they wouldn't be necessary. There was a chance of that since Abu Zubaydah had been in relative isolation for a while and might have decided to cooperate. When put in isolation, he had been left a crayon (for his safety and ours, as opposed to leaving a pen or pencil) and paper. He was instructed to pass a note to the guards when he had something to communicate. He never used the crayon. But we still wanted a fair assessment of his resistance posture before possibly introducing physically coercive measures.

Bruce and I had benefited from hours of in-depth briefings from the analysts and targeters on scene and from reading finished intelligence reports focusing on Abu Zubaydah, but we were not professional analysts and never believed or implied that we were skilled enough to evaluate the *intelligence value* of the things he or any other detainee reported. That wasn't our job, and we were the wrong people to do it. On-site were some of the CIA's most skilled career analysts and targeters, subject matter experts who had followed Abu

Zubaydah's activities and had access to intelligence materials that we did not have. Not only that, they were plugged into the CIA's and other government agencies' massive intelligence databases and could search inside them and quickly retrieve information to aid in the interrogations. Bruce and I were not the right people to evaluate how actionable what he told us was.

Our job was to get Abu Zubaydah talking again, ask the questions the analysts and targeters wanted us to ask, and then, when he began to cooperate a little, transition to having the right subject matter experts conduct their own debriefings while we sat in to monitor the way he interacted with them. It was their job, often with the real-time help of analysts at headquarters, to evaluate the quality and quantity of the information Abu Zubaydah provided, determine how actionable it was, and keep us informed so that we could adjust our interrogations.

The plan, which was approved by headquarters, became a template for future interrogations using EITs on other senior al-Qa'ida leaders. The interrogation was to start with what we referred to as a "neutral probe." It was a noncoercive questioning of Abu Zubaydah to assess his willingness to answer questions about potential attacks against the United States. The wording and content of our questions had been worked out with targeters to be sure it covered the topics in which they were most interested. The approach was to be business-like without coming across as either aggressive or overly friendly.

Because I look more like somebody's uncle than an interrogator, I was chosen to do the neutral probe. The probe had no set time limit. If Abu Zubaydah was willing to provide information that the analysts and targeters monitoring via closed circuit TV on-site judged useful, the use of EITs would be abandoned or delayed unless and until he started to resist again. If Abu Zubaydah refused to answer questions or used resistance techniques to thwart questioning, the plan was for EITs to be introduced, starting with lesser coercive techniques and ending if necessary with the waterboard. I say "if necessary" because if at any point in the escalation of EITs Abu Zubaydah started answering questions, EITs would be discontinued. This didn't happen with Abu Zubaydah, but it did later with several other detainees who quickly decided to cooperate after being subjected to only a few of the more benign techniques. Quick compliance became more common after rumors of the harsh tactics began to leak into the press.

Before starting, the team took the time to go over security procedures for the interrogation. Assignments were given to each of the guards, and they were told what to do if Abu Zubaydah attacked me in the cell. During previous interrogations when CIA and FBI interrogators had been in his cell, Abu Zubaydah had been sitting in a chair, feet shackled and hands cuffed in front of him to the cell's bars. Although he could move his hands up and down the vertical bar and shift his position in the chair to get more comfortable, he was unable to get up and move around. But this time, because we wanted to alert him to a change in tactics, when I entered his cell, he was free to move around with only his feet shackled.

Because we were to be standing in the middle of the cell talking, our staff wanted to be sure that I was protected if things got out of hand. But the guards were instructed not to intervene unless I was really in trouble. Minor contact with me, even if aggressive, shouldn't trigger a takedown. I could protect myself in the short run. I had practiced karate in the past and learned and used humane takedown procedures while working on staff on locked wards in psychiatric hospitals. I knew that with him shackled, I had more freedom of movement and could cover up and get out of reach. We didn't want to interrupt the interrogation unless it was absolutely necessary, because we didn't want Abu Zubaydah to think he could stop interrogations by aggressively acting out. It turned out this precaution was totally unnecessary.

Abu Zubaydah had a still-healing leg wound extending over most of one thigh. We had to be sure we didn't aggravate it. We reviewed the list of approved EITs with the physician at the black site to determine which ones, if any, could be used on Abu Zubaydah. We also discussed how to reduce the chances of hurting him and what we were to do in case of a medical emergency. We had gone over this before, but it was important that no real harm come to Abu Zubaydah. There was a fully stocked emergency room crash cart stationed behind a curtain just outside his cell, not more than a dozen feet from where the interrogations were to take place.

Finally, the COB made it clear that we needed to err on the side of caution. He said that anyone could stop an ongoing interrogation at any time for any reason. Bruce and I were to stand down immediately if any member of the team raised a concern. We would clear it up later. No interrogation I was involved in, however, was ever stopped unexpectedly. Sometimes someone would send in a note with additional questions to ask, or a request for more details on a topic, and at other times we were given background information that could be incorporated into questioning, but I was never interrupted during any interrogation because of medical or security concerns.

As the time to start the first interrogation approached, the COB; the law enforcement interrogation expert; the physician; the psychologist; a handful of debriefers, report writers, and targeters; and a double handful of security personnel gathered outside Abu Zubaydah's cell to watch on closed circuit TV.

## Interrogations Begin

Abu Zubaydah seemed startled when I walked into his cell. I could tell he was wondering who I was. Although I had been watching him for almost six months, he had never laid eyes on me. He seemed nervous, maybe because he didn't recognize me or maybe because he wasn't seated and cuffed to the bars as was typical when someone entered his cell. It was probably both.

As I approached him, he circled the cell like a cat, staying at least an arm's length away from me, making intense eye contact. He initially glared at me and then softened his gaze when he figured out I wasn't there to attack him.

From the outside the cell seemed white and bright; it looked very different standing inside it. The lights shining into the cell created a shadow barrier that made peering more than a couple of feet beyond the cell bars almost impossible. I had been in a bad rock band when I was a kid, and the feeling was similar to being on stage trying to look out into the audience. It was also warmer than I had expected. I figured it was because of the lights.

I started by asking him what he would like me to call him. He said, "Zayn." Then I said, "I understand, Zayn, that you and al-Qa'ida have declared war on the United States. In your diary and your discussions with my friends who questioned you before, you mentioned several different attacks you'd like to see take place in the United States." I listed the attacks.

He said yes in a matter-of-fact fashion.

I went on, "You even said you would like to see a nuclear bomb set off in the United States. And you talked about sending Abu Ameriki [the nickname he used for José Padilla, an American-born al-Qa'ida operative] to KSM so that he could later join others KSM already had on the ground in the United States and set off a dirty bomb. But you only gave us vague information, held back details about how he was traveling, and claimed you didn't know his real name. We caught him and know that's not true. And you talked about other attacks, but each time you gave only vague information, or claimed you didn't remember important points, or tried to distract us with dead ends and stuff you made up."

We continued to circle each other in the center of the cell. He was listening intently. I could see he was wondering where I was going with this.

I said, "Washington thinks you are holding back important details that could help us stop operations in the United States and save innocent lives. That's what we want . . . information to stop operations inside the United States. We know you don't have all of it, but you have some of it and Washington thinks you're deliberately keeping it from us."

He just looked at me and shrugged. He seemed to be saying, "So what?" with his body language.

"Zayn," I said, "in every man's life there are moments of opportunity that open and close. Moments of choice when the decision you make forever changes what happens to you. This is one of those moments. I want to be sure you understand that, because you only have until I walk out of this room to determine what happens next. If you work with us and try to provide full and complete answers, even if you don't know everything, we will improve your conditions and nothing bad will happen. But if you jerk us around, if you try to hide information or disengage like you did when my friends tried to talk to you, you won't like what happens next. The decision is yours."

I then asked him one of the questions the targeters and analysts had developed. He shook his head and said, "I don't have anything for you." We continued to circle each other. I don't know how long this went on, but I gave him ample time to change his answer. I encouraged. I told him I was disappointed. He made a "what did you expect?" face. I asked the same question again in a different way. He indicated that he understood what I wanted. I reiterated that although I knew he might not know everything, he knew something that would help us answer this question, some small detail, a snippet of conversation, something he had overheard or been told at a meeting, travel arrangements he had made, or documents he had forged.

Nothing. I got no response from him. I asked another question. Again he just looked at me blankly. This went on a bit longer, and I realized he was pushing the test button, testing to see if I was bluffing, something that trained resisters do to distinguish real threats from bluffs. I shrugged and said, "It's your choice. You can stop this anytime. The next time someone comes in to question you, they're going to ask you this question." I told him the question and said, "How you answer will determine what happens next."

Then I think I signaled the guards, and they brought in a large wooden black box. It was about as big as a wooden crate one would need to ship a full-sized American refrigerator, only taller. It was big enough for him to stand in, but if you were claustrophobic, you would not want to be placed in it. Abu Zubaydah stared at it.

Following the headquarters-approved interrogation plan, I told Abu Zubaydah, "This is your new home." I motioned, and the guards placed him inside.

Abu Zubaydah was given a lidded bucket he could use to go to the bathroom in and sit on if he grew tired of standing. He was left in the box overnight. The box was monitored continuously by medical personnel. While he was in the stand-up box, we built a "walling wall" in his cell. A walling wall is a flexible wooden wall built of quarter-inch plywood with no studs in the middle of its span and a plywood clapper suspended inside. It is intentionally designed to have a lot of give and make a loud noise when someone's shoulders are bounced off it. It's disorienting because of the noise and the movement of fluid in the inner ear.

Early the next morning, the guards opened the box, shackled Abu Zubaydah, hooded him, took him out, and placed him against the newly built walling wall. Bruce put the rolled-up towel we used as a safety collar around his neck and pulled him forward into an attention grasp. He then bounced Abu Zubaydah's shoulders off the walling wall maybe three or four times. Each time it made a big boom. It was like when professional wrestlers throw each other around the ring. The noise is more dramatic than the effect.

After that, Bruce put Abu Zubaydah's back against the walling wall and slowly pulled off the hood. Bruce then asked him the question I had instructed him to think about at the end of the last session. This is called bridging. It reorients the person being questioned to the last session and signals that you are not going to forget what you were asking him before. It is important to start each new session with the bridging question even if your primary intent in the current session is to ask about other topics. That is the time when detainees who wish to avoid the next EIT session most often begin to answer questions on point. Once they started cooperating, we often would get the most useful information early because the detainees had the opportunity to think about the bridging question between debriefings. Of course, it also gives a detainee time to fabricate a response, but in the beginning we asked questions we already knew the answers to or information that analysts could easily verify on the basis of information they either already had or could readily check.

Years later, Abu Zubaydah reported to the International Committee of the Red Cross (ICRC) that he was initially bounced head-first off a concrete wall. That did not happen. He didn't know he was against the flexible walling wall. Because he was hooded when his shoulders were bounced off it, he didn't know it was there. I think he assumed it was the concrete wall because concrete was what his cell walls were made of when he was put in the box and he hadn't seen the walling wall yet. The notion that he was rammed headfirst into a concrete wall is an exaggeration. The guards were there to protect

Abu Zubaydah from us as much as to protect us from him. The COB, medical personnel, and operational psychologist would have stopped the session immediately and reported us to headquarters if we had done that.

Abu Zubaydah's answer to the bridging question was vague and meaningless. It was clear that he still wasn't ready to provide any new information. He continued to claim ignorance or answer with vague generalities with no information value. Therefore, Bruce used a few of the other EITs, such as the facial hold and facial slap and a stress position that wouldn't irritate Abu Zubaydah's injury, while asking questions and demanding answers. When Bruce was convinced Abu Zubaydah would not be forthcoming, he ended the session with the same bridging question I had left Zubaydah with at the end of the previous session. Abu Zubaydah was put back in the stand-up box.

Bruce and I then went for a long walk. This would become our habit after sessions using EITs, especially the ones involving waterboarding. We didn't like using EITs, and we used the walks to think about what we were being asked to do and consider whether we were making the right decision in continuing. I often felt that I was balancing my sense of morality against the cost of innocent lives. Because there was credible intelligence that another wave of catastrophic attacks was imminent, I couldn't bring myself to soothe my conscience by putting the lives of others at risk. Neither, I think, could Bruce. But we had a line, and we checked every day to be sure we hadn't crossed it.

Later, after headquarters approved, the decision was made to move on to waterboarding. Although I did not know it at the time, I have since been told that every time there was a significant escalation in interrogation techniques, Washington had to give its okay.

With the exception of the short description the CIA sent to the Justice Department for approval, I have yet to see an accurate depiction of how waterboarding was carried out in this program. I've read numerous accounts in the press and seen several videos of journalists being waterboarded, but none of them accurately represented what was done in our program.

Ever since he had been moved from the hospital to the black site, physicians had kept Abu Zubaydah on a diet of mostly red beans and rice. Medical personnel wanted ten hours to pass after a meal before he was waterboarded. They also required us to waterboard him on a full-size hospital gurney, one of the wheeled ones used in surgery suites and emergency rooms. They reasoned that in case of medical emergency, he would already be on a gurney for treatment. It was awkward, but the gurney could be reclined to a 45-degree angle. The guards had practiced lifting the head end of the gurney with a volunteer roughly Abu Zubaydah's size strapped to it to ensure that Zubaydah's head could be raised quickly and safely to a vertical position to clear his sinuses after longer pours. It was doable, but it took a lot of people. One guard timed how long the water was poured and counted off the seconds with his fingers. Other guards were positioned at various spots around the gurney for lifting and security.

Bruce poured the water out of a one-liter plastic bottle, and I controlled the duration of the pours by standing at the top by Abu Zubaydah's head, raising and lowering a black cloth to cover his face. When I lowered the cloth, Bruce was to pour. I would watch the guard count out the seconds. When I raised the cloth, Bruce was to stop immediately. The legal guidance said we could pour water for twenty to forty seconds, allow the person to breathe unimpeded for three or four breaths, and then lower the cloth and pour water for another twenty to forty seconds, and so on, for twenty minutes. That would have been one waterboarding session with multiple applications or pours of water.

However, it quickly became apparent that twenty seconds was

too long for the shortest pour. During one of the longer pours, Abu Zubaydah seemed slow to expel the water from his sinuses. After the guards raised him to a vertical position, I waited a couple of heartbeats and then pressed on his chest, and he immediately cleared. Shortly after that, to our surprise, even though more than the recommended ten hours had passed since his last meal, Abu Zubaydah threw up undigested beans and rice. (This prompted medical personnel to switch him to a diet of Ensure.) As they had practiced, the guards immediately raised the gurney so that Abu Zubaydah wouldn't breathe in any thrown-up food.

It was an ugly sight. Abu Zubaydah had beans and rice stuck to his face and in his chest hair. Because the fluid around his lips was kind of thick, it bubbled as he breathed in and out. We wiped it off with a hood and waited what seemed like a long time to see if medical personnel were going to intervene. When they didn't (although one stuck his head in the door for a confirming glance) and we were sure Abu Zubaydah was breathing properly, we did one or two more short pours so that he didn't get the idea that a dramatic display would stop the procedures. Then we took him off the waterboard.

I decided on the spot to shorten the pours. It seemed to me that most of the pours should not be longer than three to ten seconds, with no more than two pours lasting twenty seconds and only one pour lasting forty seconds. I didn't think it was safe to take full advantage of the length of time Justice Department guidance would have allowed us to pour water on the cloth or to use as much water as was permitted. I reasoned that if the Justice Department approved a pour of twenty seconds, it should not object to ones much shorter than that. When I had the chance, I checked with a CTC attorney, and he agreed.

Critics of the program assert that there was some evil motive behind my shortening the length of time water was poured on the cloth. They assume the end result somehow made the experience rougher on the detainees we waterboarded. But that is not the case. We did not exceed the total number of pours the Office of Legal Counsel's guidance would have allowed. In addition, by shortening the pours, we actually allowed the detainees to breathe more often and used less water than the OLC required.

It has often been alleged that we waterboarded Abu Zubaydah eighty-three times. This is nonsense. Eighty-three is the number of times Bruce tipped the bottle and poured water. Abu Zubaydah later told the ICRC that he was waterboarded five times. That is closer to the correct number of times he was strapped to the gurney and subjected to the technique.

During the waterboarding session we told Abu Zubaydah that we wanted information to stop operations inside the United States. We wanted to know what the plots were, when they were going to happen, who was involved, and where the attacks were going to occur. We said he could stop what was happening to him immediately if he showed us he was willing to provide information that could help locate the people involved.

We paused at several points during the session when Abu Zubaydah said something. We would listen to what he had to say and then ask, "Is what you're telling me going to help us stop operations in the United States?"

He would say, "No."

"I thought not," one of us would say, and we would go back to waterboarding him.

In that first session, Abu Zubaydah was so panicked that we didn't think he would provide reliable information on the waterboard. We weren't expecting him to. The program was not designed to extract information while the EITs were being administered. It wasn't pour water, demand a confession, pour water, ask a leading question. That was not how it worked. We weren't looking for a false confession and had to avoid asking him leading questions because we did not want him making up what he thought we wanted to hear.

The waterboard induces fear and panic. It is scary and uncomfortable but not painful. I know because I was waterboarded in July 2002 during practice and preparations for using the waterboard as one of the enhanced interrogation techniques. Both Bruce and I thought it was important that we experience what Abu Zubaydah was going to experience so that we could better assess his reaction. We knew Abu Zubaydah would dread the next session and wanted to plant the idea that there was a clear way to avoid it. He could simply start answering questions before it began. It was like dealing with someone who dreads going to the dentist. Apprehension builds in the hours between waterboard sessions. The closer it gets to the next one, the more he looks for ways to avoid it. We wanted to be sure he understood there was a clear way to stop the next session before it began. Abu Zubaydah's highest level of apprehension occurred when he was hooded and stood against the walling wall just before the next session started; that was the time he would be most apt to offer useful information he had been withholding. Thus, when the waterboard session ended and before he was left in his cell, we said, "The next time we come back, we are going to ask you this question," and then we told him the question. We then said, "Take some time, pull yourself together, and think about it. Because if you answer our questions the next time, this won't happen again."

This was the pattern. We would do one interrogation session in the morning using EITs without the waterboard and one session in the afternoon with the waterboard. Because of concerns about the next wave of attacks, the early interrogations always started with a focus on attacks inside the United States and for the first few days remained there. But headquarters started sending intelligence requirements that, though still related to attacks on the U.S. homeland, focused on locational information for al-Qa'ida operatives in general, their leadership structure, and their capabilities. We also questioned him about potential overseas attacks on U.S. interests or allies. We showed Abu Zubaydah photographs of terrorists to identify and asked him how he would go about locating those people if he were to escape or be set free.

We started sprinkling these questions into our interrogations. After about seventy-two hours, Abu Zubaydah gradually started answering them, but he did more than that. Over time, where he previously had pleaded ignorance or provided short vague answers lacking detail, he started putting his answers into a larger context, providing background and unsolicited details on the topics we were asking about. He acknowledged knowing very well people he previously had described as mere acquaintances and described his interactions with them beyond the narrow focus of the question, often walking us through conversations he had had with them while providing personal details about their background, relatives, known associates, and training. He started providing fuller and more complete answers about al-Qa'ida's leadership and structure. Headquarters started sending more and more intelligence requirements that focused on al-Qa'ida's organizational structure, its key members, their decision-making processes, their operational intent, and their current capabilities.

As Abu Zubaydah began to offer up information that the targeters and analysts on-site judged valuable and wanted more of, we asked for permission to stop using EITs, especially the waterboard. To our surprise, however, headquarters ordered us to continue waterboarding him. None of us at the black site liked hearing this. For several days in a row we questioned the necessity of continuing the EITs, but every day we received cables, phone calls, or e-mails instructing us to continue waterboarding Abu Zubaydah. At one point Bruce and I pushed back hard and threatened to quit. We were told, "He's turning you; you are not turning him." The officers we were dealing with—midlevel CTC officials—really pissed us off by saying, "You've lost your spines." They insisted that if we didn't keep waterboarding Abu Zubaydah and another attack happened in the United States, it would be "your fault."

Faced with this, we did two things. The COB, our leader at the black site, conveyed our concerns to the chief of station (COS), the CIA officer in charge in the country in which we were stationed. And Bruce and I dialed back the intensity of the EITs we were using.

The COS had been keeping up with developments but wanted a better sense of our concerns. He wanted to observe Abu Zubaydah being waterboarded. When he visited the black site, I recommended that we suit him up in the head-to-toe black garb worn by the guards and have him in the room when we waterboarded Abu Zubaydah. Bruce objected. He pulled me out of the meeting and told me that to him it seemed voyeuristic, unnecessary, and demeaning to Abu Zubaydah's dignity. I agreed. It was all those things. But I feared that watching Abu Zubaydah being waterboarded on a monitor wouldn't convey the intensity of it. It was just too sterile, like watching a video game. I thought the COS needed to be in the cell, where he could hear Abu Zubaydah, smell the smells, and feel the spray of water and snot when Abu Zubaydah cleared his sinuses. But I had another, more compelling reason. Because the sessions were being recorded, I wanted somebody important on those tapes with us, especially if they were going to try to force us to continue. Bruce didn't buy my first argument, but he accepted the second.

After he observed Abu Zubaydah being waterboarded, the COS set up a videoconference with the leadership at the CTC so that we could discuss the issue. Those of us at the black site thought that those at headquarters didn't have a good idea what waterboarding was really like. They talked about it as if it were some kind of sterile, impersonal procedure. Therefore, to prepare for the conference call, the criminal investigator at the site spliced together a video of what a typical waterboarding session looked like and then added in multiple scenes of Abu Zubaydah clearing water from his sinuses taken from several different sessions.

Jose Rodriguez chaired the videoconference. My take was that he was trying to be an honest arbitrator of the issue. He seemed focused on preventing another attack inside the United States and wanted to do it in the most straightforward way possible. He was being assailed by advocates on both side of the argument but seemed objective and not locked in on any single approach. We showed the videotape and voiced our opinion that we didn't need to continue using EITs, especially waterboarding. Not surprisingly, some in the room with Rodriguez objected. One or two objected vigorously. They insisted we continue waterboarding Abu Zubaydah for at least thirty days. That was when it dawned on me that my answer months before to Jose Rodriguez's question about how long it would take for me to believe a person subjected to EITs "either didn't have the information or was going to take it to the grave with them" had come back to haunt us. I pointed out that that comment was made before waterboarding was incorporated into the list of potential EITs and didn't apply anymore. Bruce and I told them we would not continue routinely waterboarding Abu Zubaydah. We asked them to send their "most skeptical" analyst or targeter and some high-ranking person whose honesty and integrity they trusted to observe a waterboarding session and then subsequently question Abu Zubaydah without EITs.

Those of us at the black site believed that if they came and saw in person the kind and quality of information Abu Zubaydah was providing, they would agree that we didn't need to continue harsh interrogations. For our part, Bruce and I firmly believed that Abu Zubaydah would go beyond just answering their questions and would recognize what they were looking for and volunteer unasked for details and clarifications they might not have thought of.

The videoconference ended with them agreeing to send the people we requested and our obtaining permission to suspend waterboarding Abu Zubaydah until the visitors arrived, at which time we would waterboard him for what Bruce and I agreed between ourselves would be one last time. We didn't want to waterboard him again, but we believed if we didn't, we probably would be replaced by other people who would not be as reluctant to use coercion as we were.

The officers we requested from headquarters arrived, headed by a highly respected senior operations officer and accompanied by the person who had been most skeptical about stopping the harsh interrogations in our back-and-forth communication with headquarters and during the videoconference. There were others. I don't remember all of them, but one was a CTC senior attorney. I was glad to see him.

We waterboarded Abu Zubaydah with them in the cell, unmasked and on camera. It was ugly and hard to do. After it was over, we washed Abu Zubaydah with warm water, cleaned him up, and told him we never wanted to do that again. He cried and promised to work for the CIA. Everyone, even those observing, was tearful.

Later in the day, after Abu Zubaydah had a chance to recover, the senior officer in charge of the visitors and the most skeptical person took turns questioning him. They spent hours with him. They came out seemingly pleased with the information they obtained, saying he was a "treasure trove" of knowledge. They agreed we should stop EITs because the information we could get without them was too important and could be combined with other intelligence and used to stop attacks. They spent several more days questioning Abu

Zubaydah, having in-depth conversations with maps and charts and photographs. Then they left.

About a week passed. Abu Zubaydah was answering questions. He was providing information on Ramzi bin al-Shibh, one of KSM's operatives, who he said was probably in Karachi, Pakistan, working with KSM. Bin al-Shibh was later caught and provided information that helped us capture KSM. Abu Zubaydah was providing fuller and more complete answers to questions about terrorists who could move in and out of the United States with relative ease, such as Jafar al-Tayyar, a U.S. citizen with pilot training who had lived in Florida. During this time, Abu Zubaydah was also providing information that helped lead to the capture of Hassan Ghul, whose information about Usama bin Ladin's courier helped lead to the location and killing of bin Ladin.

We were told his answers were being verified and more often than not were truthful. Then we received notification that headquarters was considering restarting EITs on him. We were confused. He seemed to be trying to answer our questions, and I hadn't seen him employ any of the resistance techniques he had used earlier. It seemed obvious that the analysts at headquarters were bothered by something they hadn't shared with us.

They were. It turned out that when Abu Zubaydah was captured, he had several videotapes in his possession with short scenes of him claiming credit for attacks. Initially they did not tell us about the tapes, perhaps thinking that knowledge of their existence would somehow color our interrogation.

I believe that it was these tapes that were prompting headquarters to reconsider EITs.

Abu Zubaydah needed to clearly and credibly explain the purpose of those tapes. We told him that headquarters was thinking about going back to the "bad times," which is what he called the harsh interrogations, unless he came clean about why he had made the tapes and what he intended to do with them.

Abu Zubaydah quickly and convincingly explained their origin. He said that he had been captured about two weeks before his planned departure from Pakistan for Iran, where he intended to set up his own jihadi group, which would be like al-Qa'ida. Although he had no problem with al-Qa'ida wanting to attack the United States, what he was most interested in was focusing on attacks against the Jews in Israel. Al-Qa'ida, he said, didn't seem very interested in that. Abu Zubaydah told us that al-Qa'ida leaders insisted that if you destroyed America, you would "cut the head off the snake." Not happy with that strategy, he was planning on setting up his own organization so that he could target Israel instead.

The most difficult part of setting up your own terror cell, he explained, was obtaining funding. He claimed to have $500,000 but said that wasn't going to be enough. For him to raise more money, he reasoned, donors needed to see him in the news claiming credit for terror attacks. At the same time, he knew the United States was hunting him and feared that having his face on TV would make it easier for the Americans to capture him. He then came up with the idea of filming lots of short videos of him claiming credit for attacks and then getting plastic surgery to change his appearance. He speculated that if he was on TV with Abu Zubaydah's old face claiming credit for new attacks, his surgically altered new face would make it safer for him to move around and avoid capture. Immediately after he made the videos, he had plastic surgery. But, he said, the Pakistani doctor who did it was, in his words, a "quack," the operation was botched, and he got an infection that made him go blind in one eye. The surgery was intended to soften his Arab features, but you could still recognize him from photographs. He was disappointed. The officers writing reports passed his explanation back to headquarters, and we received no more threats of restarting harsh interrogations from them.

Some human rights groups have publicly accused the CIA of blinding Abu Zubaydah, speculating that he now has to wear an eye patch because of injuries incurred during some brutal interrogation gone wrong. The truth is, however, that Abu Zubaydah's pirate look was the result of his own attempt to become a terrorist Internet celebrity while hiding in plain sight. Abu Zubaydah is blind in his left eye because he wanted to be famous and came up with a comic book scheme to make it happen. He wanted to be a supervillain, the face of terror on the Internet, raising money to attack and kill innocent victims while living the high life safely, protected by a new face. As often happens with people driven by twisted ambition, it backfired on him.

We used EITs on Abu Zubaydah for a little over two weeks total. We didn't use them again. After that, Bruce and I spent over seventy days questioning him using noncoercive, rapport-based, and social influence approaches before I left the black site and Bruce stayed to continue the mission without me. Headquarters wanted one of us to take a break so that we could rotate being at the black site. I was told to go home first because in the previous seven months I had spent less than nine days at home.

I left feeling good about what we had accomplished. I knew Abu Zubaydah was continuing to hold back some information—they all did—but he was cooperative enough that headquarters seemed pleased with the information he was providing. The targeters and analysts told me that his information had increased their understanding of the enemy significantly. They said they had combined his information with intelligence from other sources and were using it actively to disrupt future attacks and capture terrorists who were still at large. I believed them. I had seen Abu Zubaydah progress from using resistance-to-interrogation techniques to thwart questioning to answering questions with details beyond the scope of what was being asked. I was certain he would be pivotal to helping us capture the terrorists who had attacked us on 9/11.

# CHAPTER 3

# The *Cole* Bomber

On October 12, 2000, the guided missile destroyer USS *Cole* was at anchor in the Yemeni seaport of Aden refueling. A small boat pulled alongside the warship, and when it got close—too close—an enormous explosive charge was detonated, killing seventeen American sailors and injuring thirty-nine. The billion-dollar warship nearly sank thanks to a few thousand dollars of explosives and several young Arab men willing to martyr themselves.

ABD AL-RAHIM AL-NASHIRI was the amir, or commander, of the *Cole* attack. As a reward for his success, al-Qa'ida promoted him to its chief of operations in the Arabian Peninsula, commanding cells of radical jihadists spread throughout the region, all of them plotting terror attacks.

It took a little more than two years, but al-Nashiri finally was captured in the United Arab Emirates (UAE) in November 2002.

When apprehended, al-Nashiri was in the final stages of completing operational plans for al-Qa'ida suicide bombers to crash a small plane into another Western warship, this one anchored in Port Rashid in the UAE.


**SINCE I INITIALLY** had been deployed immediately after Abu Zubaydah's capture, I had been away from home more than 206 days. This stretch had been broken only once five months earlier, and then for less than nine days. Now I was home again, looking forward to a longer break, but that wasn't to be.

I was home less than a week when my summons to CIA headquarters came about midday. "Drop whatever you're doing and report to CIA headquarters immediately," I was told by the voice on the phone. "Be prepared to deploy to some undisclosed location for an unspecified period of time." Unlike my first deployment for the CTC, this time I had a chance to bring functional shoes and more than one pair of pants.

On arrival at CIA headquarters, I was told they had captured al-Nashiri and wanted me on the rendition flight that was taking him from where he was being held temporarily to a black site. "You can use the flight to get a sense of what he's like," my briefer said, "and start interrogations as soon as he arrives at the black site."

Being on board the renditions flight also would give me a chance to talk to those holding him, providing an opportunity to discuss how he had reacted to his initial questioning and to hear firsthand what he had told them.

At headquarters, I was introduced to a subject matter expert who had targeted al-Nashiri. She too would be on the rendition flight and stay for his initial interrogations. Her job was to guide those of us interrogating al-Nashiri through the maze of chatter and threat reporting, pull the information we needed from the CIA's enormous resources, and write the cables and reports headquarters wanted. She was to receive intelligence requirements sent by headquarters and provide us with enough background details to put them in context. Her most important job was to take what al-Nashiri said and turn it into raw intelligence. A dark-haired, scary-smart ball of energy— that's how I remember her.

Another person on the rendition flight who would stay during al-Nashiri's initial interrogations was our linguist. Al-Nashiri's English was poor, and so it was important to have a translator skilled enough to do real-time simultaneous word-for-word translations. Word-for-word translations are critical because many indicators of deception are flagged by *how* things are said as much as by *what* is said. As an interrogator, I didn't want a translator to tell me what he or she (the interpreter) thought al-Nashiri meant. I wanted a precise translation. Our linguist for this mission was superb. He was about ten years older than I, with silver hair and wise eyes, and was quick to smile. I told him what I needed.

"No problem with simultaneous word-for-word translations," he said. "And I spent years moving money around the Middle East, so I know the dialect and slang of Saudi Arabs of Yemeni descent. I can catch weasel words and highlight inconsistencies."

Perfect, I thought.

When it came time to hand over al-Nashiri, an SUV and chase cars sped across the asphalt taxiway toward our aircraft. On arrival, al-Nashiri was helped out of the vehicle transporting him. His hands were cuffed. He wore Arab dress, consisting of a white thoub, a one-piece gown that covers the whole body, and a shumagg, a red and white scarflike head cover. The only thing missing was the ogal, the heavy black rope band that sits on top of the head to hold Arab headgear in place. It was missing for safety reasons.

Arab officers who were dressed similarly flanked al-Nashiri and slowly walked him across the tarmac toward our plane, head scarves flapping in the wind. I was surprised at how small he was. I had expected the *Cole* bomber to be imposing, but he was just a little man in Arab dress.

The handover was done in silence. Our crew, wearing black ski masks, took physical control of al-Nashiri by placing him in a grappling hold that I won't describe here for security reasons. I don't want our enemies to be able to train to defeat it.

They checked al-Nashiri for weapons, traded out handcuffs, and then stripped him. Medical personnel on the flight performed a quick exam and cavity search and then photographed al-Nashiri to document his physical condition at the handover.

Al-Nashiri was re-dressed in a dark sweatshirt and sweatpants. His eyes were covered with a blindfold. Earphones attached to a cassette player that was playing music were placed over his ears to limit what he could hear during the flight. Then he was hooded, feet shackled, and led, almost carried, onto the plane, all without anyone talking. The only noises were the wind, the sound of vehicles idling, and bird calls off in the distance.

Then something happened that set back our interrogation of al-Nashiri.

As I was getting ready to board the aircraft, the CIA officers handing over the detainee tried to give me a letter-size envelope with a photocopy of an address book he had had with him when he was captured. In it, al-Nashiri had handwritten names and phone numbers with cash amounts penned next to them in the margins. The CIA officers had made a copy of that address book to send along so that the interrogation team could start questioning al-Nashiri about what was in it as soon as we reached the black site and started the interrogations.

The address book wasn't in code, and so anyone able to read Arabic could translate what was there. But you couldn't deduce what the money was for or how it fit into the bigger picture of al-Nashiri's various attack plans. Nor could you infer where the jihadists listed in that address book currently were or what they were doing. Al-Nashiri would have to provide that information, and it would be much easier, once interrogations started, to keep him on track if we could point to a name and question him about the notes he had scribbled in the margin next to it.

However, security personnel on the aircraft refused to let me bring the photocopied pages of the address book on board even though once they were out of the envelope, there were fewer than a dozen loose pages of ordinary copy paper. They were adamant, insisting that it was against regulations. They told me they couldn't let me bring the photocopy paper on board because it might be "a potential explosive hazard."

Bullshit, I thought. For years early in my air force career, I was an explosive ordnance disposal (EOD) technician. I know the difference between copy paper and explosives. The local CIA officer holding the loose pages stood there, looking at us as if we had completely lost our minds, saying something like, "It's just paper. It's been in our custody the whole time."

I thought the security guys were being unnecessarily cautious and said so, but the mission commander concurred with them, and the copy of the address book was left behind. In my opinion, that refusal set back the interrogations by several days while the address book circuitously made its way via official channels first to CIA headquarters and then, after multiple frantic requests, back across the world to the black site where we were questioning al-Nashiri.

·    ·    ·

**WHEN I GOT** off the plane after the first leg of the journey at an intermediary stop, Bruce was waiting on the tarmac, but I didn't recognize him. He was kitted up with protective gear and weapons. His hair, usually short, was long and scraggly. He had a scruffy full beard and wore a headdress and overvest that made him blend with the locals so that he wouldn't stand out so much as an American.

I walked right by him, a man I'd worked next to for fourteen years. I would have kept going if he hadn't called my name. Even then, after we made eye contact, I didn't know who he was until I recognized his voice when he greeted me.

Because of the threat level and because al-Nashiri had been captured in the act of putting together a terror attack, headquarters didn't want us to wait until he was settled in at the black site days later to find out if he was willing to answer questions. If he was, they wanted us to start servicing intelligence requirements right away. Therefore, while we were waiting for the follow-on aircraft, I conducted the neutral probe to assess whether al-Nashiri would be willing to answer questions without us having to use EITs.

I had been told al-Nashiri was uncooperative before being handed over to the CIA. He mentioned a few attack plans but refused to provide actionable details. Those holding him said he taunted them and tried to bargain for his release. But people can and often do change their minds, even terrorists, and I had no interest in getting rough if it was unnecessary. We always preferred not to have to use EITs.

I questioned al-Nashiri in a long, narrow makeshift interrogation room. It was part of a complex of rooms and cells situated inside a big steel building on some dusty back road that I couldn't find again if I had a map to the place and a GPS. The rooms were plywood boxes plopped down inside a giant windowless shed. Twenty feet or more of open space reared up between the top of the enclosed box that made up the room and the tin roof barely visible in the over-head gloom. The interrogation room had plywood walls and halogen lamps on yellow tree stands, the kinds of lamps you might see in an auto mechanic's garage or on a construction site. Dust was every-where. You could see it drifting in the beams of the halogen lamps.

I positioned al-Nashiri against one of the makeshift walls and pulled the black hood off his head. He blinked, looking up at me, eyes adjusting to the bright light that backlit me and hid the others in the room. I folded the hood and placed it around his neck like a shawl.

"What would you like me to call you?" I asked in a neutral tone.

"I'm Abd al-Rahim al-Nashiri," he said. "I'm also called Mullah Bilal, Bilal, and Abu Ahmad. I am the amir of the *Cole* attack. Allah be praised, we killed many American sailors." A thin smile crossed his face. It might have been nerves.

"Yes," I said. "Yes, you did. But that's not what I'm here to ask you about. I want to know about the other attacks you have planned. Someone told me you arranged to have explosives delivered for the attack on another warship, the attack you were working on just be-fore you were captured. I want to know where you were getting the explosives, who was delivering them, and where the explosives are now. And I want to know about other attacks you have planned, the ones against Americans."

"I told those other people holding me that if they took me to the Saudi border, gave me a car, and let me go, I would tell them where the explosives were as I drove away," he said. "I make you the same offer. I would shout it out the window as I drive off. I promise."

"Not going to happen," I said. "The people that handed you over to us told me you made that offer to them. They wouldn't do it, and I won't either. What I will do is give you the chance to avoid a lot of discomfort and distress later by answering questions now about the attack you had planned against the warship in Port Rashid or by telling me about some other attack. For example, who was bringing you the explosives? How were you planning on obtaining an aircraft? Now that you are captured, who will try to carry out the attack? That's a lot of questions, I know. But it will give you a sense of what I'm interested in."

"Just let me go," al-Nashiri said. "I can find my own way out of—" and he mentioned a country.

"What makes you think you're there?" I asked.

"The way it smells," he said. "I lived here. I know this place."

"I don't think you know where you are," I said, not willing to confirm or deny the location of our intermediate location. "And I'm not letting you go. It's just not going to happen," I said, realizing the interview was going nowhere and starting to transition into my "you-don't-have-a-lot-of-time-to-make-a-decision" pitch.

"I want information to stop operations," I said. "You have until I walk out of this room to show me that you're willing to answer questions in a civilized way; after that, you're not going to like what happens next."

"If you're not going to let me go, I have nothing to say to you."

"The next time someone talks to you," I said, moving into the bridging question, "he will ask about the Port Rashid attack. He will want to know who was working with you. Where that person is now. And what happened to the explosives. Answer any one of these questions and nothing bad will happen to you. Refuse and you will bring unnecessary misery upon yourself. It can be avoided."

The guards returned al-Nashiri to his cell. I followed them back. Although he wasn't in my custody, I felt responsible for him. I wanted to see where he would be spending the night. I didn't like the place; it resembled a horse stall more than a cell. I made sure he had water and plenty of blankets. I then told the indigenous guards that he was

not to be fooled with: no disciplinary action, no visitors, and no taking him out of his cell unless there was a genuine emergency. Then
I checked that his cuffs and shackles weren't too tight and left him.

Later, while the subject matter expert and I were standing in the
makeshift interrogation room discussing the report she was going to
send back to headquarters that evening, Bruce told me that another
detainee with an amazing resistance posture was being questioned in
a nearby room. Bruce said the detainee was refusing to acknowledge
who he was despite being confronted with a driver's license bearing
his photograph that the detainee had had on him when captured.
Bruce said the detainee was highly skilled at resisting interrogation
and tough. He steadfastly refused to give up any information while
maintaining a polite and apparently cooperative demeanor. Bruce
said the detainee was so good, he might have been resistance-trained.

As I was leaving the shed, I stopped by the room where the detainee was being interrogated. He was sitting on the floor with his
back against the plywood wall, his wrists and ankles raw and bloody
underneath handcuffs and shackles. He looked bad. Not sick so
much as just not right.

"How are you?" I asked.

"Very well, thank you," he said in perfect English. "And you?"

"I'm fine. Is there anything I can do for you? Anything I can get
you . . . or bring you?"

"No, thank you. I'm fine." He said it as casually as if we were
acquaintances who happened to bump into each other in the parking
lot of a coffee shop.

The CIA officer handed me the license with the detainee's photo
and said, "He says this isn't him. He's been insisting on that for days."

I wasn't there to interrogate the detainee, but I took the license,
looked at the photo, and showed it to him. Pointing to his picture, I
asked, "This isn't you?"

"No," he said. "That's not me. He looks like me, but I don't know who he is."

"It sure looks like you," I said, tilting my head to one side. "And you had it on you. Kind of suspicious, don't you think?"

"I know; it seems odd. I can't explain it, but it's not me. I don't know where they got that," he said, his voice calm and pleasant.

I didn't want to get into a prolonged exchange with the detainee. I just wanted to see firsthand his resistance posture, and so I handed the license back and asked if I could speak to the CIA officer questioning him outside the cell.

I was wondering why, if the agency was sure of the detainee's true identity, the focus was on getting him to admit who he was. My background in resistance training told me that focusing on getting him to confess his identity was providing the detainee with the opportunity to protect information that was more important. The focus gave him a chance to keep away from sensitive topics, to make interrogations nonproductive by keeping the focus on getting him to admit who he was. As a resistance technique, the goal is not to convince those questioning you that you're telling the truth but rather to convince them that you are not going to change your answer. And he definitely wasn't going to do that.

As I thought about it and listened to the CIA officer discuss the case, I realized that was indeed the goal of the detainee's resistance posture: to convince his questioners that he wasn't going to change his answers and to use his refusal to identify himself as a deliberate technique to circle away from sensitive areas and refocus the questioning on getting him to admit who he was. When asked about something he should know, given his identity, the detainee would claim there was no way he could know that kind of information since he wasn't that person.

I was told that the detainee displayed the same cordial but defiant resistance posture no matter what question they asked him. The thinking seemed to be that if they could get him to admit who he was, it would break his resistance and he might be more willing to answer other questions. We briefly discussed my impressions of the detainee's resistance posture; they matched what Bruce already had shared with the CIA officer. I did not offer any suggestions for how he should be interrogated. That was not why I was there.

"I think you need to get a medic down here to look at his wrists and ankles," I said as I was about to leave. "He doesn't look right to me."

The CIA officer said that he thought the same thing and that Bruce had mentioned it as well. He said he would ask the medic to stop by when he got a chance.

By coincidence, late that same afternoon I saw the medic as I was walking up the steps into the aging historic building used as CIA headquarters. I recognized him from another assignment. After a bit of small talk, I said, "When you get the chance, you might want to stop by the cells and check Gul Rahman's wrists and ankles. They look bad, and he doesn't look quite right."

"I can't. I don't have time for that," he said, shaking his head and looking over my shoulder into the distance. "I have hundreds of people to take care of and no real help. I'm swamped. I barely get any sleep as it is."

We exchanged words, and as I became more insistent, he flared and said, "I'm not here to provide medical care for fucking terrorists!" It was clear he felt overwhelmed and understaffed.

A few days later Gul Rahman was dead. (I mention him by name only because his death has been declassified and I don't want readers to think I'm talking about an unreported death.) Reports say he died of exposure after he had been mistreated by the indigenous guards.

It's easy in hindsight for people like me to postulate about what should have been done and criticize those who were there doing the real work. But I'm not going to do that, because Rahman certainly did not look like he was about to die when I saw him. Otherwise I would have pushed harder to get him seen. Maybe, in hindsight, I should have, but I didn't. When I saw him, he looked like he needed medical attention for his wrists and ankles. And I thought, based on the concerns Bruce and I raised and the things the CIA officer in charge of the facility had said, that Gul Rahman would be seen by medical personnel.

The description of Bruce's activities at this black site is an example of how Feinstein's Democratic staffers cherry-picked documents to create a misleading narrative. Their report leaves you with the false impression that Bruce did not raise concerns about the grim conditions or the brutal treatment of detainees at that site. I know that isn't true.

Bruce wrote a multipage report advising both headquarters and the host country COS that conditions at that site needed quick and drastic improvement. He raised concerns about the unsupervised brutality, recommended that trained interrogators be sent to the site, suggested that the CIA provide blankets and space heaters, cautioned that an American presence should be at the holding facility, especially at night, and advised that the guard force be changed from indigenous personnel, who may have had a beef with the detainees, to CIA security officers.

Bruce and I tried to brief the chief of station, but the COS would not meet with us. I also know Bruce discussed these recommendations when he returned to headquarters and met with the deputy chief of the CTC, who asked him in a good-natured way at the start of that meeting if he was the psychologist "creating a stir" by complaining about conditions at that black site. The deputy chief of the CTC heard Bruce out and showed interest in and concern about what he had to say. Later, Bruce outlined his observations and concerns to the CIA inspector general, John Helgerson. These documents should have been available to those putting together the Democrats' SSCI study.

But you don't get that impression when you read the Senate Select Committee on Intelligence majority report. Their selective use of cited source documents and the way they framed the narrative make it seem that Bruce recommended that conditions be made harsher rather than more humane. The opposite was true.

Feinstein's report also makes a big deal out of the fact that Bruce made interrogation recommendations. Of course he did. Although this site eventually would be brought under the control of the newly stood up Rendition, Detention, and Interrogation Group—a branch that consolidated the CIA's interrogation efforts under the supervision and control of one section—it was not yet part of that section, not part of the interrogation program for which we were working. That was why headquarters sent Bruce there: to provide recommendations for interrogating some of the detainees they were holding there and to question one in particular.

Two important facts were left out of Feinstein's report. First, Bruce raised concerns about the treatment of detainees and recommended that *if they were planning on using* EITs *at this site,* they should get the appropriate training and stick to interrogation techniques reviewed by the DOJ and approved by headquarters. Second, at the time of Gul Rahman's unfortunate death, this black site was not one of the enhanced interrogation program's facilities. It was under the control of the chief of station, the senior CIA officer for the country where it was situated. Headquarters simply arranged for us to hold al-Nashiri at the site temporarily while we waited for a follow-on flight to our final destination. CIA leadership moved the management of this troubled site under the newly created Rendition, Detention, and Interrogation (RDI) Group specifically to address the grave safety and management concerns raised by the detainee's death. Feinstein's report makes it seem like this black site was always an RDI facility and smears the people who were sent in to clean it up with mistakes that were made before they took over.

For me, on the ground at the time, I could tell it was headed for some sort of trouble. Bruce and I spent hours the day I flew in with al-Nashiri cataloging potential problems, and I know he reported them before Gul Rahman's death.

**EARLIER ON THE** day I arrived, we drove straight from the airport to where the detainees were being held. As evening approached, it became necessary to find a place to sleep. That was not an easy task. The place was crawling with CIA officers, and every spot where someone could sleep was crammed with personnel. People were stacked so tightly that in some cases they might as well have been sharing the same bed.

Bruce and I finally were assigned sleeping quarters in a converted broom closet where three army cots had been crowded into a space hardly large enough for two. We were almost on top of each other in our sleeping bags. We had to walk on the beds to enter and leave the room.

It was uncomfortable, but not as uncomfortable as the sleeping arrangements made for our linguist. He was assigned to sleep under the pool table in the bar, which remained open until after midnight. The next day, when our usually good-natured linguist showed up, he was a mess. Half his shirt was not tucked into his pants, his eyes were red, and his hair was askew. He complained bitterly about the noise in the bar.

"Horrible racket," he said. "Loud music and people shouting all night. They were playing pool right on top of the table I was under, trying to sleep. They stepped on my hands and kicked me in the head. I didn't get any rest at all. I had to scrunch up in a little ball. Noise and feet . . . all night long . . . noise and feet. Finger pain. Finger pain."

Bruce and I started laughing. The mental image of our digni-fied linguist lying under a pool table in one of the most popular bars in that region of the world, trying to sleep in all that racket while trained killers and intelligence officers from all over the world stepped on his fingers, seemed like something out of a situation com-edy on TV or a movie. Before he walked up, we had been bitching to each other about sleeping in that damn broom closet, but now we realized we had been given the cushy quarters.

Our laughter did not amuse the linguist, who familiarized us with a couple of Arabic cusswords and showed us one or two instruc-tive finger gestures.

Sometime on the second day, the aircraft we would use for the last leg of the rendition arrived. We watched it drop out of the sky, gathered our stuff, and followed the security convoy that took al-Nashiri to the plane.

Once there, al-Nashiri underwent the same preflight loading procedures as before. He was strip-searched, medically examined, cavity-searched, and reshackled for rendition. The security staff from the holding site had already blindfolded him, put on headphones, and hooded him.

A problem developed when we asked the mission commander about loading our bags. The commander said that we were not au-thorized to get on the plane. He said something about a new inter-rogation branch that was being stood up and said we weren't part of it. I told him that leaving us behind had to be a mistake because we were al-Nashiri's interrogation team. Headquarters had specifically ordered us to be on that rendition flight with al-Nashiri. I argued that because of the importance of interrogating al-Nashiri, it made no sense for him to arrive at the black site without us, thus delaying the interrogations. The mission commander still refused. I asked him how we were to get to the black site if not on the rendition aircraft.

"Don't know, don't care," he said.

I suggested that he contact headquarters for clarification.

"Given the importance of questioning al-Nashiri as quickly as possible," I said, "there will be a shit storm back home if the rendition aircraft leaves us, al-Nashiri's interrogation team, stranded, delaying interrogations unnecessarily."

He said that people stuck where we were were always trying to scam rides off of them.

"We aren't trying to scam a ride," I said. "We are just trying to do our job the way headquarters told us to. Leave us here and I'll make sure that headquarters knows where to direct that shit storm."

Eventually, the mission commander agreed to let me and Bruce on the plane but didn't want to take the subject matter expert or the linguist. I refused to get on the plane without them, and finally, after a lot of bickering, we were all allowed to board.


ONCE AT THE black site, we reviewed the intelligence requirements and then submitted a detailed interrogation plan and waited for approval to proceed from headquarters.

While we were waiting, Bruce and I talked with Abu Zubaydah about waterboarding. By then he had been cooperating for several months, and even though I hadn't seen him for a couple of weeks, I was confident he would help if he could. I thought he was the best source available to help us fully understand how Islamic terrorists were likely to respond to the waterboard and how we could avoid using it, if possible. We told him that we didn't like doing it. We asked him to help us come up with some way to get the brothers to provide information we could use to stop attacks, information they were trying to protect, without the use of waterboarding or other harsh interrogation techniques.

"No, no," Abu Zubaydah said adamantly. "You must do this for all the brothers. If you don't and he talks, the brother has sinned. Allah will punish him."

"I'm not following," I said, thinking I had misheard him. "You think we should use harsh techniques more often?"

"No," he said. "Not more often; only enough. Allah does not expect more of a man than he is capable," Abu Zubaydah explained. "He knows our limitations. Allah does not expect me to lift a mountain and is not disappointed when I can't. There is no sin. Once a brother has held out as long as he can and cannot hold out any longer, he has fulfilled his obligation to Allah and there is no sin in answering questions."

"Are you saying we need to push brothers to the point that they can't hold out any longer each time we want a question answered or it's a sin for them to tell us what we want to know?" I asked, not liking the idea.

"No," Abu Zubaydah said. "A brother doesn't have to hold out as much as he can each time. Allah does not expect me to go around trying to lift mountains when I know in my heart I can't. As long as the brother knows he will eventually be forced to give up information, he can answer questions and still keep faith with Allah."

I said, "This sounds like a justification for using hard times [Abu Zubaydah's term for EITs] on all the brothers."

"Not so," Abu Zubaydah said. "That would be a mistake. The line is different for each brother. Some brothers are incapable of withstanding any hard times. They will talk without pain. Other brothers can stand a great deal to protect secrets. Allah will look into their hearts and know. If a brother who can take more pain to protect secrets doesn't, then Allah will know and he will punish him. You must only use as much as Allah would expect to help the brother and no more. If you use more than you need to, Allah will know and he will punish you."


**AT THE START** of the first enhanced interrogation al-Nashiri was given the opportunity to answer the bridging question before any EITs were used. He refused. He also refused to answer any questions generated by the intelligence requirements. He would not talk about attacks he was planning against American interests inside or outside the United States, but he did say he would talk about the *Cole* attack. He seemed proud of and almost bragged about the number of Americans he had killed. But we weren't there for a confession. When it became clear that he had no intention of cooperating, we began to use the EITs.

At some point, following the headquarters-approved plan, al-Nashiri was waterboarded. But not without difficulty. He was a really small guy. Security personnel had trouble securely strapping him to the large hospital gurney that the medical personnel wanted us to use as a waterboard at the time. When the guards stood the gurney up on end so that he could clear his sinuses, al-Nashiri would slide down, and his arms and hands would almost slip out from under the wide Velcro bands designed to hold him in place. We were concerned that he would fall off the gurney and get hurt. We were all feeling uncomfortable, but Bruce was the first to state it aloud.

The interrogation team discontinued waterboarding al-Nashiri after three sessions. Problems strapping him to the gurney were not the deciding factor. There was another, more compelling reason we stopped without trying to find an alternative method of securing al-Nashiri to the gurney.

We didn't have to, because al-Nashiri started offering up bits and pieces of information before the next EIT session started, and we began switching to noncoercive social influence techniques to question him. His address book finally had arrived at the black site, and al-Nashiri started to open up about who the jihadists listed in the book were and what the money he had written in the margins next to the names was for. Although not fully cooperative, he gave us enough help to convince us that the harshest of our approved tactics no longer were needed.

Because Abu Zubaydah was being held in a nearby cell and by that point was answering questions quite helpfully, we were able to ask him about the people al-Nashiri named and the attack plans al-Nashiri disclosed. We would leave al-Nashiri's cell, walk over to Abu Zubaydah's, and ask him, "Who is this brother? Tell us about his activities." If we had photographs of al-Nashiri's men, we could show them to Abu Zubaydah—without sharing with him what al-Nashiri had offered up—and compare what he had to say with what al-Nashiri told us. Often Abu Zubaydah knew the men. He had trained some of them. He was forthcoming and provided us with information we could use to get al-Nashiri to elaborate more fully on some areas of interest to headquarters.

As our questioning of al-Nashiri continued, he discussed a number of attack plans. His answers were often so vague about actionable details that some at headquarters didn't want to abandon EITs altogether; however, his answers were not so vague that Bruce and I thought the harshest EITs were necessary. We recommended against using them, and headquarters gave us permission not to use them.

I think al-Nashiri reasoned that since we had his address book, there was no point hiding things he imagined we could find out anyway by using available leads. It provided him with a face-saving way to answer questions less evasively and gave us a chance to use social influence techniques to take him outside the circle of things he wanted to talk about. Getting him comfortable talking about things he thought we could find out with enough effort or already knew made it easier for al-Nashiri to answer questions about topics he preferred not to discuss. Our job was to use that comfort to move him gradually outside the circle of things he was willing to talk about and farther into areas he was trying to avoid.

**HERE IS AN** example of how he would combine bits and pieces of a real threat (the Port Rashid plot) with ridiculous assertions to delay dealing with topics he wanted to avoid.

"One idea," al-Nashiri said, "was to use the attack on the warship in Port Rashid as a practice run for flying a small airplane into a U.S. aircraft carrier. We'd pack the plane with explosives and then get a couple of *shahids* [martyrs] to crash it into the carrier deck."

We had discontinued EITs days before, and on this particular day we were asking al-Nashiri about potential attacks against U.S. interests. He had mentioned a list of plots in various stages of completion, including planned attacks on the Diplomatic Quarter in Riyadh, Saudi Arabia. (Subsequently there were successful terrorist attacks there in May and November 2003. Combined, there were 56 people killed and 282 injured.)

"An aircraft carrier?" I said, trying to keep the incredulity out of my voice. "Have you ever seen the complement of warships that protect a U.S. aircraft carrier? It wouldn't be like the Japanese kamikazes in World War II. Carriers have over-the-horizon radar, defensive missiles, Phalanx guns, and fighter jets flying continuously. They're usually accompanied by many other warships. Once you violated their protected airspace, they'd shoot you out of the sky. And your idea is to have a couple of brothers fly a small plane past all these defenses and into a carrier?"

Al-Nashiri smiled sheepishly. "I never said it was a *good* idea. Just one of the ideas we talked about as possible future plans. We hadn't got past thinking about it."

"It's not like the *Cole* attack. How would you even get brothers to volunteer for a mission with so little chance of success? It seems more like straight suicide than martyrdom."

"Lots of brothers volunteer as martyrs. No problem getting someone to fly the plane. I just ask."

"So let me see if I understand. You have a bunch of al-Qa'ida jihadists who want to go head-to-head against one of the most powerful warships on the planet and the battle group accompanying it, using just a small plane packed with explosives as a weapon?"

Al-Nashiri smiled. "It seems silly when you put it like that."

"If you promise to fill it up with al-Qa'ida operatives, I think I can put you in contact with a U.S. government official who might get you a larger plane. Maybe something big enough to hold several hundred brothers. It would be like chartering a private aircraft straight to paradise. All you need to do is tell us where the brothers are so we can pick them up and give them a ride to the airport."

"Not a good idea, like I said . . . just something we talked about." Al-Nashiri was laughing and shaking his head.

"Ah," I said. "We both know this carrier attack was not something you were seriously working on. Just a distraction for you and me to talk about. Let's talk about something more practical, maybe a little further along, like your plan to attack the Diplomatic Quarter in Riyadh, Saudi Arabia."

We got the information about who was going to do the attack and the general targets, but the timing was to be determined by emerging circumstances in the target area. After al-Nashiri's capture, his terror operatives fled deeper into hiding and changed their security practices, and Saudi officials were unable to disrupt the attack before it occurred. They were, however, on heightened alert and were able to respond quickly at the scene of the attack.

ONE THING THAT al-Nashiri made clear was that until Usama bin Ladin went into hiding and stopped directly communicating with operatives in the field, al-Nashiri was his go-to guy for carrying out maritime attacks. According to al-Nashiri, one plot that bin Ladin had him working on was a plan to sink multiple civilian oil tankers in the Strait of Hormuz, a narrow opening connecting the Persian Gulf with the Arabian Sea. Al-Nashiri's task was to find and outfit a large cargo vessel that could be used like an aircraft carrier to launch multiple explosive-laden small boats to be piloted by suicide bombers who would each ram an oil tanker. The idea was to trigger economic chaos in the international oil market by creating an ecological disaster that clogged the Strait of Hormuz with burning oil tankers and millions of gallons of spilled crude oil.

Al-Nashiri told me he found a cargo ship and outfitted it. He said his jihadi brothers were unable to pilot it because of its size and because they weren't familiar with the controls that operated it. He said he hired a crew of Yemeni pirates to sail the vessel for him. But that didn't work out, because while his operatives were still trying to find the small boats to use to ram the oil tankers, the pirates he had hired took the cargo ship out for a test run and never came back.

"They stole your ship?" I said, hardly believing what I was hearing.

Al-Nashiri shrugged. "They were Yemeni," he said, as if that explained everything. "They can't be trusted."

Al-Nashiri said the October 2002 attack on the French oil supertanker *Limburg* off the coast of Yemen was a remnant of that larger operation.

Al-Nashiri said that bin Ladin provided a lot of hands-on guidance. For example, he had given al-Nashiri exact specifications for the cargo ship he tasked him to purchase. Al-Nashiri said bin Ladin would work out the details of the terror attacks and then trust al-Nashiri to carry them out. Al-Nashiri said he wasn't so good at coming up with ideas and that made it hard for him after bin Ladin went underground. My impression of al-Nashiri was that he was very concrete in his thinking and had trouble adapting to unanticipated events when left without supervision and guidance from bin Ladin.

Al-Nashiri was captured in the UAE. He was living with a Chechen "escort" as a girlfriend and driving a new high-end BMW paid for with Allah's money: donations intended for jihad. I asked him about this because his big-spender lifestyle was so different from the simple lifestyles usually adopted by Islamic jihadists. He said that was the point. His spending and running around with an escort was intended to hide his al-Qa'ida affiliation. He said he even put on a Speedo swimsuit and frequented a large water park as part of his disguise.

"Really?" I said. "You spent Allah's money to play on a Slip'N Slide?"

He said, "Maybe I was casing the park for an operation."

I said, "Not really."

"No," he admitted. "I like water parks."

You can see that he was somewhat engaging. We thought that with patience and a knowledgeable debriefer, al-Nashiri could be nudged without physical coercion into providing fuller and more complete answers.

But we didn't get a chance to see if our impression was accurate.

Provoked by fears that it would soon be compromised, headquarters decided in a matter of a few weeks—maybe just days—to hastily close the black site where we were and move the detainees to a new site, one that had just been built by the recently created Rendition, Detention, and Interrogation (RDI) branch.

We scrambled to get the detainees ready to relocate. The COB, in concert with headquarters, decided that I should be on the rendition flight that moved them. I was told to help the new interrogation team any way I could. I thought I was going there as an interrogator.

Before I departed, the COB handed me a pouch containing a computer with our black site's intelligence reports and cables on it. She told me what it was and asked me to hand carry it to the new black site.

As before, I had trouble getting the pouch on board the rendition aircraft.

I didn't have a dog in the fight about taking the computer versus leaving it behind. I was just the guy who wasn't supposed to allow it to leave his possession. Take it. Leave it. I didn't care. But since the COB was someone I respected and didn't want to disappoint and they might need the information on the computer at the next site, I wasn't going to leave it without a fight. Finally, someone—maybe the COB or another CIA officer—interceded with the mission commander and I was allowed to bring it on board.

I was displeased with how roughly the rendition team handled Abu Zubaydah and al-Nashiri as they prepared them for transport. I thought they were manhandled more than they needed to be, particularly since by that time Abu Zubaydah was cooperating and al-Nashiri was starting to make progress. I mentioned this to the mission commander, and he told me to mind my own "fucking business."

Later, after more rendition flights, I came to appreciate that the job of the mission commander and the security team on that plane is to relocate the detainees without injury or incident. Having a well-rehearsed standard set of safety procedures is one way of doing that. Establishing overwhelming total control right away discourages detainees who might otherwise become belligerent from acting out.

My acute displeasure with how Abu Zubaydah was being handled brought home to me for the first time the fact that I was starting to feel protective of him. In many ways, I felt that he had mostly held to his agreement to work with us and that unless and until he showed that he was going to become belligerent or stopped cooperating, we owed it to him not to treat him as if he had just been captured every time we moved him. But I had little say about it, because I wasn't in charge and it wasn't my decision to make. And maybe it's good that it wasn't.

# CHAPTER 4

# There's a New Sheriff in Town

I had just walked through the door of the new black site when a dark-haired man I guessed to be in his midfifties, dressed in black battle dress uniform bottoms and a tight-around-the-middle T-shirt, walked up to me. He had the body of an aging special operator, hard at one time but starting to go soft.

"There is a new sheriff in town" was the first thing he said to me. "I'm calling the shots now. Your services as an interrogator are no longer needed." He went on to identify himself as the chief interrogator for the newly formed Rendition, Detention, and Interrogation group of the CTC's special missions department.

What a dick! I thought. Struggling to keep that thought to myself, I stuck out my hand and said, "Hi. My name is Jim."

He shook it, squeezing a little too hard and standing a little too close. I squeezed back. As we stood there eyeballing each other, the chief interrogator told me he had worked interrogations with anticommunist rebels in Latin America. He said he had participated in interrogations and was familiar with coercive interrogation techniques.

Well, there you have it, I thought. But sensing that I would be better off keeping quiet, I just looked at him, waiting. That was when he picked up a worn paperback, a murder mystery by Michael Connelly, and handed it to me, motioning dismissively with his head toward a long wooden table centered in a large, open dining room. "Take a seat someplace out of the way. And if I want your opinion, I'll come find you and ask for it."

It was laughable. I knew he was trying to bully me with this hackneyed and obviously rehearsed tough-guy dismissal. I wondered how much adolescent dick checking I'd have to put up with from this guy. But I was careful not to say that out loud, because I didn't want to get drawn into a food fight with the CIA's chief interrogator, somebody who probably had friends back at headquarters who would, if things got ugly, take his word over mine. But I still bristled, and it probably showed, especially in my eyes.


**I FIGURED MY** involvement with CIA interrogations was ending. That was fine by me. The new Rendition, Detention, and Interrogation Group had been set up successfully. I hadn't expected to be a long-term part of the program. After all, my first deployment for the CTC was supposed to be for only two weeks. True, those two weeks turned into several months and my role had shifted dramatically from advisor to interrogator. But standing there, I figured that with the new branch operational and the detainees rendered to the new black site where the interrogators from that branch were situated, the handoff was complete. The only thing left was for me to return home and try to piece together my old life.

"No problem," I said, tossing the paperback onto a chair. It skittered off the cane seat and tumbled to the tile floor under the table, earning me an annoyed look from the chief interrogator.

I glanced around for the driver who had dropped me off earlier. I wanted to secure my ride back to the airport before he left. I saw the driver standing near the front door chatting with security personnel and caught his attention. To the chief interrogator I said, "I haven't been home for weeks, it's almost Christmas, and I have no desire to be here. So I'll get out of your hair. Just get me back to the plane and I'll catch a ride back to the States."

"No," the chief interrogator said, "you are not leaving. You have to be on-site in order for us to do interrogations. So you are not going anywhere." Then he said something that didn't make sense to me, and I never did sort it out. It sounded like he said, "You are the only one on-site certified to use certain pressures."

"Then I'm not going to sit off to the side. I'm going to participate."

"No," he said, his face starting to flush. "You're going to stay out of my fucking way. Headquarters says you have to be here. Headquarters didn't say that I have to let you do anything. You can watch, but don't interfere."

That was when he noticed I was carrying the pouch, the one containing the computer from the last black site. I handed him the pouch, relieved to be rid of it.

"What's this?" he asked suspiciously, hefting the weight of the pouch in one hand and then passing it to someone hovering behind him.

"It's the interrogation database from the last site," I said. "The COB wanted me to give it to you so you would have the cables and intel reports from the earlier interrogations . . . just in case your communications gear won't let you search the agency's databases yet."

They opened the bag. "Whose computer?" the chief interrogator said, suspiciously eyeing the new laptop. "Yours?"

"No," I said. I then explained that it was an agency computer supplied by the chief of security at the black site I'd just left. I further explained that a communications technician from the abandoned site had loaded the database on the laptop's hard drive specifically so that I could hand-deliver it to them.

I told him I was just the delivery boy.

I thought the laptop issue was resolved: computer delivered, purpose explained. But weeks later, the chief interrogator told CTC security that I had put the highly classified database on my personal laptop and smuggled it to the new black site. By the time I heard about it, the hallway talk was that I had been caught trying to smuggle that laptop home.

That was, of course, nonsense. But this nonsense, I'd find out later, was part of his effort to discredit me and the genesis for an evolving series of allegations. Some asserted that I had copied Abu Zubaydah's interrogation videos; others, that I had stolen the black site's database and squirreled it away on a hidden hard drive that I successfully smuggled home. These false rumors took on a life of their own, and over the years I often had to address them in one form or another during official investigations involving other matters. Sometimes the bogus stories even showed up in media reports and were treated as true.

"We don't need this," the chief interrogator said, gesturing toward the computer. He made it clear that he was less concerned with what the detainees "did say" and more interested in what they "will say."

That was when the chief interrogator told me he intended to restart enhanced interrogations of both Abu Zubaydah and al-Nashiri. To "start all over from square one" he said, using an approach he had employed while working in Latin America.

I objected, especially when it came to Abu Zubaydah. I stressed that the chief interrogator should check with headquarters first. I told him that Abu Zubaydah was providing information that targeters and analysts judged valuable. I argued that he should not restart harsh interrogations because they were in my opinion no longer necessary to service the intelligence requirements headquarters was sending in regard to Abu Zubaydah. I was also concerned that if physical coercion was used on Abu Zubaydah without his provoking it, he would view the rough treatment as a betrayal and stop answering questions.

I also objected to restarting enhanced interrogations for al-Nashiri, but not as vigorously. Although he was being somewhat helpful at that point, he was not fully cooperative. (I later learned that the chief interrogator told headquarters that I recommended restarting EITs for al-Nashiri, but that is simply not true. I think this was part of a larger effort on his part to cover his ass, as I will discuss below.)

I didn't think additional EITs were necessarily required for al-Nashiri because the last few times I had questioned him, he had provided physical descriptions of operatives listed in the phone book that was captured with him. He explained what the cash amounts written next to the names were for and revealed plans for his still-at-large operatives to use truck bombs to attack the Diplomatic Quarter where Western diplomats and their families lived in Riyadh, Saudi Arabia—all without the use of harsh measures. But it was slow going. Interacting with al-Nashiri was like dealing with a stubborn, pouting, petulant, entitled child; you had to work at it. But when confronted with information gathered by technical means or gleaned from materials captured with him, he eventually would give up information analysts judged useful, though not complete, without the use of EITs.

At the previous black site, we had used enhanced measures to create an opening for the use of noncoercive social influence techniques and were using that opening to shape gradually how fully and completely al-Nashiri answered questions.

Headquarters was still on the fence about whether enhanced measures should be restarted with al-Nashiri. The reason was that his answers were often so vague, it was clear he was holding back.

For example, although al-Nashiri would talk about his plans to attack the Diplomatic Quarter in Riyadh, he insisted he could not provide specifics. He insisted that he couldn't remember the location of the safe house where he stayed in Riyadh, not even the neighborhood, although he had been there for weeks. He also insisted that he could not recall which mosque he attended for Friday prayers, although he said several times that he went to the same mosque with the same people. Al-Nashiri maintained that none of this information was relevant. He said that because his men knew he had been captured, they would change safe houses and delay attacks in Riyadh. Al-Nashiri claimed that his men would determine the timetable for attacks and the specific targets on the basis of the way things unfolded on the ground in Riyadh and that he had no way of knowing those things. For these reasons, the analysts and targeters thought, as did we, that al-Nashiri was still withholding actionable information that could be used to disrupt attacks or capture his men. Some at headquarters thought that if he didn't quickly become more forthcoming, we should restart enhanced interrogations.

I had all this in the back of my mind while the chief interrogator and I were debating the wisdom of restarting enhanced interrogations on both detainees. I told him I could see an argument for restarting EITs on al-Nashiri but thought we had been making some progress at the last black site without them.

At some point, the chief interrogator became exasperated with me. He said that he was the CIA officer in charge of interrogations and I was "a fucking contractor with no real say in what happened at this black site or anywhere else in the world as far as CIA activities were concerned."

"Understood," I said. "I have been told that many times. Even signed documents acknowledging that."

I then reiterated that I felt compelled to be clear with him that I thought that it would be a mistake to restart enhanced interrogations on Abu Zubaydah and that if he did and Abu Zubaydah subsequently shut down, I would report my objections to headquarters, specifically to the chief of the CTC, Jose Rodriguez.

"It won't matter," he said. "No one at headquarters cares about your opinion."

"Then why am I here?" I asked.

Shortly after that encounter, I watched the chief interrogator's first interrogation of al-Nashiri. Before it started, the chief interrogator introduced me to three men. All were newly minted interrogators who had just graduated from the CIA's first interrogation course. Until then I wasn't even aware there had been an interrogation course. He said he had handpicked all of them and had taught portions of the course himself. They were at the black site, he said, to obtain "practical experience" using enhanced interrogation methods on al-Nashiri and Abu Zubaydah.

"What if EITs aren't needed?" I asked.

"Oh, we're going to need them," he assured me.

The chief interrogator told me I wasn't allowed in the interrogation room, and so I watched this first interrogation through a small glass window in the door.

In the room where interrogations were to be held, a cheap white plastic table had been set up like a desk facing the center of the room. Three flimsy lawn chairs were positioned behind it. The chief interrogator and two of his recent graduates were sitting in the chairs, with the chief in the middle and the other two flanking him. A fourth interrogator moved around the room, ready to pitch in when the chief interrogator gave directions. There was no chair for the detainee.

Al-Nashiri, hooded and shackled, was brought into the room by one of the guards and positioned, standing like an errant schoolboy, across the table from the chief interrogator. The chief interrogator leaned over the table, removed al-Nashiri's hood, and introduced himself as "the man in charge." He instructed al-Nashiri to always address him as "sir." He then asked al-Nashiri if he understood. Al-Nashiri nodded, said "Yes," and shrugged, separating his hands, palms out, as far as his shackles allowed, but didn't speak further. That was typical of the way al-Nashiri sometimes responded to questions.

The chief interrogator screamed that al-Nashiri needed to answer when he was spoken to and say "sir" when addressing the chief interrogator. When al-Nashiri didn't respond immediately, the chief interrogator suddenly threw the table aside and grabbed al-Nashiri in an attention grasp. When he released him, two of the other interrogators put al-Nashiri in a stress position. They made him put his forehead against the wall and walk his feet back so that he was leaning at a forward angle, back straight and forehead against the wall in front of him. When his neck and shoulders looked like they were beginning to tire and he started to wobble, two of the interrogators held his arms out to his sides and leaned into him, pressing his forehead against the wall. Once he started to squeal, the interrogators pulled him away from the wall, forced him to his knees, and bent him over backward until his upper back and shoulders were touching the floor behind him, all the while screaming at him to answer the questions and address them as "sir." When it became apparent that al-Nashiri was limber enough to sit easily in a kneeling position with his back on the floor, the interrogators put a broomstick behind his knees. This time when they pushed him backward, al-Nashiri started to scream.

I was shocked, but not by their general approach: I recognized that. I surmised that much like many old-school military training instructors might, they were trying to condition compliance by focusing on absolute obedience to small demands. I had never asked al-Nashiri to address me as "sir." But it was a conditioning approach that sometimes was used to establish dominance right away. You see it used a lot, often poorly, in military and paramilitary settings.

It was the specific physically coercive techniques they were using that distressed and concerned me. I did not believe those techniques had been approved by the Justice Department. I was also concerned that the way the techniques were being applied placed undue strain on al-Nashiri's knees, back, and neck muscles. I was expecting medical personnel on-site to stop the interrogation. But that didn't happen.

I was sorting through my recollection of how the original authorization concerning stress positions had been worded to figure out if it was possible that these techniques were covered by it, when the chief interrogator stood al-Nashiri up and cinched his elbows together behind his back with a leather strap until they touched. Then the chief interrogator and one of the newly minted interrogators started lifting al-Nashiri's arms behind him, toward the ceiling. Al-Nashiri bent over and screamed.

I *knew* this had not been approved. I had seen less intense versions of the first two stress positions before—minus the broomstick behind the knees—during SERE training. I had even experienced them. Maybe I was wrong and more SERE techniques had been approved that I didn't know about, but the last technique and the use of a broomstick, no way.

The higher the chief interrogator lifted al-Nashiri's arms, the more al-Nashiri squealed and struggled. I became fearful that he would dislocate al-Nashiri's shoulders, and so I stuck my head into the room to stop the interrogation. It was headquarters policy that anyone could immediately stop interrogations at any time for any reason. Because of that policy, I fully expected them to stop. That is what we would have done at the black site I had just left.

"Get out!" the chief interrogator shouted at me. He sent the guard over to escort me out of the room.

"The things the interrogators are doing have not been approved by the Justice Department, and they should stop," I whispered to the guard when he was close enough to hear me. "I think they are going to dislocate al-Nashiri's shoulders. Headquarters policy is to stop interrogations when someone raises a concern about safety."

I had no idea what the guard thought. He was completely clothed in black, with his eyes hidden by mirrored goggles. I saw a tiny version of myself, angry and pointing at the chief interrogator, reflected back at me in the lenses. The guard nodded, walked to where the chief interrogator was standing glaring at me, and whispered something in his ear.

I mouthed "What?" and gestured, opening my hands, palms up. The chief interrogator pointed to the door, hissed for me to get out, and instructed the guard to escort me completely out of the interrogation room.

The interrogation was being observed by medical personnel and several others on closed circuit TV. I was surprised medical personnel had not intervened and said so. I expressed my concerns to them and the guards. I got a "so what can you do?" look from the medic. The guards said they were worried, but their hands were tied because they had been told the chief interrogator called all the shots. No one made any move to stop what was happening. It was clear that everyone there except me thought that what the chief interrogator was doing was authorized, believed they did not have the authority to stop him, or simply didn't want him angry with them.

In spite of my protests, during the remainder of that interrogation session and several sessions to follow, I watched the chief interrogator use a variety of physically coercive measures on al-Nashiri that I believed were not on the list of approved techniques. They included the two stress positions discussed earlier: dousing al-Nashiri with cold water while using a stiff-bristled brush to scrub his ass and balls and then his mouth and blowing cigar smoke in his face until he became nauseous. In place of waterboarding, one of the navy SERE schools used the exact same cigar-smoke-in-the-face technique I observed the chief interrogator and his newly minted apprentices use.

The chief interrogator was very angry at me when he came out of al-Nashiri's first interrogation. He got right up in my face and started hollering, "What the fuck is your malfunction?"

"You are doing things that are not approved," I said, talking over him. "I'm trying to look out for you as much as al-Nashiri."

"You are not allowed to interrupt interrogations," he said. "If you do it again, I will have the guards restrain you."

It got even uglier after that, but I was confident that if I could talk to someone running the program back at headquarters, this rogue disregard for what was and wasn't authorized would stop. I told him I wanted to call back to headquarters and talk to the chief of the CTC, Jose Rodriguez; he said I couldn't. I told him I wanted to talk to the CTC lawyers who had worked out the approvals for the techniques with the Justice Department; he told me I wasn't allowed to call anyone, "especially the fucking lawyers." I told him I wanted to send an e-mail back to my contract manager; he told me I couldn't. I told him I wanted to leave the black site. I would pay my own way home. He said I couldn't do that either.

I wished Bruce was with me as a witness to what was going on, but I assumed he was back home by then. I felt like I had fallen down a rabbit hole. The flagrant disregard for both Justice Department approvals and headquarters guidance was out of character for the carefully controlled program I knew Jose Rodriguez and the leadership at CIA had in place. I knew they wouldn't tolerate it if I could just let them know what was happening.

Later that night I was summoned to the first of several acrimonious meetings with the chief interrogator and the COS of the country we were in. The COS chewed me out. They readdressed the subject of restarting EITs on Abu Zubaydah, and again I threatened to share my objections with headquarters and make it clear that I had recommended against it. I was told again that it wasn't my decision to make and that I had no say.

As I was being dressed down, I realized for the first time that in their view I was at the site to function as a psychologist monitoring interrogations, not as an interrogator, as I had earlier assumed. No one had told me about this change in roles. If they had, I would have objected.

I knew this new role would raise ethical questions. I was being told that I was there to provide psychological monitoring for interrogations involving detainees I had interrogated myself: a less than ideal situation. How could I objectively monitor interrogations when I had interrogated the same people earlier? To make matters worse, I was being told that I had to do that monitoring without speaking to the detainees or letting them know I was there.

I thought briefly about refusing, but that would not have stopped the interrogations. Since no other psychologist was on-site, it would just mean that there would be no psychological monitoring. From what I had seen earlier, someone needed to monitor what the interrogators were doing, at least until I could get back to headquarters and report what I was seeing.

Thus, I found myself in an ethically troubling situation in which I had to choose the least bad among several bad choices. I had to put aside my pride about being shabbily treated and accept the role of psychologist until I could get back to the States and resolve the issue.

Retreating to the corner where the chief interrogator wanted me, closing my eyes, and sticking my fingers in my ears wasn't going to help. It was me or no one, and so I resolved to be cognizant of the difficult ethical issues raised by my shifting roles and accept the challenge.

The ugly meetings with the chief of station and the chief interrogator only got worse. They told me that the "gloves were off," a phrase I had heard many times, and accused me of being a coward and a "bleeding heart who felt sorry for terrorists trying to kill us."

Not so, I told them. I said that I didn't think the techniques they were using had been approved by the Justice Department and they needed to seek clarification from CTC attorneys. I was told they were going to "keep the lawyers out of it."

"The lawyers will know anyway because the site has to document the techniques interrogators use in their reports to headquarters," I said.

"Headquarters is interested in results, not what we do to get them. Headquarters is there to support our activities. We don't have to ask permission for what we do."

"I don't think that's true when it comes to interrogations," I said. "I need to hear that from the lawyers."

"Not going to happen," one of them said. Then I was ordered not to have any communication with headquarters while I was at the black site and told I wouldn't be allowed to leave until they decided I could. I couldn't sneak around and contact headquarters behind their back, because all communications gear was locked in a secure room under twenty-four-hour guard.

"I am a U.S. citizen," I said angrily, "and as of right now you're holding me against my will in a foreign country. I will eventually get back home, and when I do, I will report you."

They said nobody at headquarters would believe me, because I was a contractor and the agency would take the word of a "blue badger" (i.e., an agency employee) over the word of a troublemaker with a green badge every time. The implication was that since they controlled what was communicated back to headquarters, they could make it appear in e-mails and cable traffic that I was a vindictive troublemaker, something I discovered later that they did with some success.

"Our story is the communications aren't good enough for you to contact headquarters. And there's no way we can get you out of here until the next time we rotate personnel. They will believe us, not you. So stop interfering and stay out of the way." They then said that as soon as I left the black site, they would see that I would "never work for the CIA again." That was the only thing they said that pleased me.

The meeting ended with them telling me to get out because they had to discuss the next day's interrogations and my input wasn't needed. This contrasted significantly with interrogation planning at the first black site where I had done interrogations. At that site, the planning sessions always included the medics, the psychologists, security personnel, the linguist, the COB, analysts, and subject matter experts. I don't know who else attended the planning sessions at this black site, but I know the person tasked with monitoring the psychological aspects of the interrogations—me—wasn't in attendance.

At this new black site, with the role of psychologist thrust on me, I had no idea what sort of guidance the site was receiving from headquarters or what the site was communicating back to them. I wasn't allowed to read incoming or outgoing cable traffic or e-mails and was excluded from all calls. I wasn't allowed to send back any reports or make any inquiries. Normally the psychologist added a paragraph or two to the daily update, but I wasn't allowed to do that either. When I asked about writing a final trip report, the chief interrogator said it would "serve no purpose."

To this day I have no idea what, if anything, was communicated back to headquarters regarding my concerns about the interrogation techniques the chief interrogator was using.

In contrast to the expected role of the psychologist on-site during interrogations, I no longer was allowed to speak to or have any contact with either Abu Zubaydah or al-Nashiri, but I watched as many interrogations as I could and observed them in their cells on closed circuit TV.

I was relieved to see that although the interrogators were cold and brutish toward Abu Zubaydah, they did not use coercive physical pressure on him. They did shave his head and beard again and take away all the amenities he had earned at the last site, including the diary we had let him start keeping. The loss of the diary was a big deal to him. I felt bad about it. Several times over the years various players would take away Abu Zubaydah's diary. He was told early on that as long as he was cooperative, he could keep a diary. I thought we needed to live up to that agreement. Therefore, as often as we could, as long as he was cooperating, Bruce and I would advocate for getting it returned or allowing him to start a new one. But that wasn't always easy, and it wasn't going to be easy this time, because the chief interrogator told me "hell would freeze over" before he would let Abu Zubaydah do something that brought him enjoyment and comfort. We eventually got Abu Zubaydah's diary returned, but it took several months.

The chief interrogator and his new recruits started Abu Zubaydah's interrogations the same way they had al-Nashiri's, by demanding that he call them "sir" every time he spoke to them and answer every question. Abu Zubaydah quickly caught on to the routine and seemed to be adjusting, if somewhat begrudgingly, to his change in circumstances.

In contrast, as the days passed, al-Nashiri looked more and more unhappy and acted more petulant and sulky. In my opinion, he wasn't developing a mental health disorder, but he was miserable and it was affecting him in ways I thought might be counterproductive for gathering intelligence. I reported my observations to the chief interrogator and recommended that they back off the intensity of what they were doing. By the time I left the black site, al-Nashiri seemed to have almost stopped directly answering questions and was simply enduring the interrogation sessions. He was talking, but not much. He squealed and struggled when they used the techniques. Because I was not allowed to read outgoing interrogation cables, I didn't know if they were getting anything useful from him.

I did not want to be there. I continued to raise concerns and as a result continued to have run-ins with the chief interrogator, his newly minted interrogators, the COB, and the COS. Finally, after one of al-Nashiri's interrogations, the chief interrogator had me escorted away from the interrogation room and restricted to monitoring, huddled around a closed circuit TV with the remaining security guards and medical personnel.

This run-in happened after I saw the interrogators use the stiff brush I mentioned earlier to scrub al-Nashiri. Agency security personnel were not involved. The chief interrogator enlisted the help of a giant man from Ground Branch, the CIA's paramilitary force, to hold al-Nashiri while the chief interrogator scrubbed him, alternating between his ass and balls and then his mouth and face for a while, and then scrubbing his whole body. Months later, the chief interrogator would tell his bosses and the CIA inspector general that he was using the brush to clean al-Nashiri because he stank and needed a bath. But that was a smoke screen. It's true al-Nashiri smelled; however, I never heard that scrubbing detainees with stiff brushes during interrogations was part of their personal hygiene plan.

I was kept at the black site a little more than a week before I was allowed to leave and return to the States. I might have been kept there longer, but the chief interrogator and I were at each other so often that I'm sure it was producing morale problems even though we were trying to keep it out of sight of those around us.

I realized during those squabbles that the chief interrogator and I had very different ideas about how EITs, if employed, should be used to acquire actionable intelligence. To me, his position seemed to be: apply EITs until the detainee tells you what you want to know, then apply them a little longer to see if he changes his story. If the story remains the same, what the detainee was saying was probably true. Over time, I've come to realize that some agency personnel, many members of our government, the press, and the general public share this assumption. Hurt them and don't stop until they tell you what you want to know. And then continue hurting them, because if they are lying, they will change their story.

I did not then and do not now see it that way. My belief is that using physical coercion in that manner increases the risk of detainees fabricating information to stop the discomfort, as several detainees did when questioned by foreign governments before the CIA established its own interrogation program.

WHEN I GOT back to the States, I went to CIA headquarters to report my concerns and complain about being held incommunicado. I was still new to the agency and, because of the program's highly restricted nature, not sure with whom I could discuss my concerns. I reported what happened to a senior CTC attorney who had worked on the authorization for EITs, and then worked my way to the offices of the Rendition, Detention, and Interrogation Group and eventually was interviewed by the CIA's inspector general.

The RDI Group chief seemed to know who I was and ushered me to a small conference room, where the two of us sat down alone with the door shut. I started describing what the chief interrogator and his interrogators had done and voicing my concerns about use of unauthorized techniques. I was angry, agitated, and a little loud. The deputy branch chief, whose office was next door to the conference room, overheard, came in, and sat down next to me. He looked about my age, thin, pale, and sickly.

I continued. When I started describing how the chief interrogator used a broomstick behind al-Nashiri's knees, blew cigar smoke in his face to restrict his breathing, scrubbed him with a stiff brush, and strapped his elbows behind his back and lifted his arms toward the ceiling, the RDI branch chief's face flushed bright red. At the time, I couldn't tell if he was mad at me for reporting this or mad at the New Sheriff, his chief interrogator, for doing it.

I was about to ask, but before I could, the deputy chief spoke up. He told me the chief interrogator was a hero and mentioned a couple of impressive operations he had been an important part of in the past. The deputy chief called me a "pussy" and said that it was a mistake from the start to involve me because I was a psychologist and a bleeding-heart liberal who cared more about the feelings of a "fucking terrorist" than about the safety of the American people. I had no business being involved as far as he was concerned because I wasn't part of the agency. "The gloves are off," he said.

This was not the first time such comments had been directed at me, but I was still taken aback by the force with which he said it and the anger in his eyes. I told him I didn't have a problem with the rough treatment of terrorists; I had waterboarded Abu Zubaydah and al-Nashiri. But I did have a problem with interrogators using techniques that weren't authorized by the Justice Department. I had a problem with being cussed out by the COS and having my legitimate concerns ignored. And I had a problem with being held against my will and not allowed to communicate with headquarters or home.

The deputy chief told me that he too was a psychologist who had left the profession and become an operations officer and that he knew all too well what people like me thought. He then launched into a litany of criticisms of psychologists and other mental health providers, criticisms that ironically sounded very much like my own list of things I don't like about liberal psychologists and their ilk regarding national security concerns. Oddly, I found myself agreeing with most of what he had to say; it was just that I didn't think those criticisms applied to me. I wasn't trying to stop their program; I was trying to keep everyone out of trouble. I didn't want to stand by while detainees were being abused, and I didn't want any detainees hurt. And I knew it wasn't what the chief of the CTC, Jose Rodriguez, wanted.

I was about to protest and tick off my reasons for rejecting his criticism when the chief of RDI held his hands up, interrupting his deputy, who was getting increasingly loud and increasingly angry. I was starting to get hot too.

"Listen," the chief of RDI said to me, red-faced but in a calm, controlled voice. "I'm glad you came to me. I'll look into it. If there are problems, we will correct them."

He then asked his deputy to give us a minute. After the deputy left, the RDI chief told me his deputy was dying of cancer and it was his last week at the agency. The chief said that because of 9/11 his deputy had wanted to work right up to the end, but now he was too sick to continue and had only a short time left to live. He asked me to take into account how ill his deputy was and overlook some of the insulting things he had said to me.

# CHAPTER 5

# Drawn Back In

January 2003. After the dustup with RDI's chief of interrogation, I thought my involvement in the CIA's enhanced interrogation program had ended and I was getting my old life back.

But it wasn't over. Unexpectedly, I was asked to return to CIA headquarters. The officers who called me in acted as if nothing had happened. They wanted to talk to me about which directorate I should work out of and schedule my next deployment.

**IT WAS SURREAL.** It was less than three weeks since some of their colleagues essentially were holding me prisoner at a black site and others were calling me a bleeding-heart pussy who cared more for the terrorists than I did for protecting America. Now they were acting as if none of it ever happened, as if that was how business was normally conducted.

They didn't want to talk about any of the previous unpleasantness. They just wanted to discuss bureaucratic details. At issue for them was the fact that I worked out of the department that housed the CIA's operational psychologists in a completely different directorate from the one housing CTC's new Rendition, Detention, and Interrogation (RDI) Group, the office that wanted me to deploy. RDI schedulers didn't like having to ask the science and technology guys if I was available for deployment. RDI wanted me to work directly out of their shop so that they would have more control over when I was deployed for them and how long I stayed overseas.

Why in the world would I allow myself to be drawn back into that program? My wife didn't know the details, but she knew I had been fuming when I got back from the last trip. Once I was home, I called Bruce and told him we ought to cut our ties with the program. Now they were asking me to come back.

I didn't dismiss the notion out of hand because of what I learned about al-Qa'ida's leaders and their aims during my initial foray into the dark world of interrogating terrorists for the CIA. Khalid Sheikh Mohammed was still on the loose, and the chatter about a second wave of imminent terror attacks, possibly involving a nuclear device, was absolutely believable. Moreover, compared with when I first got involved, I had a visceral, firsthand understanding of the motives of those attacking us.

For months, almost daily, I had spent hours in a cell with one of the most dangerous men on the planet. We argued. We laughed together. We stood close enough to smell each other's breath. I watched his eyes flash with reverence when he told me about his brand of Islam's unending obligation to destroy our way of life. He said Allah had given them dominion over the earth and commanded them to convert, enslave, or kill everyone or die trying. The only way he could avoid hell and ensure his place in paradise was to devote his life to destroying our way of life.

You only have to look at the actions of ISIS a decade later to get a clear picture of the sorts of things these jihadists had in mind for the United States—and the rest of the world, for that matter.

Their goal has always been to replace our freedoms with a draconian medieval way of life that stopped evolving fourteen hundred years ago. They live in a religiously dominated world where it is normal and even desirable to burn churches, raze irreplaceable antiquities, destroy great works of art, treat women as property and sell them as sex slaves, throw gays off tall buildings, and publicly slaughter people who aren't like them while little children watch or even take part in the beheading, stoning, shooting, and burning of helpless victims.

That's not how I want to live, and I don't think other people should be forced to live like that either. Therefore, when the CIA asked me to help again, I felt the urge to put aside my pride and petty grievances and pitch in.

At the same time, I knew that if I refused, there was a possibility I could get some of my old life back. If I went back to the dark side, that chance would disappear completely. I knew I would be required to do things—harsh things—that some would view as unethical, maybe even monstrous.

I'm not Islamophobic, as some would have you believe. I reject that. I'm not afraid of their culture or their religion. I love the Arab culture. Parts of the religion would be beautiful if you could get the Islamists who want to impose Sharia (Islamic law) on the whole world out of it. As for those members of Islam who are not trying to destroy our way of life, I don't give a damn what they do. It is none of my business. And it shouldn't be.

But when people decide that their god requires them to kill my countrymen, kill my family, and destroy my way of life and they set out to do just that, I do care. They have my full attention.

We're fools if we don't take them at their word and stop them while we can.

I decided my obligation was to try to balance the law, my duty to my fellow Americans, my desire to help, and the ethical code the American Psychological Association would have psychologists follow. For me, this balance favored fighting those who would destroy our way of life. I'm not ashamed of that.

I was then and I am now willing to use any lawful and authorized means that has a chance of success as a weapon in that fight.

This includes what I know about psychology. As I considered my choices, I believed it would have been immoral and unethical for me to have ignored my obligation to use what I know to defend our citizens and our way of life against enemies whose stated goal is to destroy us, especially when that enemy initiated the fight and has the power to stop the violence any time they choose simply by ceasing to attack us.

In my mind, nothing in my ethical code requires that I put the temporary discomfort of a handful of terrorists ahead of saving the lives of thousands of innocent Americans. For some people that is a hypothetical question; for me it was a real choice.

Thoughtful people can disagree with my moral calculus; I accept that. But after thinking about it, I was willing to redeploy. I would do it again today under similar circumstances.


**BACK AT HEADQUARTERS,** I met the chief of the Special Missions Department (SMD) and his chief of RDI, the same man I had talked to after my dustup with the New Sheriff. I asked what was being done about the unauthorized techniques I'd reported. They assured me my concerns had been passed to the appropriate authorities and were being investigated. The chief of interrogations had been admonished to use only the techniques approved by the DOJ on which he was certified, and then only after actively seeking approval from headquarters. Furthermore, to ensure understanding of the guidelines, personnel traveling to black sites were now required to read current guidance from headquarters each time on arrival and sign a logbook acknowledging that they had. Previously, I was routinely briefed on the guidelines before deployment, but I liked this new policy. Things were evolving rapidly, and it was now easier for me to make sure I was following the latest guidance.

They then asked me to move my work center from science and technology to RDI in the Clandestine Service's Counterterrorism Center. I told them that I was afraid that if I did what they requested and worked out of RDI—the office where the chief interrogator had a desk—he and I would soon be at each other's throat. The SMD chief suggested that since Bruce and I were seldom in the building, we should work out of his secure area, sharing one of the desks set aside for visitors, well away from the New Sheriff, who would be in a different part of CIA headquarters.

I was assured that neither Bruce nor I would ever be asked to deploy with the chief interrogator. I also was told that we would not work for him.

And that was how it worked out. As time passed, we specialized. Bruce and I had essentially nothing to do with low-level and mid-level detainees. We focused instead on high-value detainees (HVDs), the handful of the most important terrorists in CIA custody, a small group that eventually included KSM. The chief interrogator would spend more time working with midlevel detainees but occasionally became involved in HDV interrogations, not without controversy.

In winter 2003, the chief interrogator had been admonished not to use a broomstick or wooden dowel anymore during interrogations. A few months later, Bruce and I observed him teaching aspiring interrogators to place a wooden dowel behind the knees of detainees in stress positions. It was part of a lesson in an interrogation course he was running for the CIA. He even demonstrated its use in front of the class.

Bruce and I had been asked to "sit through" the course by the chief of RDI. When we saw what the chief interrogator was teaching, we immediately left the room and reported it to the chief of RDI. Later that day, the chief of RDI and the chief of SMD came out to where the interrogation course was being held and told the chief interrogator to "knock that shit off." But he didn't.

In July 2003 the New Sheriff was removed from the interrogation program because he once again used a wooden dowel behind the knees on a detainee he was interrogating. That incident was reported after the staff psychologist assigned to RDI told me he had seen the chief interrogator use the dowel. He asked me for my advice. I told the psychologist to report it immediately. He did, and the chief interrogator was promptly removed from the program, a sign that CIA leadership was cleaning house of rogue elements.

We were all shocked to hear that just a few weeks after his departure he died of an apparent heart attack.


**BUT I'M GETTING** ahead of myself. In early 2003, I was asked to return to the black site where the chief interrogator and I had had our dustup. When I got there, I was surprised to find out Bruce had been there ahead of me. He was rotating out as I was coming in.

The people at the black site were crackling with tension. A few weeks previously, a CIA officer with no interrogation training had tried inappropriately to frighten al-Nashiri into giving up information on imminent threats by threatening him with a handgun and a drill. The officer had approval from the more senior COB in charge of the site, but not from headquarters. They never would have permitted it. The threats didn't work, and Bruce had been sent in to clean up the mess.

The incident had an emotionally disconcerting effect on CIA personnel on-site, especially the security personnel, many of whom had worked with us at the first black site. One senior security guard told me he "feared the wheels had come off" and was glad when Bruce showed up to put them back on.

What that security officer said is an indication of how most of the CIA officers and contractors working at black sites felt. They wanted clear rules and firm guidance. There was tremendous pressure to get the information necessary to stop the next wave of attacks. There were a lot of moving parts. The work was exhausting and emotionally charged. Nobody wanted to do anything wrong. The people working at the sites wanted to know the left and right limits and had to be able to predict what the officers beside them were going to do next. They also wanted to know that headquarters had their backs.

Headquarters responded quickly. The incident was investigated, the officers involved were disciplined, and the lessons learned were incorporated into headquarters policy and operating procedures. Rather than being an indication of a failed and corrupt program run by incompetents, as it has been portrayed by some in the media, the way this incident was handled indicated to me that accountability was important to the CIA's leadership. It also illustrated the importance of adhering to a set of DOJ-approved EITs rather than allowing officers to freelance, making up techniques on the fly to ramp up the pressure. Preventing this sort of freelancing was the reason I recommended that the CIA use SERE-derived interrogation techniques in the first place.

.   .   .

**I WAS SENT** to the black site as an interrogator to advise two new interrogators who were already there questioning Ramzi bin al-Shibh. He was one of KSM's key terror operatives and a core member of the 9/11 plot. He originally had been penciled in to crash one of the planes into buildings during the 9/11 attacks, but he had visa problems and couldn't get into the United States for pilot training. He ended up facilitating the attack instead.

Bin al-Shibh was captured in late 2002 thanks in part to information obtained from Abu Zubaydah after aggressive interrogations. A cooperating Abu Zubaydah told us how he would go about locating and capturing a senior al-Qa'ida facilitator, Hassan Ghul, who the CIA believed had knowledge that could help locate Usama bin Ladin. That strategy was passed to Pakistani authorities, and they implemented it, ultimately raiding Hassan Ghul's apartment, where they missed Ghul but found bin al-Shibh hiding there and arrested him instead.

At the time of his capture, bin al-Shibh was the leader of a cell, under KSM's operational control, plotting to crash hijacked aircraft into Heathrow Airport and into buildings in London's financial district.

I had not met the two interrogators before. They both had been handpicked by the chief interrogator and were very different from each other. One seemed unnaturally obsessed with a communication and persuasion system called neuro-linguistic programming (NLP). Some would say it was a largely discredited pseudoscience, but he thought it was magic. He insisted on incorporating it into his interrogations, to no good effect. He drove me crazy with incessant talk about which way eyeballs were moving. He would even try to manipulate me by touching me (called "anchoring" in NLP) while saying words he wanted to plant in my head, as if working a Jedi mind trick. He wasn't very good as an interrogator and eventually was removed from the program for some infraction; it was another case of CIA leadership doing the right thing.

The other interrogator was a seasoned intelligence officer who stayed with the program until it closed. I call him the Preacher because in the early days during enhanced interrogations he would at random times put one hand on the forehead of a detainee, raise the other high in the air, and in a deep Southern drawl say things like "Can you feel it, son . . . can you feel the spirit moving down my arm, into your body?" and "There's fire in the lake!"

I asked him one time what that was all about. In a heavy drawl, he replied, "I do it to make it tough for the detainees to predict what I'm going to say or do next . . . to make them think I could become unhinged at any moment."

I don't know if it worked like that on the detainees, but I know it had that effect on me. For my part, I thought detainees needed to be able to predict exactly what you were going to do as an interrogator, both when they lied and when they told you the truth.

But he was skilled and got results. He worked well with bin al-Shibh, who soon started providing bits and pieces of useful information—"squirts," the Preacher called them—while still trying to protect the most important stuff.

After he became more cooperative and the EITs were stopped, bin al-Shibh continued to provide information to interrogators and debriefers that was judged useful by analysts and targeters. Sometimes it was in response to a simple, direct question. Other times it was through elicitation or by leading him to believe that other detainees had already told us about the topic.

The last approach worked best when we led him to believe we were comparing his responses with those of other detainees to see how truthful his answers were. Since we often did compare their responses and confronted the detainees with inconsistencies, this ruse sometimes worked well in situations in which we had some information and could make it seem we knew more than we actually did. Most parents with teenagers know exactly how this is done and the risks of getting caught doing it.

Some of the insights bin al-Shibh provided about KSM during the early interrogations contributed to KSM's capture. For example, after exposure to EITs, bin al-Shibh told the interrogators and debriefers that "the best way" to find KSM was to find KSM's nephew, Ammar al-Baluchi.

A few days later, when shown a photograph of the confirmed 9/11 financier Ali Abdul Aziz Ali, bin al-Shibh identified the person in the photo as the man he knew as Ammar al-Baluchi and had referred to when indicating the best way to find KSM.

According to CIA analysts and targeters, bin al-Shibh's photo identification was a breakthrough. It was not the whole picture, but it filled in part of the puzzle that helped the CIA capture KSM.

This vignette illustrates one of the most effective questioning strategies we used with the detainees to help track down terrorists the CIA was hunting. As you might imagine, there was a lot of high-level interest in locating and capturing terrorists still at large, and detainees frequently were asked where these "brothers" were. The detainee would typically deny knowing, and headquarters would send back a blistering message saying it was "inconceivable" that the detainee didn't know that information and demanding that the pressure be ramped up.

One day we were asking Abu Zubaydah where Hassan Ghul was situated. He denied knowing where he was. Headquarters was unhappy with that answer. When pressed, Abu Zubaydah wasn't willing to speculate. He said he wasn't that long out of the "hard times" (EITs) and was uncomfortable guessing where Hassan Ghul might be because he was afraid that if he named a place and we went there and looked and Hassan Ghul wasn't there, we would think he had lied to us and the "hard times" would come back.

That was when one of us, either Bruce or I, hit upon the idea of asking Abu Zubaydah how *he* would go about locating Hassan Ghul if he had to find him and had no idea where he was. Abu Zubaydah said he would contact one of Hassan Ghul's well-known associates (a person I can't name). Pakistani officials "reinterviewed" the associate, he disclosed the location of Hassan Ghul's apartment, and when they raided it, Pakistani officials captured Ramzi bin al-Shibh, together with several other terrorists. We routinely used this questioning strategy with detainees, with good results.

**SHORTLY AFTER I** arrived at the black site to help with bin al-Shibh's interrogations, I also checked on Abu Zubaydah and al-Nashiri and sat in on some noncoercive debriefing sessions. Abu Zubaydah had settled in and was working well with a debriefer.

Headquarters was very interested in al-Nashiri's well-being. Because al-Nashiri had been subjected to unauthorized techniques, headquarters took the further use of EITs off the table. That was a good move, in my opinion.

Al-Nashiri's debriefer was a smart, capable female targeter who was patiently trying to get him to answer questions of great interest to the analysts back at CIA headquarters. She was attractive and had a caring but no-nonsense approach. Al-Nashiri liked working with her. Sometimes he would answer her questions; sometimes he acted like a petulant child.

A staff psychologist was on-site to provide psychological monitoring and evaluate al-Nashiri's mental health. But since I was there, headquarters asked me for my opinion as a psychologist about al-Nashiri's emotional state. I gave my opinion, but in retrospect, I probably shouldn't have.

It put me in an awkward dual role and later allowed critics of the program to create a false narrative. The narrative went something like this: Bruce and I would determine a detainee's psychological fitness for interrogation, then we would interrogate that detainee, and finally, after we finished roughing him up, we would evaluate how he was doing emotionally. That would have been unethical, because we would be checking our own work to see if we had done any mental harm. We didn't do that, but that narrative became part of the myth about our activities.

The narrative is just not true. The assessments to determine the psychological fitness for interrogation of Abu Zubaydah and al-Nashiri were conducted by staff psychologists from headquarters, not by us. Also, a senior staff psychologist was present throughout our interrogations of Abu Zubaydah and al-Nashiri at the first black site. That psychologist was there to monitor the detainee's mental health and our activities and then send assessments of both back to headquarters. Like everyone, he had the power to stop interrogations for any reason, but he never did.

As of January 2003, Bruce and I were not issuing psychological reports of record. Instead, staff psychologists who were never involved in interrogations conducted psychological evaluations of the detainees we interrogated. They were the ones who issued the psychological reports of record.

But occasionally, because of manning issues, where we happened to be in the world, or exigent circumstances, one of us would be asked to provide an assessment of a detainee we had never interrogated, and we would do that. There was no dual role, but it created the appearance of impropriety. By May 2004, as more resources finally became available and more psychologists were briefed on the closely held program, the CIA changed its policy. Headquarters stopped asking us for psychological opinions. We were glad to stop giving them. After that we were deployed strictly as interrogators.

Some psychologists in the agency objected to our conducting interrogations not simply because of a potential for a dual relationship (although I'm sure that was part of it), but primarily because it was somehow "unfair" for someone who was an experienced psychologist to conduct interrogations. Here is how I found this out.

The agency required that anyone conducting interrogations undergo a psychological evaluation, including me and Bruce. When I showed up in the psychology department of the Office of Medical Services (OMS) for my evaluation, I was ushered into the office of the chief psychologist. I could sense as soon as I sat down that he was hostile. He told me he thought it would be a waste of his time to conduct a psychological assessment of me. Because of my years as a clinical psychologist, he was certain I knew how to take psychological tests and could manipulate the results. I told him I would be happy to take any test he had in mind or honestly answer any question he asked as long as it didn't involve something classified.

The chief psychologist said it wasn't necessary and then proceeded to tell me he was going to file an ethical complaint within the agency and to outside resources because he thought it was inappropriate for a psychologist to conduct interrogations. I thought he was going to object to the issue of dual roles, which we were trying to resolve, and there was a little of that. But mostly it seemed that he thought psychologists had some unfair advantage in questioning detainees because of their background in assessing and influencing human behavior. He dressed me down. I sat there and listened because of the possibility that he was just trying to provoke me so that he could use my outburst as grounds to disqualify me. Today I see

the irony in one group of critics squawking about my not being qualified to question detainees and another squealing that I had an unfair
advantage.

I reported the chief psychologist's threat to file an ethics complaint to the chief of special missions, who in turn requested that an
outside senior psychological consultant provide an opinion on the
ethics of using a psychologist as an interrogator. Because the consultant's opinion dealt with ethics and not the agency's interrogation
program, it was not classified. It emphasized the need to clarify roles,
identify conflicts of interest, and try to balance conflicting ethical
demands. Although it did not explicitly address it, my takeaway was
that the easiest way for us to resolve any ethical dilemma was to avoid
providing any mental health services to detainees. That opinion was
one of the reasons Bruce and I finally were allowed to discontinue
performing psychological assessments as part of our routine duties.
We would have preferred to make a clean break early on.

Years later, I asked the chief of the Special Missions Department why he wanted our input on how the detainees were doing
emotionally since he had staff psychologists performing the assessments of record. He said that because interest at headquarters was so
high and there were so few people involved, he was trying to collect
as much feedback as he could from anyone and everyone who had
contact with the detainees. My feedback and that of Bruce went into
the mix with the reports of record from the staff psychologists and
physicians, feedback from interrogators and debriefers, and reports
written by other CIA officers as just another piece of data. Relying
solely on us or even heavily on us would have been inappropriate, but
since we were psychologists and had spent so much time with the
detainees—literally thousands of hours—completely excluding our
input would not have been the correct thing to do either. According to the chief of SMD at that time, our opinions carried the same

weight as those of other interrogators; it was just that we had more insight into how the human mind works.

**MY CONTACT WITH** Ramzi bin al-Shibh lasted well beyond his initial harsh interrogations. Off and on through the years I was involved with the program, bin al-Shibh and I crossed paths many times. I spent a lot of time at various black sites doing what RDI called "maintenance visits." Really they were daily visits with the detainees on-site to keep their morale up.

At that time, detainees were held in isolation except for contact with guards, debriefers, medical personnel, and on occasion the COB, who were all business. Every contact they had focused on the business at hand. The detainees got lonely. When they did, their intelligence production fell off. We couldn't put an ad in Craigslist for a companion. We also couldn't let the guards spend social time with them because we didn't want our security staff in a position in which these charismatic enemy fighters could potentially develop a compromising relationship with one of them, endangering others.

The interrogators already had a relationship with the detainees. It may sound strange, but after all the time spent together from EITs through debriefings, across multiple renditions and moves among various black sites, the relationship the interrogators developed with the detainees over the years was surprisingly cordial. It was kind of like the bond that develops between recruits and tough drill sergeants.

Once headquarters approved the activities, we watched movies with some of them, read books, did calisthenics, played basketball, and engaged in a host of other activities you wouldn't normally associate with interrogators. We even listened to complaints about how they were being treated by the people in charge of the black sites and often acted as their advocate on-site.

I had this kind of relationship more or less with all of the thirteen or so high-value detainees except two: Walid bin Attash (who helped select and train some of the 9/11 hijackers) and Ramzi bin al-Shibh. Ramzi never gave his militancy a rest. If there was a fledgling hunger strike or a brouhaha about female guards or a serious problem with the female debriefers, bin al-Shibh was at its core. He complained about everything. He objected to the halal food because he couldn't inspect the slaughterhouses, objected to his clothes, objected because he didn't have a head scarf, and objected to haircuts, claiming that tufts of hair were left in scraggly patches to demean him. He objected . . . and objected . . . and objected.

In day-to-day interactions, I got along better with al-Nashiri than I did with Ramzi bin al-Shibh. Al-Nashiri could be cantankerous when he had a migraine, but bin al-Shibh was a nearly constant pain in the ass. Dealing with him day after day was exhausting.

One time when Bruce and I were passing through a black site, the COB approached us about a problem he was having with bin al-Shibh. It seemed bin al-Shibh was complaining that the CIA was either drugging his food or deliberately shaking his cell at night as part of some devious mind-control experiment.

Consistent with headquarters policy, the COB looked into his complaint. He looked into food preparation, had bin al-Shibh examined by medical personnel and staff psychologists, made sure nobody was messing with him, did a walk-through of his cell, and after exhaustive investigation found nothing. He wanted to know if we could do anything to help get bin al-Shibh back on track because his accusations and complaints were disrupting debriefings.

Headquarters policy was that EITs were *not*, I repeat *not*, to be used to punish a detainee for acting out or force detainees to comply with administrative procedures. And to his credit, in a debriefing, bin al-Shibh would still address questions between his sulking and accusations. Thus, any discussion of EITs would have been inappropriate.

But that was not what the COB had in mind. He wasn't even thinking about physical coercion. He was perplexed by the complaint and really wanted to know what was going on. He said bin al-Shibh actually seemed to believe what he was saying. The COB wanted us to look into the mystery because we both had worked extensively with bin al-Shibh and were used to his antics.

Bruce and I interviewed bin al-Shibh about his concerns. Since we had just arrived at the site and he didn't know any better, we told him that headquarters had sent us there to figure out what was bothering him and fix it. We assured him that he was very important and that we were there to resolve the issue and not try to force him to drop his complaints and live with the problem.

We did what some would call a critical incident analysis. It was a technique I used as a tool in the friend-of-court sanity evaluations for criminal cases, mishap investigations, and psychological autopsies I performed in the military. The essence of it is to reconstruct the target of the investigation's thoughts, feelings, and actions at critical points as key events unfold.

Rather than just describe his complaints, we asked him to put the incident in the context of his day, to create a time line, and to walk us through key events. The analysis indicated that bin al-Shibh felt dizzy and the room started shaking with what felt like a low hum running through his body, mostly after his evening meal when he lay down to sleep. But it also happened sometimes when he lay down to nap during the day, though not always. He said he was convinced that either he was being drugged or the CIA monitored his cell and threw a special switch that made it vibrate when they saw that he was trying to rest. Those claims sounded so crazy, I thought about giving him a special tinfoil hat to make it all go away.

We knew no one was deliberately messing with him, and so we considered the possibility that he was suffering from a hypnagogic sensory experience, some kind of tactile sensation that occurred just as he was falling asleep. We made a note to discuss it with the medical personnel and the psychologist to see if they thought it needed to be ruled out as a possibility. Then, at Bruce's suggestion, we went back to bin al-Shibh's cell and asked him to walk us through his evening activities. Bruce played the part of bin al-Shibh, and bin al-Shibh told Bruce what to do next.

During the walk-through, when Bruce lay down on bin al-Shibh's bed, his eyes widened and he looked at me, puzzled. "This bed is vibrating," Bruce said. "I can't believe it. But I can feel some kind of deep hum."

I thought Bruce was messing with me, but when I lay down, I felt the same thing. The vibration was there, and it was not something you could ignore. It made it feel like the room was spinning. I could imagine that after a while it might make a person nauseous. It would certainly keep me awake, but oddly enough, you couldn't feel it anyplace else in the cell.

Bin al-Shibh said, "See, I told you. The CIA is doing mind-control experiments on me." We assured him they weren't, but he just pursed his lips and shook his head in disgust.

Bruce and I left bin al-Shibh's cell and met with the COB, who was waiting outside, monitoring on closed circuit TV. The three of us went looking for the source of the vibration. For security reasons I can't describe the cell or how it was affixed inside the building, but we found the source. It was an engineering problem localized to that cell, and it happened only when a large piece of equipment situated nearby was running.

There was nothing that could be done to fix the problem, and so the COB had bin al-Shibh moved to a different cell, well away from the source of the vibration. Before he was moved, we tested the new bed to be sure it wasn't vibrating.

Bin al-Shibh's response was to incorporate me and Bruce into his accusations. Thereafter, when the topic came up, he would assert that Bruce and I had stopped by the black site because the mind-control experiment was over and we wanted to assess the effects it had had on him. He said we attempted to hide the experiment by trying to make him believe it was just a mechanical problem.

I write about this not just because it provides insight into bin al-Shibh's personality but also because it illustrates the great lengths to which CIA personnel went to address detainees' concerns. Bin al-Shibh was a constant complainer. Even so, rather than dismiss his complaint out of hand, the COB persisted until he found an answer and resolved it.

Each of the detainees had his own set of idiosyncrasies, but there was one who was the most challenging and most important—that was KSM.

# CHAPTER 6

# KSM: From Confrontation to Compliance

One of an interrogator's jobs is to get inside the mind of the person being questioned. In the case of an Islamic terrorist such as Khalid Sheikh Mohammed, it's important to understand the core beliefs and motivations that underlie his involvement in violent jihad and figure out why he's trying carefully to protect some pieces of information but not others.

Let me show you what I mean by giving you a peek at what I believe was going on inside KSM's head as he waited for interrogations to start at the black site.

**KSM IS SITTING,** back against the wall, chained to the floor of a damp room in the basement of an aging building. It is dank and smells of dust and mildew. Dingy white paint covers the walls and ceiling. Sunk into the cracked concrete floor is a steel eyebolt to which KSM's leg shackles are chained. On the ceiling is another eye-bolt. He almost doesn't notice it and wonders what it's for.

A little less than an hour has passed since KSM's first contact with an interrogator at this new place. The man said he wanted information to stop operations inside the United States. KSM had that information but had no intention of providing it. KSM had a different set of priorities.

KSM's hands are shaking, but he's confident he'll be all right. This is the third or fourth place the Americans have tried to question him. He won the battles of wits and wills at the other sites, and he is sure he will win this one, too. He believes that even if things get rough, he can hold out until it is too late for the CIA to do anything about the upcoming attacks. Soon they will know.

As he waits, KSM sorts through his priorities. The most important is protecting Sheikh Usama. Whatever happens, KSM is willing to die rather than tell the American infidels anything that will help them locate the sheikh.

His next priority is to protect information that could help the infidels stop future terror attacks against the United States. KSM has several in the works. Some of them could rival 9/11 in death and destruction. It's important that preparations for them continue.

KSM needs to be especially careful not to give up information that could be used to capture or kill brothers working on these operations, such as Hambali's plan to crash hijacked aircraft into the tallest buildings on the West Coast. KSM also wants to protect the jihadi brothers and sisters he already has on the ground inside the United States. There's Iyman Faris, a jihadist working on a plot to cut the suspension cables on the Brooklyn Bridge with specially designed explosive tools and collapse it during rush hour, when it is packed with cars and people. Because the technology is unfamiliar, some have made fun of this plot, asserting that it is far-fetched. But with my background in explosive technology, I can tell you those tools really exist and with enough of them, properly placed, you can bring down a suspension bridge. Then there is Uzair Paracha, who has been working with KSM to smuggle special explosive devices into the United States to blow up gas stations along the East Coast.

KSM has thousands of other details in his head about al-Qa'ida's strategic plans, operatives, and activities. Although this information could help the Americans, it is less important to him. He can hand out these details like candy to the interrogators if necessary, using them like a relief valve to take the pressure off if things get too intense.

He has been in custody only a few days. He runs through a quick mental list of throwaway items: abandoned plots, long-dead brothers, things the infidels should already know from other captured detainees. He can use these things, he thinks, to stall, to give the brothers a chance to "adjust themselves": a chance to change their e-mail accounts, wipe their computers, destroy their cell phones, abandon safe houses, and flee deeper into hiding.

The door to his cell opens. Enormous men enter dressed completely in black. Not a bit of skin showing. Eyes covered with mirrored goggles. He sees himself in them. KSM tries to talk to the guards, but they act as if they don't hear him. Without speaking they undo his leg chains and stand him up against the wall. This part of the wall is different. It is covered with burlap and bounces a little when the guards press his back against it. They put a black hood over his head. Then KSM hears the door open and footsteps approach in the dark.

Bruce walks toward KSM. What he sees resembles a hooded troll. KSM is short, with a grotesque potbelly. His body, what can be seen of it, is covered with finger-length black hair that KSM sheds like a cat losing its winter coat.

Bruce is carrying a rolled-up towel duct-taped to form the protective collar that we used to prevent whiplash when bouncing someone off a walling wall. He slowly moves the rolled towel over KSM's hooded head and cinches it the way he would if he was adjusting his grip on the towel before walling KSM. Bruce then lets it go and carefully repositions the rolled towel on KSM's neck and shoulders.

Bruce slowly pulls the hood off KSM's head. KSM closes one eye and blinks up at him. The look on his face says, "This guy is scarier than the first one."

KSM's eyes widen when Bruce takes hold of the rolled-up towel and says in a cadence and voice quality that sounds like vintage Clint Eastwood, "When my friend spoke with you the last time, he told you we wanted information to stop operations inside the United States." With each pause in the Eastwood-like cadence, Bruce adjusts the rolled towel. Cinching it. Releasing it. Both hands working the grip.

"My friend said the next time someone spoke to you, he would ask you for that information. I'm that someone. We want information to stop operations in the United States. This is your last chance. Give us what we're asking for and nothing bad will happen to you."

KSM mutters something about being the mastermind of 9/11, voice deliberately low, hoping to distract Bruce with information about an old operation that would be useful for a court case but not as valuable for disrupting new attacks. We had been told not to be distracted by this.

As soon as the mention of 9/11 leaves KSM's mouth, Bruce pulls him forward in an attention grasp, using the rolled towel to support his neck. KSM's naked potbelly swings out away from his body and bounces off Bruce's upper thighs.

Bruce leans into KSM's ear and softly says, "Is what you're telling me going to help us stop operations inside the United States?"

KSM shakes his head, not speaking. Not looking at Bruce.

"No?" asks Bruce. "I didn't think so."

Then Bruce bounces KSM off the walling wall several times, careful to keep KSM's feet on the ground and protect his neck and the back of his head. The fluid sloshing around in KSM's inner ear starts the room swimming. Suspended inside the hollow walling wall, the plywood clapper slams back and forth each time KSM's shoulders are bounced off the wall, making a hell of a racket, adding to the disorienting effect. The noise is thunderous. The experience is disorienting but not painful. I know because Bruce and I had it done to us many times as part of our resistance training.

When the walling stopped, Bruce once again stood KSM against the walling wall, held him until he was sure he could stand unassisted, and then carefully and gently arranged the rolled-up towel around KSM's neck as if he were smoothing crumpled clothing on a child.

"Let's start again," Bruce said in a low, pleasant voice.

This is how KSM's first enhanced interrogation session began. After that, Bruce and I and the Preacher interrogated KSM in rotating shifts around the clock, sometimes alone, sometimes in pairs, sometimes all three of us. Since KSM had already resisted intense physical pressure at another site, we escalated more quickly than we might have otherwise because his confidence and defiant attitude rendered less coercive measures ineffective.

Over the next three weeks or so we followed the interrogation plan approved by headquarters, escalating from less physical techniques such as the attention grasp to waterboarding. As it turned out, the waterboard wasn't effective on KSM and we weren't willing or authorized to do the kinds of things that would make it work. He beat it by using two strategies. First, he sometimes swallowed the water, prompting the physician monitoring the interrogations to require the use of normal saline instead of bottled water to avoid a potentially dangerous condition known as hyponatremia or water intoxication. The second thing KSM did was somehow open his sinus passages and let the water enter through his nose and pour out of his mouth as fast as we poured it on the cloth. I don't know how he did it. It looked like a magic trick.

KSM also figured out that there were limits to how long we were allowed to pour water during any single application. Once he discovered this, he would use his fingers to count off the number of seconds water was being poured and then gesture with a slashing motion of his left hand for us to stop as we approached the upper limits. I don't know how he did this either, but it was remarkable.

I was also impressed with how little the reality of being waterboarded seemed to upset him. At one point, early in his interrogations and before he had been exposed to much sleep deprivation, we momentarily left the room where he was being waterboarded so that he couldn't overhear us as we spoke with a subject matter expert. The physician, the guards, and the COB remained in the room but didn't interact with him. When we returned a couple of minutes later, KSM was asleep, strapped to the waterboard. Snoring!

**KSM'S RESISTANCE FINALLY** was overcome with a combination of walling and sleep deprivation. It wasn't that he broke and suddenly spilled his guts. It was the result of a gradual conditioning process that I will explain here publicly for the first time.

First a little background.

To appreciate the problem Bruce and I faced, you have to step back and consider it from our perspective. It was a year and a half since the 9/11 attacks; while Americans were struggling to get their lives back to normal, at the CIA things were still in a state of emergency. They were struggling to counter the threat of more mass-casualty attacks at home while undertaking high-risk operations to find, capture, or kill those who had blindsided us on 9/11. They needed to build liaison partnerships in other parts of the world and redirect massive amounts of money and resources. The threat level had not changed significantly since 9/11. In many ways it was the worst-case scenario.

- The CIA had reliable intelligence indicating that a catastrophic terror attack, possibly involving a nuclear device, was in the works and could occur at any moment.

- The CIA was under tremendous political and psychological pressure to do "whatever it took" to stop the next attack.

- In order to stop it, CIA needed perishable, time-urgent information.

- KSM, a senior al-Qa'ida leader with the blood of thousands of Americans on his hands, almost certainly had that information and was refusing to provide it.

- Previous efforts to question him had revealed that KSM was a hard-core jihadist, psychologically resilient, highly skilled at protecting information, and tough enough to withstand earlier efforts to coerce it out of him.

- KSM wanted to see future attacks succeed; knew that if he provided the information the CIA wanted, the attacks could be stopped; and was demonstrably willing to endure significant hardship to protect what he knew.

For many at the CIA it felt like a ticking time bomb scenario. It was actually worse from my perspective. I had been on a bomb squad, I had worked hostage negotiations and armed standoffs, and I never feared as much for those around me as I did during those first chaotic months after 9/11. The threat of another catastrophic attack was palpable. You could feel it in the briefing rooms and see it taking its toll behind the eyes of CIA officers scrambling to do all they could to make up for having missed the first attack by stopping the next one.

KSM had demonstrated that tea and biscuits weren't going to get him to provide the information necessary to stop attacks. After KSM was captured and before he was rendered out of Pakistan, two CIA officers had tried to question him using standard debriefing and rapport-building techniques. One CIA officer went so far as to dress head to toe in traditional Pakistani clothing for tea and "respectful conversation." Later, KSM described him to me and Bruce as a "clown," saying the officer was "a fool" if he thought KSM was going to inform on his "brothers" because someone put on Pakistani garb and served him tea and treats.

You weren't going to bully the information out of him, either. Here is how I know. KSM was not moved directly to where we interrogated him. The rendition stopped for several days at another remote black site, where KSM was interrogated by a third CIA officer, the same chief interrogator I had reported earlier for using unapproved EITs.

During this stopover, the chief interrogator and KSM got into what a senior agency psychologist who observed it called "a battle of wills," a contest that, according to the psychologist, KSM won. The battle of wills was over KSM's refusal to address the chief interrogator as "sir" each time KSM spoke to him, something that never occurred to me or Bruce to ask any detainee to do.

The psychologist told us that with each refusal, the chief interrogator used more and more physical coercion and became more and more obsessed with "breaking KSM's will." So much so that forcing KSM to call him "sir" became the single-minded focus of the last several interrogation sessions before KSM was moved to our location.

The senior agency psychologist (who was not an interrogator but had been resistance-trained in SERE school) told us that in his view, KSM had deliberately drawn the chief interrogator into this battle of wills to derail the interrogations and protect information. KSM avoided answering questions about future al-Qa'ida attacks and operatives still at large by refusing to address the chief interrogator as "sir," knowing his refusal would irk the chief interrogator, who would stop questioning him and try to bully him into compliance. Winning that battle of wills strengthened KSM's confidence that if he just held out long enough, he could keep his secrets.

In my opinion, we would never get the information the CIA needed to stop future attacks by trying to beat it out of him, though there was pressure from some to do just that. It would have been wrong, and it would have been ineffective. You might be able to coerce him to capitulate one time, to squirt out one piece of information. But there were too many questions that needed to be answered, too many unknowns that the analysts and targeters needed to piece in their link charts and analytical formulations, for beating it out of him to be a successful long-term strategy for stopping future attacks. We needed him to cooperate.

But how do you do that? How do you get a terrorist who is willing to suffer to protect information to start cooperating?

CIA senior leadership tasked us with getting KSM to comply. Accomplishing that required two things. First, because we wanted KSM to cooperate during questioning when no EITs were being used, we had to condition him so that the mere *thought* of being deceitful triggered fear and emotional discomfort. Second, to keep his cooperation going, we had to condition him to experience a sense of relief when he did cooperate. This required us to use two very different naturally occurring learning processes.

The first process we used is called classical conditioning or Pavlovian conditioning, after Ivan Pavlov, the man who first described this learning phenomenon. Here is a simple textbook description of how classical conditioning can be used to get a previously neutral stimulus (such as the sound of a buzzer) to evoke fear. In this scenario, the person is hooked up to a machine that delivers mild but aversive shocks. The buzzer sounds, and a shock is delivered. After a few presentations (or pairings) of the buzzer with a shock, the sound of the previously neutral buzzer starts to evoke fear. Eventually the sound of the buzzer alone evokes a conditioned fear response even if the shock doesn't follow. In the end, the success or failure of the conditioning process depends on the timing of the buzzer and the shock. The shock has to occur within a few moments after the buzzer sounds or the buzzer won't come to elicit fear.

To condition KSM and the other detainees to experience fear and emotional discomfort when they thought about being deceitful, we had to time the application of an aversive EIT such as walling to start when they were thinking about withholding information and stop when they were thinking about *anything* else. We couldn't know for sure what they were thinking, but we could judge from their behavior when they were looking for a way out of the situation. If they showed any sign, no matter how small, that they were genuinely looking for some way to cooperate, we would reinforce that. But the primary objective at this point was to pair the naturally occurring discomfort and distress of the EITs with the urge to deceive. *Pair* in the sense that I'm using the term means to be sure that both occur at approximately the same time. *Contiguous* is the word psychologists use to describe this relationship. It worked best when the effort to be deceptive occurred first and EITs were applied a few heartbeats later.

It's a more complicated version of the classical conditioning process described in the previous paragraph, and again, timing is critical.

To tap into the second naturally occurring learning process and condition KSM and other detainees to experience a sense of relief when they cooperated, we had to orchestrate events so that they could escape or avoid the adverse consequences of being deceitful when and only when they actually tried to cooperate, even if in the beginning that cooperation was minuscule. This is called *avoidance conditioning* by psychologists. It is one of the hardwired, natural ways humans learn to escape uncomfortable situations. We learn to avoid things that cause us discomfort and distress and seek out those which make us feel better.

After conditioning, detainees still can resist providing information, much as people who are afraid to go to the dentist still can force themselves to go. But the thought of trying to withhold information causes acute distress and anxiety. After their conditioning was complete, the high-value detainees Bruce and I worked with generally feared holding back. When they did hold back, the emotional distress displayed in their body language alerted us that they were trying to hide something.

Some interrogators understood the conditioning process better than others and were more proficient at getting the timing right. Overusing or underusing EITs or using them at the wrong time disrupted conditioning for the desired response. Some interrogators, such as the chief of interrogations, didn't even try to condition compliance. They simply tried to keep the pressure up until the detainee broke.

Contrary to what has been reported in the press, in the early days of the program, Bruce and I were not involved in the CIA's initial interrogation training. In fact, we didn't even know about it at first. The training was handled by a CIA employee who formerly had been a SERE instructor and the chief interrogator. We didn't know what they taught, but whenever Bruce and I worked with a new interrogator, we explained the need for timing in the conditioning process. On the basis of their reactions, I got the impression that timing wasn't emphasized in the early CIA interrogator courses with which we weren't involved.

When the Counterterrorism Center leadership learned that some of their personnel in the field were going beyond what they were authorized to do, they took steps to rein them in. As the haul of captured bin Ladin operatives grew (in part because of intelligence gained in our earlier interrogation of people such as Abu Zubaydah), there was a need for more interrogators.

By then the chief interrogator had been removed from the program for cause, and in 2004 Bruce and I were asked to become involved in CIA interrogator training. We made a point of explaining how to use the conditioning process in the interrogation courses we taught. We believed the uneven effectiveness among interrogators trained in early CIA interrogation courses, and the fact that some of those interrogators resorted to unauthorized techniques to break a detainee's resistance, was a result of not understanding the powerful learning principles that underlie the enhanced interrogation process and overfocusing on EITs rather than the way they should be applied.

In addition, not every detainee responded to the EITs with the same emotions or emotional intensity. Remember, KSM fell asleep on the waterboard moments after we stepped away from him. That's why for some detainees walling was enough but with others we had to try a variety of EITs before we found a combination that was effective. Some people's nervous systems are naturally slower to form the learned associations that are the neural machine language of emotional conditioning; that's just how it is.

Early on, KSM didn't display many signs of cooperation, and

it wasn't because he didn't understand: he spoke excellent English. In the beginning when he did act cooperatively and we stopped the EITs, what he offered was usually a detail about a dead person or a decades-old terror plot or a piece of perishable information well past its use-by date. To condition him not to do this, we applied EITs (usually walling) as soon as it became apparent that he was being duplicitous.

As the interrogations progressed and the conditioned associations formed, KSM shifted his priorities from protecting information to trying to find answers that would allow him to avoid EITs. As protecting information became less of an immediate priority, KSM started looking for ways to provide just enough truthful information to avoid EITs but still protect his most important secrets.

Gradually KSM began to offer bits and pieces of better information, as expected, at the beginning of a new session, before EITs were applied. As this new phase started, he initially offered information that in his mind had a lower priority than protecting Sheikh Usama or his own attack plans. But that meant answering questions instead of rocking, chanting, issuing threats, and taunting interrogators. It also meant that information became available to analysts that though it was not a top priority for KSM to protect was useful for expanding our understanding of al-Qa'ida, targeting al-Qa'ida operatives, and aiding in the interrogations of other detainees. It was also the initial opening for us to begin using social influence techniques.

We got useful information in this phase, but we wanted his answers to be more full and complete. We also wanted him to work directly with the subject matter experts, who could debrief him more proficiently than we could.

About this time, KSM adopted a resistance technique I've seen many times with savvy resisters. Bruce and I call it hiding in the truth. This technique involves telling a version of the truth that is uninformative and not responsive to the question, usually by leaving out critical details, emphasizing irrelevancies, or using language ploys to link details that are accurate standing alone but misleading when presented together. Watch politicians on the Sunday talk shows to see this technique in practice. I've seen this tactic trip up skilled interrogators and debriefers.

**EVEN SO, ONCE** KSM started looking for ways to answer questions, we could gradually back off the use of EITs and shift to social influence strategies to shape his cooperation. In the beginning of this phase we couldn't back off completely, because withholding information by hiding in the truth and other, less subtle resistance ploys had to be discouraged if we were going to move him to the debriefing stage. But at the same time, we didn't want to go back to full-on EITs that took him out of the moment, so to speak. At this stage, forcing him to deal with the question being asked was critical.

I had thought about this problem when helping the CIA put this program together. Earlier in this chapter I explained how the repeated pairings that occur in classical conditioning can result in something as benign as the sound of a buzzer evoking a reflexive response such as fear without any adverse event happening. We took advantage of this learning phenomenon to create an opportunity to use fewer EITs later by making the rolled-up towel we used to protect the detainees during walling an object that evoked fear.

Here is how we did that. In the limited time EITs were in play (detainees usually started trying to cooperate about seventy-two hours after EITs began), Bruce and I always started every interrogation with the same conditioning ritual. The detainee would be standing against the walling wall, hooded. The interrogator would enter the room and slowly and gently run the rolled towel over the top of the detainee's head from the forehead to the back of the neck. We then would spend several minutes adjusting it, as if searching for the perfect grip. We did this because we wanted the towel to become a fear-inducing object: an omen of what might happen next, a harbinger of what was to come if they didn't cooperate. Once that Pavlovian association was formed, the towel represented a potential adverse consequence and elicited a conditioned fear response without our having to resort to the physical discomfort of EITs.

We put the towel around the necks of detainees each time they were questioned and used it to wall them if necessary. Later, when the detainees were in the beginning stages of transitioning out of EITs—sometimes cooperating and sometimes holding back—we would carry the towel into the room with us, put it around their necks, and slowly pull off their hoods. If they started answering questions, we would make a show of removing the towel, saying something like "I guess we won't be needing this today. But I'll put it over here just in case." If they started lying to us or being duplicitous, we would put the towel around their necks using the same slow ritual and wall them.

Later, as their cooperation increased, we would walk in, pull off the hood, show them the towel, and ask, "Am I going to need this?" They would usually reply "No," and we would say, "Okay. I'm going to take you at your word." And a noncoercive interrogation would begin.

Gradually we went from placing the towel in a detainee's sight line on a nearby table to making a show of moving it out of the room. At that stage, when detainees started holding back, we'd glance in the direction of the towel before actually moving toward it. More often than not, that was all it took to get them back on track. Finally, when detainees were in full debriefing mode, the rolled towel never made an appearance.

At some point, generally about midway in the conditioning process described above, a debriefer usually joined the interrogators in the room, taking turns asking questions and taking notes but not participating in the rough stuff, if any even occurred. This was done to ease the transition from interrogators asking all the questions to debriefers directly questioning the detainees. Over time, the interrogators asked fewer questions and the debriefers asked more. The debriefers were, after all, the subject matter experts who wrote the intelligence reports. It was better for them than for me to ask the questions.

Even after detainees were as compliant as they were going to be and debriefers were asking most if not all of the questions, it was useful to have an interrogator in the room. Debriefers came and went every few weeks, but there was a small number of interrogators dealing with the high-value detainees, and they stayed longer and spent thousands of hours with the detainees. They knew a detainee's idiosyncratic mannerisms, signs he was trying to be deceptive, and the sorts of debriefer behaviors that made questioning specific detainees such as KSM easier or harder.

CRITICS OF THE enhanced interrogation program allege that the CIA started using physically coercive EITs on KSM too quickly. They say that the CIA didn't give him ample opportunity to demonstrate his unwillingness to answer questions before getting physical. This is simply not true. KSM was given multiple opportunities to answer questions before he arrived at the black site where interrogations with EITs started in earnest.

For example, while he was still in Pakistan, where he had been captured and was awaiting rendition, CIA officers attempted to question KSM. He responded with taunts and by rocking back and forth, chanting verses from the Koran, and refusing to cooperate. Furthermore, after leaving Pakistan, KSM was held briefly at a second location before he was transported to the black site where those of us in the primary interrogation team were waiting. At this second location, KSM was given another opportunity to talk. Again he refused and was (in my opinion) unfortunately subjected to a short regime of physical coercion, some of which was not approved by the DOJ. Finally, when KSM arrived at our location, we started at square one. We gave him a third opportunity to talk during our neutral probe, and again he responded with taunts and veiled threats. KSM had plenty of chances to talk before things got rough. He simply chose not to. If he had cooperated at any point, KSM would not have been subjected to harsh interrogations. It is as simple as that.

**THE TYPICAL NONCOERCIVE** debriefing went like this. The guards would escort the hooded detainee into the debriefing room and sit him in a chair. One of the interrogators would come in, take the hood off, and make a bit of small talk to ascertain the detainee's mood and disposition that day. We would ask how the detainees had slept and if they needed anything. If they did need something or had complaints, we told them we would come back after the debriefing and figure out what we could do to address the issue. Most important, we would ask them if they had thought of anything overnight they would like to tell us. Often, this was when one of the detainees would offer clarifications and volunteer to discuss new information about al-Qa'ida operatives and plans. We would get a quick sense of what it was and then alert the debriefer so that he or she would know to inquire about the topic.

Then the debriefer entered the room. Early in a detainee's debriefing phase, interrogators would stay for the entire debriefing.

Later, as the detainee became more compliant and the debriefer more proficient with that detainee, we would excuse ourselves once it was clear that the detainee was cooperating and monitor the debriefing on closed circuit TV. After the debriefing was over, interrogators would stop by the debriefing room for what we called a fireside chat and follow up on any concerns raised by the detainee before the debriefing.

In the beginning, before the CIA implemented a training course, CIA sections sent their "best and brightest" to be debriefers, and these individuals were, with few exceptions, excellent. Later, when promotions and the logistic demands of supporting both the war on terror and the war in Iraq forced the parts of the agency that provided officers to be less discriminating, debriefers varied greatly in their skill and approach. Some debriefers were excellent, most were competent, and a very few were train wrecks.

I recall one CIA officer who showed up to debrief Hambali, the leader of the 2002 Bali hotel bombings, dressed entirely in black jungle fatigues, hell-bent on interrogating rather than debriefing Hambali. The officer raised a fuss when the interrogator on-site told him that his approach probably would shut down Hambali and lead to fewer rather than more answers. Finally, the COB ordered the officer to change both his clothes and his approach, but the debriefing was still contentious and went nowhere.

Most marginal debriefers were not that obvious. Some floundered after trying to trick a detainee into revealing information that the debriefer suspected he was hiding, and failing to elicit that information. These debriefers would get angry when the detainee didn't fall for the trick and then accuse the detainee of lying, often claiming that it was "inconceivable" that the detainee couldn't recall someone in the background of a crowded meeting from years before, as if memory worked like a videotape, accurately recording exact details of conversations and peripheral events.

But the good ones were really good: cordial, businesslike, able to provide context to aid recall without asking leading questions. They took the time to establish rapport and tailor questions to a specific detainee to understand that particular detainee's response style. This made the questioning easier and allowed the debriefer to figure out if a detainee who didn't engage was trying to hide information or just having a bad day. They tended to stick to open-ended questions to avoid leading the detainee and didn't get into a huff if the detainee seemed to have a bad attitude.

Some debriefers would enter the room weighed down with maps or charts or photographs or technical intelligence that had been cleared to share with the detainee, others with just a simple notepad and pen. Most often the debriefer had a list of intelligence requirements with possible questions for reference and notes fleshing out important points.

Debriefers and subject matter experts worked tirelessly, away from their families for weeks, living under virtual house arrest, often writing reports or debriefing detainees late into the night. When new captures occurred, like the interrogators and others at the site, the debriefers would work all night and long into the next day, taking advantage of the flood of new information that previously captured detainees felt the sudden urge to "clarify" or correct once they were confronted with a capture photo of someone new. Debriefers also fed information to interrogators questioning the new arrival. If the new captive offered a piece of information, debriefers and interrogators often could check the databases and query other detainees immediately.

CONTRARY TO THE false claims made in Feinstein's report, after enhanced interrogation, KSM and other high-value detainees in the program provided enormous amounts of unique intelligence that, as the CIA's official response notes, "helped the US disrupt plots, capture terrorists, better understand the enemy, prevent another mass casualty attack, and save lives." Information gained from those detainees also aided U.S. law enforcement efforts to capture and prosecute terrorists operating inside the United States.

For example, information obtained from KSM after enhanced interrogations was used to disrupt a second wave of terror attacks aimed at crashing hijacked aircraft into multiple buildings on the West Coast and across the United States. KSM's reporting was a critical link in the capture and detention of Hambali (mastermind of the 2002 Bali hotel bombings that killed two hundred people) and the seventeen non-Arab students his terror cell was grooming to be pilots and provide the muscle to subdue passengers on the hijacked airplanes that would crash into the Library Tower in California, the Plaza Bank in Washington State, the Sears Tower in Chicago, and possibly other places.

Also, information obtained from KSM after enhanced interrogations led to the arrest of Iyman Faris, an al-Qa'ida sleeper inside the United States tasked with attacking the Brooklyn Bridge during rush hour. The CIA has reaffirmed that KSM's reporting "informed and focused the investigation" for FBI and law enforcement officials questioning Faris.

In addition, information obtained from KSM and others after enhanced interrogations played a key role in disrupting terror attacks against Heathrow Airport and the Canary Wharf financial district in London, England.

Moreover, information obtained from KSM and others after enhanced interrogations contributed to the identification of Jafar al-Tayyar, an al-Qa'ida operative who was also known as Adnan Gulshair el Shukrijumah. Significantly, he held a U.S. passport. Before his identification, al-Tayyar could travel in and out of the United States with ease and had been dispatched by al-Qa'ida to surveil nuclear power plants, the homes of past presidents, historical landmarks, dams, subways, bridges, and buildings for attack planning. He was named in a federal indictment for plotting suicide bomb attacks on New York's subway system. After identification by KSM and Abu Zubaydah, Shukrijumah had to go into hiding. He was reported killed by Pakistani forces in December 2014.

Additionally, information obtained from KSM after enhanced interrogations led to the identification and arrest of the U.S.-based Pakistani businessman Saifullah Paracha and his son, Uzair. They were working with KSM to smuggle explosives into the United States and advance KSM's plot to blow up gas stations along the East Coast.

Finally, KSM was critical to finding bin Ladin.

That's five plots disrupted and several terrorists detained or killed, including bin Ladin. There are many other examples, but cataloging them is not my purpose in this book. If you're interested in what really happened and want more details about the kinds of intelligence obtained from the CIA's detention and interrogation program that kept Americans safe, there are many sources to consult. For example, you can read the CIA's comments on the SSCI report on the Rendition, Detention, and Interrogation program, paying special attention to the twenty case studies included in the back of the document. You can read the SSCI Minority Views, starting on page 29 and running through page 73. Or you can read *Courting Disaster* by Marc Thiessen or *Hard Measures* by Jose Rodriguez.

# CHAPTER 7

# KSM—Devil and Diva

Although stopping future attacks was our prime mission, once the detainees became compliant, we did obtain intelligence about past atrocities that was valuable. Here is an example from one of our post-debriefing chats.

"You looked uncomfortable during parts of your conversation with the lady," Bruce said, referring to KSM's just-completed de-briefing with a weapons of mass destruction (WMD) subject matter expert.

In these chats we would discuss a detainee's actions and body language during an interrogation or debriefing that had just ended. We would say to the detainee, "Now that the questioning is over, let's take a few minutes to relax, put aside any friction between us, and discuss what that was like for you."

Then we would have a direct and sometimes surprisingly open and intimate discussion with the detainee about what he thought and felt while being questioned. If we thought it would help nudge him toward being more compliant the next time he was questioned,

Bruce and I would share our reactions to what he said and how he acted during questioning.

The chat was also helpful in getting additional information. Detainees often elaborated on something they had said or provided additional details they forgot to include when initially questioned. It wasn't really a chat, of course; it was part of our interrogation process.

"We noticed that several times when you were talking to the lady, you seemed about to say something and then decided not to. You would glance down and look away. Sometimes when she asked you questions, you were lost in thought. You know the hard times are over; there's nothing that you can say that will offend us. What's bothering you?"

"Go get the lady who asks the questions so she can take notes," KSM said. He sounded nervous.

While Bruce stayed with KSM, I ran to the communications center where the WMD subject matter expert was writing up her report for the day.

"KSM says he has something important to say and he would like you there," I said.

When the two of us got back to the briefing room and settled into our chairs, KSM launched into a gory and detailed description of how he beheaded the *Wall Street Journal* reporter Daniel Pearl in Pakistan in February 2002. Although some suspected his involvement, up to that moment we had no idea that he had committed that horrendous murder personally.

This was not the first time this topic had come up while KSM was in CIA custody. Soon after capture, while he was still in Pakistan, a CIA officer had asked him what he knew about the Pearl killing, but KSM had simply replied, "Not yet."

I don't recall the exact words KSM used when the debriefer, Bruce, and I questioned him that day, but the picture they painted in my head caused me to tear up. At first, KSM's hands shook and his voice was hesitant. I think he expected us to punish him. But then, as he got into the story, it was obvious he enjoyed the telling and experienced pleasure reliving parts of it. At one point he got out of his chair and used hand gestures to illustrate how he cut Pearl's throat.

One of us asked him "Was it hard to do?" meaning, "Was it emotionally difficult?"

KSM misunderstood the question. "Oh, no," he said, hardly pausing, "No problem. I had very sharp knives. Just like slaughtering sheep. The only hard part was cutting through the neck bone." He then went into an ugly matter-of-fact description of the technique he used to decapitate his victim.

I was disgusted and horrified. We all were. Each of us struggled to hide his or her outrage. We wanted him to complete the story and needed him to continue cooperating in debriefings, and so we let him talk, asking questions when he glossed over important details. The creepiest part for me was that he kept referring to Pearl as "Daniel" in a tone of voice that suggested they were good friends.

KSM told us how the British-born radical Pakistani cleric Ahmed Omar Saeed Sheikh arranged for the kidnapping and later turned Pearl over to al-Qa'ida after discovering Pearl was Jewish. KSM walked us through the grisly details: where he took Pearl, how he killed him, how he dismembered the body and stacked the pieces in a narrow hole in the frozen ground. I will not describe it further, but it is the stuff of nightmares.

When we mentioned to KSM that there were some in Washington who wouldn't believe him, he seemed taken aback. He pointed to his hairy arms and hands as if their appearance should make identification obvious. "You can't see my face in the video that we released, but you can see my arms and hands," he said, running his right hand over his left forearm. He then made a slashing motion and stopped midway, posing to show us how his arms and hands would be visible in the video.

Later, after KSM was returned to his cell, one of the guards who had overheard his gleeful confession said, "That guy needs to die. Real bad!" I knew what he meant. It wasn't a threat. The guard meant that the world would be a safer place if monsters like KSM were not among us.

The report went back to CIA headquarters and immediately generated controversy. As predicted, some were skeptical. A rumor subsequently spread that KSM had confessed to cutting Pearl's throat during waterboarding. That's not remotely true. This conversation about Pearl took place weeks or months after he was subjected to enhanced interrogations for the last time.

Headquarters wanted definitive proof that it was KSM who had cut Pearl's throat. They needed to be sure it wasn't a false confession. Therefore, Bruce, the COB, and KSM reenacted the beheading, careful to re-create KSM's arm and hand positions exactly as they were in the video. They used a pillowcase stuffed with bags of sugar to approximate the size and weight of Pearl's head. KSM got into the task, providing direction, correcting camera angles, and arranging and rearranging his hands and arms around the stuffed pillowcase until he had the position just right. Throughout the reenactment, KSM smiled and mugged for the camera. Sometimes he preened.

CIA and FBI officials compared the pattern of veins and other morphological features of KSM's forearms and hands to those of the person murdering Pearl in the video. They matched. It was definitely KSM.

When the news came back, KSM was in good spirits. "See, I told you," he said. "I cut Daniel's throat with these blessed hands."

.   .   .

**KSM WAS A** diva, and when new debriefers came on board, he inevitably would test them. He would listen to the questions they asked, and if he concluded that they were not familiar with what he had said previously on the topic, he would complain, "Why do you send these people to question me when it is obvious they don't know what I said before? How can we advance our discussions if I have to start at the beginning every time?"

Fortunately, this seldom happened. Most debriefers were very well prepared, sometimes too well prepared. Once, in an effort to put KSM on notice, a newly arrived debriefer warned at the beginning of his first debriefing with him, "I've been studying you for so long that I know more about you than you do."

KSM immediately replied with a twinkle that became a glare: "Then you should be able to answer your own questions and I can go back to my prayers." KSM then sat there, acting like offended royalty, until I leaned in to reframe what the debriefer had said.

"KSM, I think my friend meant that as a compliment. What he's saying is that you are so important to him and he has studied you for so long that he feels like he knows you even though you two have never met."

KSM was not fooled by this bit of flattering verbal hocuspocus. He looked at us and made a face that said, "Oh, really? Come on, now!"

At the same time, however, KSM liked to see people go out of their way to flatter him, especially when they were forced to do so to keep him talking. That bit of awkwardness was in itself flattering to him. Accepting the pretense that it was a compliment and knowing that it galled the debriefer to go along with it allowed KSM to save face and continue with the debriefing with less friction.

There was often friction. For example, one debriefer was hot to show KSM that he wasn't going to take any guff from him. He started interrupting KSM with assertions about what he was thinking during the incident about which the debriefer was asking.

KSM finally said, "Why do you waste your time talking to me when you think you already know the answer?"

After that, KSM, who was normally quite talkative, answered the questions exactly as asked without elaborating or offering any details that were not requested. It was a missed opportunity, an example of why establishing rapport and tailoring the questions to the specific detainee's temperament was so important during debriefings. Later, a different debriefer would have to readdress the topic to fill in the details that I think KSM would have provided if the first debriefer had been less abrasive.

KSM could be difficult to debrief even when he was being cooperative. At one point, he announced to the COB of the black site where he was being held that he once again was going to travel the true path of Sufism, a mystical branch of his faith that its adherents consider the true original path of Islam. Going forward, he said he was devoting his life to this Islamic mysticism and therefore needed to establish "office hours" so that he had uninterrupted time to immerse himself in the required chanting, contemplation, prayer, and study. He posted his office hours on his cell door and flipped a hand-scrawled sign to "Open" or "Closed" to indicate when he was available for his "CIA work."

As you might imagine, this didn't go over well at the black site. Bruce and I were dispatched to sort things out. Everyone except the guards, who found it amusing, was in a snit. KSM was slowing down the debriefings, and the COB was on the verge of stripping away his amenities to pressure him to abandon the idea of office hours.

We knew from the chief interrogator's past experience with KSM that when you drew a line in the sand with him, he would dig in and out of spite refuse to budge. We could force him to sit in a room with a debriefer, but the level of cooperation he had been showing, the level that headquarters had come to expect, probably would suffer. However, the COB was in charge of running the site, and the idea that a captured terrorist could dictate his own office hours was unacceptable to him. There was a new interrogator already on-site, and some were pressing him to consider requesting the resumption of EITs to force compliance, something that Bruce and I would have recommended against and refused to participate in and that headquarters never would have approved.

Like ombudsmen or marriage counselors, we listened to both sides.

The COB's position was easy to understand. He was in charge, and KSM would do what he was told when he was told to do it. Period, full stop, end of discussion.

KSM's position was a little more nuanced. It had two main components: one religious and one practical. Regarding the religious aspect, KSM told us that his obligation to Allah in pursuing Sufism required that he immerse himself, praying and contemplating the deeper meaning of the Koran and Islamic mystical texts throughout the day. He said that if he capitulated to the COB's demands and gave up on this path without a fight, he would be turning his back on what Allah expected of him and placing his soul at risk. On the practical side, KSM said that he had lots of time during the day for prayer and contemplation but couldn't use it. He couldn't take advantage of the downtime he had available because the guards would pull him out of his cell, seemingly without warning, for debriefings, bathing, medical checkups, and the like, interrupting his devotions and not allowing him to finish his meditations or prayers.

"Often," he said, "when they pull me out of my cell, I sit in the chair for a long time waiting for the CIA person to arrive, only to have them show me a single photograph or ask me a single question and then leave. It wastes my time."

KSM also complained that debriefings tended to start sometime around midday, interrupting or forcing him to miss important obligatory midday prayers. He said this wasn't what it was like at the other black sites where he had been held before, and he didn't like it.

During this first meeting with KSM, Bruce and I reminded him that although we encouraged his spiritual devotion and understood why it was important to him, the CIA was not running a religious retreat for Sufis and headquarters would not allow him to quit cooperating. We asked him to work with us until we could find a solution. We told him we weren't going to make any recommendations right away because we wanted to see what he was talking about. He agreed to continue cooperating with the debriefers until we resolved it.

We told the COB that we wanted to get a better sense of what was going on and that we needed to observe for a while before we made any recommendations. Then we watched.

Sure enough, events during the day played out almost exactly as KSM had described them. The debriefers, who had been up late the night before writing reports, would arrive in the control center where the terminals were situated in late morning. They would either begin a new report or return to writing the one they had started the night before. In addition, some were working on bigger projects that required many days and much research to finish. It was not uncommon for one of the debriefers to say to the chief of security, "I want to talk to KSM in a little while." The guards, among the most proactive and dependable force I've ever encountered, would pull KSM from his cell, move him to the meeting room, and prepare him for debriefing.

Sometimes KSM would sit waiting for an hour or more while the debriefer finished a report or got to the point in a report at which she needed to query KSM for clarification. Most debriefers would include the follow-up query in their main session, the one in which they planned to pursue whatever issues the folks back at headquarters had decided were the most important to focus on that day. But some debriefers, intent on completing an important report, would pop into the meeting room long enough to ask a couple of follow-up questions about a photo from the day before or some al-Qa'ida operative he had mentioned or some other needed detail and then leave. KSM would be moved back to his cell. He'd then be pulled out again around noon for a full debriefing. Once we saw the debriefer pop in after KSM had been waiting long enough to become irritated, ask a question, and then tell the guards, "I'll be back in a little while to do my debriefing." Meanwhile KSM remained there hooded, chained, sitting in a chair, and waiting.

The other thing we noticed that was consistent with KSM's complaint and unique to this site was that the debriefers tended to start debriefing in earnest about the same time midday prayers rolled around. This was not deliberate but a natural consequence of starting late, finishing reports, reviewing new intelligence requirements sent by headquarters the night before, and researching the background required to service them. Meanwhile KSM, knowing they were going to debrief him that day, would be wandering around his cell, looking up at the cameras, and making "what gives?" gestures with his hands the closer it got to prayer time. More often than not, KSM would give up waiting and settle into prayer, and a few minutes later the guards would enter to escort him to the debriefing room. None of it was deliberate, but all of it was irritating to KSM.

After we understood what was going on, Bruce and I made our recommendations to the COB. Those recommendations were among the reasons some people at the CIA thought we were soft on terrorists. We recommended that the COB add structure and predictability to KSM's day. Although KSM should not be allowed to dictate office hours per se, personnel at the site could accommodate his need for time for prayer and mystic contemplation with just a few procedural changes.

To add structure to KSM's day, we recommended that each morning the interrogator on-site get together with the debriefers and anyone else who would need to see KSM and figure out a daily schedule that was tailored to whatever the unique demands of that day were. After that, the interrogator would stop by KSM's cell and tell him what to expect.

For example, the interrogator might tell KSM, "There's going to be three debriefings today: one in the morning and two in the afternoon. Unless there is an urgent requirement, you should have from now until ten a.m. for prayer and contemplation. You'll be back in time for midday prayers, but after that you'll be busy from one p.m. until late afternoon."

The schedule was still driven by the needs of the debriefers, but it was more predictable because KSM was told ahead of time what to expect.

We recommended a couple of other changes as well. We recommended that rather than pull KSM out of his cell for a brief question or clarification, the guards should escort the debriefers to the cell, where they could ask their questions through the bars. This would still interrupt his prayers or reading, but not for as long as the time required to escort him to the debriefing room and force him to wait for the debriefers to show up.

We sold this to KSM by telling him that the only way headquarters would let us cut back on how long he sometimes had to wait was for him to be open to debriefers who briefly interrupted his nonobligatory prayers or contemplation to ask a quick question and then left. We also told him that the site would try to respect his obligatory prayer schedule, but sometimes it wouldn't work out that way. We said, "As you have told us, Allah will know what is in your heart. He will know that it is us, not you, that prevents you from praying."

Using what KSM and Abu Zubaydah had taught us about radical Islam, we told KSM that sometimes he might have to wait longer than he liked for the debriefing to start. "But rather than just sitting there waiting," we said, "that might be a good time to pray or chant or contemplate the deeper meaning of Allah's presence in everything, including your current situation. Your god will know how much more difficult it is to pray or meditate while hooded and chained to a chair rather than sitting comfortably on a prayer rug. There is no dishonor in that." Afterward KSM continued to tease us about having office hours for months, but it was in jest.

Although our recommendations were implemented at the site and appreciated by the COB, not everyone there initially liked them. Some thought any accommodation of KSM's request for more predictable time to pray and contemplate the mysteries of Islam represented capitulation. They said he should be forced, with physical coercion if necessary, to do whatever he was told whenever he was told to do it; after all, KSM was a captured killer.

Bruce and I reminded them that the CIA was in the business of obtaining intelligence, not running a prison where the primary focus was to punish detainees. As long as it was possible to make minor accommodations for a cooperating detainee and as a result elicit answers to our questions that were more full and complete, that was what we should be doing. We reminded them that EITs were not authorized for use to punish detainees for acting out or to force compliance with administrative rules.

Bruce and I, along with some of the other interrogators, did a lot of this sort of dispute resolution between detainees and black site managers or other personnel, and oddly, I often found myself taking KSM's or some other detainee's side.

Here's another example. Just after moving to a new site, KSM started refusing to answer questions. I think Bruce and I were sent to the site because headquarters was expecting a new capture. We were asked to sort out the slowdown while we were there. We discovered that KSM had been promised he could fast during the day. However, the new COB was forcing him to take a multivitamin each morning after daybreak. Bruce and I immediately understood the problem: taking the vitamin after first light invalidated the religious value of the fast.

Bruce and I asked the COB why he was so insistent on forcing KSM to take the vitamin during daylight hours, since it would work just as well medicinally if he took it after sunset with his evening meal. It was another one of those "because I said so" standoffs combined with "What's the big deal? It's just a little vitamin."

Black site personnel already had taken KSM's mattress and were getting ready to take his clothes. Bruce and I suggested that they hold off. We explained the religious significance of non-Ramadan fasting during daylight hours to a Sufi as a means of demonstrating additional sacrifice and devotion to Allah and pointed out that deliberately taking anything by mouth between first light and last invalidated the fast. Thus, by forcing KSM to take that vitamin, as small as it was, we were reneging without good reason on a promise made by the CIA. It was a problem, we said, not because KSM needed to get right with his god but because it slowed down intelligence collection. The COB initially argued with us, but he could see it was a self-inflicted wound and eventually relented. Because this guy was smart and wanted the best for intelligence collection, he became one of the best COBs Bruce and I ever worked with.

. . .

**ONCE KSM GOT** comfortable in his role as a CIA collaborator, he began to view himself not just as "the brain" but also as "the professor." At one of the sites, a forward-thinking COB let KSM establish what he called a "training camp" where he lectured on Islamic jihadist ideology, terrorist recruiting, attack planning, target reconnaissance, and fund-raising for terror attacks. Since part of what we were there to do was keep KSM busy between debriefings to lessen the effects of isolation, a variety of people attended those seminars, including the COB, interrogators, debriefers, targeters, and security personnel. Often something of intelligence value would come out of them.

KSM would waddle over to the whiteboard, pick up an alcohol marker, and begin lecturing. He ran a pretty strict class. He would scowl good-naturedly and wag his finger at you if you asked a question that suggested you weren't paying attention. He would tease us about tests and term projects. He even playfully suggested that I could get "extra credit" if I helped him with an "after-school project." It was just talk.

I liked all the lessons, but I really enjoyed discussing radical Islam with him. I did not understand their brand of militant Islam with clarity until he and other high-value detainees explained it to me from their perspective. I had read about it and studied it from afar, and even though the writings used some of the same words to describe the beliefs that the detainees employed, the depth of their conviction and their absolute adherence to their faith did not come through on the printed page. That depth of conviction is one of the reasons they are so dangerous.

I don't claim to be an expert on Islam, but I have spent thousands of hours with captive senior al-Qa'ida leaders such as KSM, talking about a variety of topics, including the religious reasons they assert underlie their terror attacks. Thus, although I don't know everything there is to know about radical Islamists from an academic perspective, I do have practical knowledge of what terrorists said inspired them to attack us.

Let me share a little of what KSM and the others collectively told me. I have to warn you that their views are not politically correct. They are the beliefs of the Islamic terrorists who are trying to kill us and destroy our way of life, not mine.

KSM said that Allah has given True Muslims (their brand of Islam) dominion over the world and a holy mandate to invite infidels to convert to Islam or submit to subjugation. If the infidels refuse, True Muslims are mandated by Allah to fight an unending war until all unbelievers have been converted, subjugated, or slaughtered. We've seen ISIS trying to do this very thing in Iraq and Syria in recent years.

KSM said that America may not be in a religious war with him, but he and other True Muslims are in a religious war with America. He described it as a battle of civilizations, with the House of Islam (*Dar al-Islam*) on one side and the House of War (*Dar al-Harb*) on the other. He said that our culture, with its liberties and freedoms and decadent indulgences, is unclean and that our efforts to live our lives as we choose and to protect our way of life are an offensive attack against True Islam.

KSM and the others said that offensive jihad is actually defensive jihad, because that is the only way to protect True Muslims from the spread of our unclean culture and the seductive way of life led by infidels.

KSM insisted that violent jihad is the religious duty of every True Muslim in response to the spread of Western culture and American influence. It is the only hope of redressing injustices. True Muslims, he said, are more important than other people because they were chosen by Allah to rule the world. This justifies the use of any means necessary to assume their rightful dominion, including terror attacks. Because they have been chosen by Allah, True Muslims are entitled to freedoms and liberties that others are not. It is the duty of True Muslims to determine the destiny of infidels.

KSM said that those who do not believe as they do (Non–True Muslims) harbor harmful intentions toward True Muslims and therefore cannot be trusted. They see modern events involving America and Western democracies as a continuation of the medieval crusades to destroy them and believe that attacking others with acts of violent terror is a preemptive defensive necessity.

KSM said that American culture is a direct attack against Islam because Allah dictates how people should be governed. It is not up for a vote. Anything that questions complete subservience to the Koran and Sharia law is a threat to Islam and must be destroyed. Western democracy and freedom of thought and true Sharia law cannot coexist because Western democracy postulates that men and women have a say in how they live their lives, whereas Sharia dictates how lives are to be led according to Allah's will and as reflected in the perfect Prophet's deeds and words.

KSM said the United States is the only major obstacle to True Islam assuming its rightful place of dominion over the world and imposing Sharia law. To him and the others it does not matter that we do not want to fight them. It does not matter that we believe in religious freedom. There are no innocent bystanders. No one in the West, especially in America, is innocent. Killing women and men who are not actively fighting Islam is permissible because they pay taxes that fund those who do. It is permissible to kill babies and children because they bring comfort to infidels who resist True Islam by refusing to convert or surrender. Allowing your enemy's children to live replenishes their ranks, he said. Killing children is a weapon Allah has provided to attack and undermine the will of their parents to continue resisting True Islam.

Once, during a conversation with Abu Zubaydah about freedom, he said that Salafist Islam was the ultimate freedom. I asked how that was possible since every aspect of a person's life had to be lived according to rigid Sharia laws that were established centuries ago. He said, "Yes, exactly. I am free because I am not burdened by choices. The true path was laid out in the perfect life and deeds of the Prophet, may peace be upon him."

I asked KSM one time how come, since his brand of Islam is so violent, he calls it the religion of peace. He told me that my problem was that I interpreted the word *peace* the way Americans always do. He explained that according to his brand of Islam, peace would exist when the entire world was under Sharia law and ruled by a Muslim caliphate. He said Islam is the religion of peace because its aim is to impose Sharia law everywhere and in doing so bring peace to the world.

KSM said that to make peace with one's enemies is to convert, subjugate, or enslave them. He told me we also use the word *truce* differently. In America most people think of a truce almost the same way they think of peace: as a cessation of hostilities, living in harmony. KSM told me that when the word *truce* is used in their brand of Islam, it refers to a cessation of hostilities only until the jihadi brothers can get strong enough to attack again. It's less about working out your differences and living in harmony and more about licking your wounds, getting stronger, and preparing for the next attack.

We also talked about al-Taqiyya: the use of deception to disguise one's true beliefs. KSM, Abu Zubaydah, and the other detainees told me it was permitted, even expected, in their brand of Islam to lie, especially to infidels, to deceive Allah's enemies and promote his will in the world. They told me there are four kinds of jihad: jihad by the heart, jihad by the tongue, jihad by the hand, and jihad by the sword. KSM and others told me that al-Taqiyya, or deception, had a role in each kind. They said that each True Muslim man was obliged to take up the sword to defend Islam and that deception to distract one's enemies or put them off guard or gain some other fighting advantage was permissible.

They said that those who cannot take up the sword are obliged to promote Allah's will through jihad by the hand. Usually this refers to acts other than fighting. Again deception is acceptable. One could, for example, conduct jihad by the hand by using money collected for charity to fund jihadist terror attacks or by establishing outreach programs that are intended to promote Islam but also radicalize fighters. A third example would be establishing mosques that promote their brand of Islam in infidel territory.

Deception in jihad by the tongue can entail pretending to promote acculturation into Western democracies while behind the scenes promoting the establishment of Sharia law. KSM told me he could see Muslim brothers after 9/11 condemning the terror attacks in the media while celebrating in their hearts.

Finally, KSM said, deception also has a place in jihad of the heart. Individuals who because of adverse circumstances must say and do things that are contrary to their true beliefs and cannot engage in any of the other forms of jihad can practice jihad of the heart by struggling to keep faith with Allah while surrounded by enemies of faith.

KSM's discussions often included his thoughts about various kinds of terror attacks. He said that although the leadership of al-Qa'ida still favored large-scale catastrophic attacks, he was beginning to see the value of small-scale, low-tech attacks carried out by one or two *shahids* (martyrs). He took note of how the 2002 Beltway sniper attacks by John Allen Muhammad and Lee Boyd

Malvo created havoc and panic in the Washington, DC, area and along Interstate 95. In KSM's mind, relatively few victims had died during Muhammad and Malvo's shooting spree (seventeen dead and ten injured), but the fear and paralysis caused by the seemingly random killing of people going about their own business brought home to him the asymmetrical utility of what we now call lone wolf terror attacks.

He sat there and calmly discussed issues such as the economy of scale and cost versus impact on his enemies in the West. He was particularly pleased with the idea that those carrying out the attacks need not be official members of al-Qa'ida or funded by them; they only needed to share militant Islam's radical ideology and goals.

He said that the al-Qa'ida leaders "dreamed" of crippling America with sophisticated large-scale catastrophic attacks, but that from his perspective, large-scale attacks were "nice but not necessary." He said sufficient numbers of brothers acting alone to launch low-tech attacks could bring down America the same way "enough disease-infected fleas can fell an elephant . . . a small bite here, a small bite there. The elephant is big and powerful, but a single flea is too small for it to stop. The elephant will eventually get sick and die."

KSM then provided an example of a low-tech terror attack that could be carried out by a single jihadist, an attack that would produce devastating consequences in any city where it occurred. His idea was to have these low-tech attacks timed to occur during rush hour. I don't want to share the specifics of his idea with our enemies, and so I won't provide the details here. I will say this much: I believe his idea could be employed with devastating effect.

I realize KSM needs to be able to talk to his legal team in private, but if we ever allow him to communicate unmonitored with the outside world, we will do ourselves a grave disservice. He could easily spread his deviously simple but potentially deadly ideas.

After I spent thousands of hours with KSM discussing the nuts and bolts of his brand of Islamic jihad, KSM kiddingly told me that I should be on the FBI's Most Wanted List because I am now a "known associate" of KSM and a "graduate" of his training camp. I wasn't the only person he said this to; I know he said it to Bruce and to others, such as the COB who initiated his lecture series. It was in jest, of course, but it also served as a reminder that he was carrying that information inside his head and could impart it as easily to others as he did to us if he had an opportunity.

I once asked KSM to explain to me why if martyrdom was one of the greatest acts of worship for Allah, he had not martyred himself. For example, I said, even though you had an automatic weapon, you didn't try to shoot it out with the Pakistani police when they came to arrest you, as Abu Zubaydah had. Recognizing that I wasn't trying to be offensive, KSM said, "Allah has chosen me to arrange for others with less talent for planning attacks to martyr themselves. I serve Allah better by arranging for many *shahids* to sacrifice themselves as weapons against Allah's enemies than I ever could by giving my one and only life."

KSM AND I spent many hours discussing his allegiance to jihad and his commitment to establishing a worldwide Islamic caliphate. He suggested that I commit the Koran to memory and read Ahmad ibn Naqib al-Misri's *Reliance of the Traveller*, a fourteenth-century manual of strict Islamic law (Sharia) that codifies how Muslims should live every aspect of their lives down to which foot one should lead with when entering a room. He said his brothers will not stop until the entire world lives under Sharia law. He says they cannot—they have been commanded by Allah to kill, convert, or enslave everyone, to create a global caliphate.

KSM explained that his commitment to spreading Islam through violence went deeper than his commitment to al-Qa'ida as an organization; after all, when he orchestrated al-Qa'ida's 9/11 attacks against the United States, he had not yet sworn *bayat* (allegiance) to bin Ladin. He said he worked with al-Qa'ida because they had the same enemies and goals but he was technically not an al-Qa'ida member at the time of the attack.

He explained that he came from a religious family of Balochis with a long history of "mischief making" in support of Balochistan's independence directed at the governments surrounding that providence in southwestern Pakistan.

KSM said that the terror activities of his nephew Ramzi Yousef, who masterminded the 1993 World Trade Center bombing, and his brother, who fought the Soviets in Afghanistan, inspired him to become involved in planning and carrying out attacks against the United States. KSM said he visited Afghanistan while his brother was there for jihad. He stayed, received military training, and fought the Soviets for several months. Eventually he was summoned from the front to take up administrative duties and discovered that he was good at planning.

Later, in 1994, KSM and Yousef met in the Philippines to plan simultaneous bombings of a dozen U.S.-flagged commercial airliners, intent on crashing them into the Pacific, creating massive loss of life. We know it as the Bojinka plot. KSM said that although they weren't able to pull off the bombings because of an apartment fire that exposed the scheme to the authorities, the plotting he did with Yousef while in the Philippines served as the genesis for his idea to crash hijacked aircraft into buildings in the United States.

KSM told me he wanted to destroy our civilization. He said his 9/11 plan was to decapitate the United States by simultaneously attacking our most important financial center, our military leadership, and our center of government, the Capitol Building.

Al-Qa'ida successfully struck two of the three targets and would have taken out the Capitol Building, killing the innocent people and legislators inside, if it hadn't been for the brave passengers on United Flight 93 who sacrificed their lives to save the lives of other Americans.

KSM told me that no one in al-Qa'ida expected the World Trade Center buildings to collapse. When the buildings fell down, KSM thought about the thousands of infidels he was sacrificing for Allah and rejoiced, praising Allah and dancing with others in the street. The mujahideen, the women and the children, all rejoiced. Many sheep were sacrificed for feasts, and they celebrated with mutton and treats and strong tea. Surely it was a sign that Allah was truly on their side. He had knocked down those buildings to show how powerful he was, to call all Muslims to jihad, and to make the infidels cower.

KSM said that with time, however, he realized they would be lucky to survive. He said al-Qa'ida should have had more terror attacks ready to hit us while we were down, but KSM and al-Qa'ida leaders believed they would have more time.

KSM said, "And why not?"

Al-Qa'ida expected the United States to respond as he believed Reagan had after the 1983 bombing of the Marine barracks in Beirut, Lebanon, that killed 241 military personnel. KSM said that America turned tail and ran, pulling U.S. troops out of Lebanon. He noted that Clinton had done the same thing after al-Qa'ida bombed two U.S. embassies in East Africa and attacked the USS *Cole* in the port of Aden, Yemen. Clinton fired a few missiles at abandoned training camps, and al-Qa'ida was essentially unharmed, free to advance KSM's deadly plan for the 9/11 attacks.

KSM told me he assumed that the United States would treat the attacks of 9/11 like a law enforcement matter, as they had the embassy attacks and the *Cole* bombing. He thought the FBI would investigate by focusing on past crimes. Eventually the United States would ask the Taliban government controlling Afghanistan to extradite al-Qa'ida members, the Taliban would refuse, and al-Qa'ida would have time to launch the next wave of attacks on the U.S. homeland.

Then he looked at me and said, "How was I supposed to know that cowboy George Bush would announce he wanted us '*dead or alive*' and then invade Afghanistan to hunt us down?" KSM was referring to comments President Bush had made on September 17, 2001, while talking to reporters at the Pentagon. He acted as if he thought President Bush's reaction to the 9/11 attacks was the last thing he had expected.

KSM explained that if the United States had treated 9/11 like a law enforcement matter, he would have had time to launch a second wave of attacks. Those attacks were already in the early stages of preparation, and he would have had his people on the ground in the United States ready with follow-up attacks to harass and distract law enforcement until the larger attack could be launched. But they weren't ready. KSM said al-Qa'ida was stunned by the destruction caused by their attacks and by the ferocity and swiftness of George Bush's response.

**ONE OF THE** terror attacks KSM had in mind for the United States was to contaminate or poison water reservoirs serving heavily populated areas. Almost immediately upon that becoming known, some in the U.S. media ridiculed the idea, saying that it was impractical because the large volume of water in the typical reservoir would dilute the chemicals so much that it would take an extraordinarily large amount of poison to contaminate it.

During one of my "how are things going?" visits, I told KSM in conversation that there were those in the U.S. media who thought what he was saying about poisoning reservoirs was just empty talk intended to scare Americans and mislead the CIA. He looked at me as if I had two heads. He said dumping chemicals into the main reservoir would be foolish. That wasn't his plan. He said that he had a degree in mechanical engineering from a university in North Carolina and had worked as an engineer in a water-treatment plant in Qatar. He said he knew how to poison water coming from a reservoir and it wouldn't be by pouring chemicals into the main body of water. He described what he would do, based on his experience working as an engineer on water treatment systems. Again, I'm not going to describe it here. I'm not interested in spreading terror attack how-to tips. But it seemed plausible.

**OFF AND ON** we talked with KSM about his enhanced interrogation. During one discussion with me and Bruce, KSM said that he understood why we had been rough with him during his initial interrogations. He said that if our positions were reversed, he would do the same thing to protect his way of life.

He said that among the brothers (i.e., the Islamic jihadists), Americans are seen as militarily strong but weak in resolve and spirit. KSM insisted that the brothers eventually will defeat the United States because Americans don't have the will or stomach to do what must be done to stop them.

KSM said the desire of Americans to have the world "like them," plus things such as our Bill of Rights and adherence to civil liberties, are defects, weapons that Allah has provided to help his jihadist brothers defeat the United States by turning our weak human nature and our country's laws and freedoms against us.

Then KSM wagged his finger professorially at us and warned, "Soon they will turn on you." He prophetically predicted that the press and some members of my own government would turn on me and Bruce and others like us who took aggressive action to prevent the next 9/11 attack and save American lives.

Warming to the topic, KSM smiled and said the media, either on purpose or without realizing it, would promote Islam's cause and champion tearing down the measures put in place to protect the American people after 9/11. He said the media would promote al-Qa'ida's cause by framing the war against Islam (his characterization, not mine) as morally wrong, impossible to win, and fraught with unacceptable losses. He said the media's response was one of Allah's "gifts," one of the ways Allah preordained for Americans to set aside those things which kept us safe and prevented attacks in the immediate aftermath of 9/11.

KSM said, "Your own government will turn on you. Your leaders will turn on you. They will turn on you to save themselves. It will play out in the media and strengthen the hearts of the brothers. It will recruit more to Allah's cause because the press coverage will make the U.S. look weak and divided."

KSM said that the "real war" is fought in the minds of the American people, not on the battlefields, where America's military power could easily defeat them. "We will win," he said, "because Americans don't realize this. We do not need to defeat you militarily; we only need to fight long enough for you to defeat yourself by quitting."

"It would be nice," he said, if al-Qa'ida or like-minded Islamists could bring America to its knees with catastrophic attacks, but that was unlikely to happen; "not practical" is the wording he used. From his perspective, the long war for Islamic domination wasn't going to be won in the streets with bombs and bullets and bloodshed. No, it would be won in the minds of the American people.

He said the terror attacks were good, but the "practical" way to defeat America was through immigration and by outbreeding non-Muslims. He said jihadi-minded brothers would immigrate into the United States, taking advantage of the welfare system to support themselves while they spread their jihadi message. They will wrap themselves in America's rights and laws for protection, ratchet up acceptance of Sharia law, and then, only when they were strong enough, rise up and violently impose Sharia from within. He said the brothers would relentlessly continue their attacks and the American people eventually would become so tired, so frightened, and so weary of war that they would just want it to end.

"Eventually," KSM said, "America will expose her neck to us for slaughter."

# CHAPTER 8

# EITs: The Ultimate Payoff

We never expected the detainees to tell us *everything* we wanted to know. We gained enormous insights from what they shared with us but also learned important information when we caught them in lies. If there was a detail they would go out of their way to protect even after having become enormously cooperative, it must have been something really big, and we took note. The best example is the way the information was put together that eventually led to finding and killing bin Ladin. Here is how that success was achieved.

It was the year 2005. My clearest recollection is of several of us huddled together near the cell of Abu Faraj al-Libbi, who had become the third-highest-ranking member of al-Qa'ida, replacing KSM as the chief of external operations after KSM's capture. The conversation started in the hallway and quickly moved into a small conference room. Abu Faraj had denied that someone named Abu Ahmed al-Kuwaiti ever had delivered a message directly from Usama bin Ladin appointing him KSM's replacement as al-Qa'ida's number three. Furthermore, Abu Faraj adamantly insisted that he had never heard of anyone named Abu Ahmed. As far as he knew, there was no such man. It was an odd claim and stood out because other detainees had confirmed that Abu Ahmed was a protégé of KSM and a trusted assistant to Abu Faraj.

This was not the first time Abu Faraj had been asked about Abu Ahmed. The usually cooperative Abu Faraj had been asked several times in several different ways by various interrogators and debriefers and always gave the same answer. We were asking again, confronting him with what other detainees had said. But he remained adamant.

Abu Faraj's denial was one of those times when the context of the lie revealed clues to the truth. With each denial CIA interrogators and analysts became more convinced that Abu Faraj was lying: Abu Ahmed *was* bin Ladin's trusted courier. Abu Faraj's protection of the courier's identity meant that he was so important that if located, he might lead us to the man the CIA had been hunting since 9/11.

The fact that KSM also was lying about this man further underlined his importance. KSM's lie was different, but it conveyed the same truth. KSM said there was an Abu Ahmed who was his protégé but claimed the man had quit al-Qa'ida in 2002. We suspected that KSM was lying because of what other detainees were telling us. Then KSM screwed up. He tried to warn other detainees secretly not to talk about the courier and in doing so betrayed Abu Ahmed's importance and revealed the truth.

CIA interrogators and personnel at the black site had discovered the means KSM and the other detainees used to try to communicate secretly but had not shut it down because they wanted to monitor what was being passed between them. For security reasons, I cannot describe the method here, but when KSM used this method to order the other detainees not to talk about Abu Ahmed, it was like he was sending up a flare, marking the spot where the CIA should start the hunt for bin Ladin.

Of course, that was not what the Democratic staffers who prepared Feinstein's flawed SSCI majority report would have you believe. They want people to think that the lies told by Abu Faraj and KSM provided no clue to the importance of Abu Ahmed, that CIA analysts, targets, debriefers, and interrogators didn't recognize the importance of those lies.

The truth is that although Abu Ahmed's name was in old CIA records as a possible bin Ladin associate, there was nothing to make him stand out from the thousands of other bin Ladin associates in that database until detainees in the CIA detention and interrogation program provided the critical tip-off. After that, several astute analysts searched old records, waded through false leads, and found a partial true name for Abu Ahmed.

Some argue from hindsight that the CIA should have been able to recognize the importance of Abu Ahmed among the thousands of others in the database. But that is like a critic of a big-city police department arguing that the importance of a criminal should be recognized because his name was on a list of thousands of known associates who had kissed the hand of some crime boss.

There was a very important detainee by the name of Ammar al-Baluchi who was KSM's nephew and who helped the 9/11 hijackers get plane reservations, money, and hotel reservations. After enhanced interrogation he was the first to reveal al-Qa'ida's closely guarded secret about Abu Ahmed carrying messages between bin Ladin in hiding and al-Qa'ida operational leaders in other parts of the Middle East. He said that KSM had told him that Abu Ahmed delivered letters for bin Ladin. When confronted, an otherwise cooperating KSM denied telling Ammar that. When Ammar was asked again, however, he insisted that KSM had told him about the courier and said that KSM was lying when he denied it. Both were questioned many times about this.

I was not involved in Ammar al-Baluchi's enhanced interrogations, but Bruce was. Ammar already was answering questions when I sat in my first debriefing with him. The rough stuff was over, and we were using standard social influence techniques to get him to participate in debriefings with subject matter experts. He already had fingered Abu Ahmed as the courier by the time I arrived, and my part in his ongoing debriefings was to sit in and help the debriefers elicit his cooperation as he responded to follow-up questions about the courier and requests for other sorts of information.

Another terrorist, Hassan Ghul, provided additional insights that were vital to identifying Abu Ahmed as bin Ladin's courier. Before enhanced interrogations, Ghul said that Abu Ahmed was one of three people who *might* have looked after bin Ladin's needs and possibly passed messages from bin Ladin to the man who took over for KSM as al-Qa'ida's chief of external operations, Abu Faraj al-Libbi.

After enhanced interrogations, Hassan Ghul told Bruce and others that Abu Ahmed definitely had passed a letter from bin Ladin to Abu Faraj in 2003 appointing him as KSM's successor and that Abu Ahmed had disappeared from Karachi, Pakistan, in 2002, which was about the same time bin Ladin went into hiding and started communicating only through a courier. The information Ghul provided was more detailed, and he used fewer of what I call weasel words. Whereas before Ghul said things "might" have happened, after EITs he definitely described what had occurred, providing concrete details and the names of the terrorist operatives involved. Like Abu Zubaydah, after EITs he volunteered details beyond what one might have expected if he simply answered the questions as asked.

Then Abu Faraj repeatedly denied knowing Abu Ahmed, and the hunt was on.

After it became known that Abu Ahmed was bin Ladin's courier, another piece of the puzzle was to identify his true name. Again, detainees subjected to enhanced interrogations helped confirm Abu Ahmed's true identity.

The CIA had a partial true name for an Abu Ahmed in the database. However, the detainee who had provided the partial name had confused Abu Ahmed with his deceased brother and claimed that the Abu Ahmed he was referring to had died in 2001. Through signals intelligence, a clandestine source, and other detainees, the CIA figured out the detainee was mistaken and Abu Ahmed was probably alive.

The last detainee I interrogated using EITs, Abu Yasir al-Jaza'iri, also filled in an important part of the puzzle. Abu Yasir was the only detainee I interrogated who ever initially denied being who he was. During the neutral probe to assess if he was willing to cooperate without EITs, Abu Yasir acknowledged that that was his name but denied being the Abu Yasir who was of interest to the CIA.

When I entered the interrogation room, Abu Yasir was hooded, standing against the walling wall. In the corner of the room behind my left shoulder was a female debriefer. Although I had prebriefed her before the session, I had not worked an interrogation with her. I think it was her first time in an interrogation in which EITs might be used as opposed to debriefings with cooperative detainees. She was seated behind a large white plastic picnic table that was covered with loose papers. She looked nervous.

In our interrogation planning, we assessed that Abu Yasir's resistance was likely to be brittle, meaning that he probably would capitulate with minimal pressure and start answering questions. Therefore, we wanted to have the subject matter expert in the room, ready to go when he started talking.

I slid the rolled-up towel along the top of Abu Yasir's hooded head and around behind his neck the way we always did. I took my time adjusting my grip on the towel, following the same preinterrogation conditioning ritual Bruce and I used to start every interrogation before detainees were moved into debriefing mode.

I slowly took off his hood. He was taller than I was, lean and athletic.

"My friends tell me that you're denying that you're Abu Yasir al-Jaza'iri," I said, tossing the hood on the floor behind me.

"I'm not him," he said, but just as the final consonant in *not* left his mouth, I slapped him open-handed and with my fingers spread across his left cheek.

It startled him. Abu Yasir squealed and launched himself upward in a vertical leap and then collapsed on the floor at my feet. I caught him on the way down so that he didn't hit his head. Simultaneously, the debriefer behind me screamed and fell out of her chair ass backward, knocking over the table and scattering papers all over the interrogation room. For a few minutes it was bedlam as she scrambled around the room like a squirrel caught inside a garage before she got her bearings and scampered to a far corner, distancing herself from the action, breathing hard, clutching the fabric of her pullover to her chest in one hand.

But there wasn't much action to distance herself from. Abu Yasir was lying on the floor looking at her, his eyes wide, seemingly convinced that something really bad was going to happen because the "note-taking lady," as he called her later, had screamed, fallen over, and scrambled away.

I helped him up and brushed the dust off his back and shoulders.

"Listen," I said as I brushed him off. "I'm an old man. It's disrespectful to lie to me, and you're scaring the lady. Just look at her. I'm going to give you one more chance to clear up the confusion and then," I said, adjusting the rolled-up towel for emphasis, "if you don't, you're not going to like what happens next." I pulled him in toward me in an attention grasp.

"But it doesn't have to be that way," I said as I gently pushed him back against the walling wall. "So please, let's not do this. If we do, I'm going to get tired of bouncing you off this wall, and then those other guys you see peeking through the door will come in and . . ."

"I am Abu Yasir al-Jaza'iri," he said, breathing hard, speaking rapidly. "I have been lying to you." It was the shortest application of EITs I had ever been involved in.

In his follow-up interrogations and debriefing he told us that Abu Ahmed had a speech impediment and spoke in a mixture of Arabic and Pashtu that made it sound like he was mixing up the two languages as he spoke. Knowing about this speech pattern helped the CIA assess that he was living in the compound with bin Ladin in Abbottabad, Pakistan.

Other detainees in CIA custody filled in pieces of the puzzle, advancing the CIA's understanding of Abu Ahmed, and provided insight into bin Ladin's security practices and information about family members with whom he was likely to be living.

Walid Bin Attash, a one-legged al-Qa'ida operative who was captured in spring 2003, told us that after fleeing Afghanistan, bin Ladin refused to meet face-to-face with anyone, including senior al-Qa'ida members. Detainees told us that bin Ladin stayed inside, seldom relocated, and depended on a small group of locals to do chores, run errands, and carry messages. They said he was protected by a small guard force to avoid attracting attention.

Contrary to what some may believe, KSM was never questioned about bin Ladin's location while being waterboarded. Waterboarding was restricted to inquiries about impending attacks, not the location of a terrorist still on the run.

When questioned after EITs had been discontinued, KSM speculated that bin Ladin's youngest wife was probably with him, and a detainee named Sharif al-Masri said another of bin Ladin's wives had passed a letter intended for her husband to Abu Faraj. The pieces of the puzzle of bin Ladin's location were coming together.

The CIA describes the information about bin Ladin's courier obtained from detainees in their custody this way:

> Information from detainees in CIA custody on Abu Ahmad's involvement in delivering messages from Bin Ladin beginning in mid-2002 fundamentally changed our assessment of his potential importance to our hunt for Bin Ladin. That information prompted us to question other detainees on his role and identify and review previous reporting. CIA combined this information with reporting from detainees [redacted] signals intelligence, and reporting from clandestine sources to build a profile of Abu Ahmad's experiences, family, and characteristics that allowed us to eventually determine his true name and location.

The current CIA leadership now says that it is impossible in hindsight to know if they could have obtained the same information from the detainees who provided it without the use of enhanced interrogation or whether they would have eventually acquired other intelligence that would have allowed them to hunt down and kill bin Ladin. Perhaps they have to say that to placate their political masters on the House and Senate oversight committees.

I am under no such obligation. I spent thousands of hours with those detainees and can say with confidence that in my opinion they never would have given up the information that eventually led to bin Ladin without enhanced measures.

Feinstein and her staffers can spin it any way they want to, but they were not there; I was. They can—and do—claim that the pieces of the puzzle provided by detainees in the CIA detention and interrogation program were not necessary and contributed nothing to finding and killing bin Ladin. But in doing so, they reveal something: they are woefully ignorant about how intelligence actually is collected and analyzed or they are deliberately misleading themselves and the American people.

KSM and Abu Faraj al-Libbi weren't foot soldiers. They were hardened al-Qa'ida operatives. They were senior al-Qa'ida leaders skilled at resisting if they chose to and highly committed to protecting the secret of bin Ladin's location. KSM had been exposed to EITs and didn't capitulate. Abu Faraj al-Libbi was willing to endure them, if necessary, to protect bin Ladin. Expecting the two of them to capitulate and give up bin Ladin because someone built rapport with them would be like expecting one of our great generals, say, General Patton, to give away the secret of D-Day because the Germans were nice to him. I can't picture it.

It is possible that there is nothing anyone could have done to get KSM and Faraj al-Libbi to admit that Abu Ahmed was bin Ladin's courier. Fortunately, other detainees who had been exposed to EITs provided the tip-off, and so they didn't have to. By lying, KSM and Faraj al-Libbi corroborated what those detainees said and highlighted how important Abu Ahmed was. Detainees from the interrogation program put the CIA on the trail to finding and killing bin Ladin. Of this I have no doubt.

# CHAPTER 9

# Beyond Enhanced Interrogations

Our Land Rover pulled up to the gate outside the tall, featureless walls of an aging prison built of gray concrete and misery. The man sitting in front of me made a cell phone call. Gates at least twenty feet tall and about the width of a panel truck creaked open on some invisible mechanism that protested the intrusion. A Klaxon was bleating, the noise loud and alarming.

I stretched my neck to see around the head of the security escort in front of me. I was looking into a mantrap for vehicles, a long narrow chute maybe twenty feet wide with concrete walls that went up forty or fifty feet. Openings for firing down on the mantrap were scattered up the vertical walls. I looked up. Far above I could see a small rectangle of blue sky. I could just make out a large bird riding the thermals at an impossible height. The gates closed behind us, and I heard the locking mechanism drive home. I felt trapped. Totally exposed. There was no place to hide.

Nobody moved. Our escort said something into his phone. A door opened. It seemed small, dwarfed by the towering walls of the mantrap. It was the only opening I could see other than the gate we had come in through and the gun ports and windows well above the ground.

Then we were inside. My recollection is of a huge open space several hundred feet square rising up four or five stories. I could see platforms on each floor with cells lining the circumference along the outside wall of the building. It was a giant rusted cage.

A labyrinth of rusted steel bars and gates led to metal stairs that took us past each floor as we ascended to our destination. I could see prisoners, some in their cells and some gathered in clusters in community areas, all under the watchful eye of their keepers. There was the incomprehensible noise of too many conversations taking place at once. The harsh smell of cigarettes mingled with the scent of overcooked prison food.

On one of the top floors I was taken to an office, one of the only rooms with walls instead of cell bars. I could smell coffee. Sitting behind an ancient metal desk was a prison official. He was fussing with a coffeemaker. Sitting in a comfortable chair on the other side of the room was the prisoner I had been sent there to talk to. The topic of conversation was going to be organized crime and the smuggling of fissionable nuclear material. My job was to spend time with the prisoner and then suggest ways for our weapons of mass destruction (WMD) experts to get him to reveal where he got the small amount of material he had been caught with and more information about what he was planning to do with it.

It would be easy to imagine that most of my work for the CIA Counterterrorism Center's Special Missions Department involved conducting enhanced interrogations. Readers could be forgiven if they thought that I spent most of my time applying EITs to detainees in an effort to secure actionable intelligence. But in truth, the intense use of enhanced interrogation techniques on each high-value detainee usually tapered off on average about seventy-two hours after we started using them. We may have been authorized to use EITs for longer, but by seventy-two hours detainees usually were starting to look for ways to cooperate, and thanks to the conditioning process, I rarely had to use walling when a detainee drifted back into being duplicitous.

Over the course of my involvement with the CIA's interrogation program, I conducted enhanced interrogations on only five high-value detainees. In order of occurrence, they were Abu Zubaydah, Abd al-Rahim al-Nashiri, Ramzi bin al-Shibh, KSM, and Abu Yasir al-Jaza'iri. I estimate that there were at most four months total during which I applied any EITs even once during the day (a very liberal estimate). That's out of the seven years, nine months, and twelve days (almost ninety-five months) that I worked for the Counterterrorism Center. Do the math and you'll see that I applied EITs on fewer than 5 percent of the days I worked for the CTC. Most of the work I did as a CIA interrogator working for the CTC's Special Missions Department didn't involve EITs at all. This chapter is about what I did the other 95 percent of the time.

## My Non-EIT Work with Detainees

In addition to the five detainees listed above, I conducted noncoercive, social influence–based interrogations and debriefings of another nine high-value detainees.

Six of them had received some EITs, but they had become compliant before I first questioned them. They were Abu Faraj al-Libbi, Ammar al-Baluchi, Hambali, Mustafa Ahmed al-Hawsawi, Walid bin Attash, and Hassan Ghul. Muhammad Rahim al Afghani was never compliant.

Two of the detainees I questioned were essentially cooperative from the start and as a result required no EITs. They were Gouled Hassan Ahmed and Ibn al-Shaykh al-Libi.

The detainees I spent the least time with were Hassan Ghul, Hambali, and Muhammad Rahim. The detainees I spent the most time with were Abu Zubaydah and KSM. I spent thousands of hours with those two over the years.

I did not interrogate or debrief any midlevel or low-level detainees. Not one. And although I visited all the black sites holding high-value detainees, I never visited or worked at any of the handful of black sites holding midlevel and low-level detainees except once briefly during al-Nashiri's initial rendition, as was discussed in chapter 3.

Most of my support for the interrogation program consisted of conducting non-EIT, social influence–based interrogations and debriefings. In this fashion, I facilitated the questioning of high-value detainees such as KSM by countless subject matter experts, debriefers, and targeters over the years during which the interrogation program existed. I debriefed detainees myself, and I interviewed detainees to answer questions submitted by the 9/11 Commission.

My job supporting the 9/11 Commission was to take its list of questions and interview detainees such as Abu Zubaydah, Ramzi bin al-Shibh, and Mustafa Ahmed al-Hawsawi (KSM's bookkeeper) about the details of their involvement in the 9/11 attacks. Those interviews were conducted long after EITs were discontinued, and the detainees were more or less cooperative. The 9/11 Commission report remains the most comprehensive publicly available account of the events leading up to the 9/11 attacks and is well worth reading. A study done by NBC News in 2009 showed that more than a quarter of all the footnotes in the 9/11 Commission report refer to information from high-value detainees.

## Morale Visits

Another key task for interrogators was to perform what we called maintenance visits, an unfortunate and uninformative name for what were really morale visits intended to counteract the effects of isolation on cooperative detainees.

One thing that the critics often get wrong about the CIA's enhanced interrogation program has to do with the isolation of high-value detainees. It's true that until a detainee started cooperating, he was being questioned or was alone in his cell, but usually this lasted a few days to a few weeks at most. After they started cooperating, it was to the CIA's advantage for high-value detainees not to become depressed and withdrawn, as most people held in isolation eventually do.

The CIA took positive steps to lessen the debilitating impact of isolation. For example, the security guards stopped wearing their head-to-toe black outfits. Interrogators and the COBs of the sites would routinely visit the detainees for morale visits in debriefing rooms, in their cells, or in specially constructed movie and game rooms. In the last location, the detainee and the visitor might play board games, watch movies and recorded soccer games, discuss books the detainees were reading, help the detainees with their English, or talk about anything a detainee had on his mind. Psychologists and medical personnel would stop by for checkups and evaluations. Dentists were flown in to fix their teeth. The detainees got better medical care than those of us who were questioning and guarding them.

Don't get me wrong. They were still detained at a CIA black site, but the high-value detainees weren't left alone chained to the wall in a dark hole. In fact, they occasionally complained, as KSM did, that they didn't have enough time to themselves for solitary contemplation.

At some point, I don't recall precisely when but later in the program's life span, to further lessen the impact of isolation, cooperative detainees were allowed to spend time with other detainees. They could pray, watch movies or soccer games, or eat meals together under careful supervision. We tried to arrange it so that a detainee in a more positive mood spent time with one who seemed more down. For example, we often had Abu Zubaydah spend time with al-Nashiri.

A few detainees, such as Abu Zubaydah and Hassan Ghul, liked to work out with weights or play basketball. As the facilities improved, it was not unusual for one of the interrogators to be in the gym with Abu Zubaydah chatting about his exercise goals while he lifted weights. The CIA supplied Abu Zubaydah with dietary supplements, and at one point he got really muscular.

Hassan Ghul was very athletic and liked playing one-on-one basketball. Midmorning frequently would find one of the interrogators in the open-air gym for an hour or so of shooting hoops and playing HORSE with Ghul at his request. HORSE is a game in which a player tries to match the shot made by the previous player. Ghul was very competitive and often would bet push-ups that he could make a hard basket or that the interrogator would miss when it was his turn. I recall one instance when Ghul lost on an easy shot and in frustration threw the basketball hard against the concrete wall surrounding the court. He was standing too close, and it ricocheted off the wall and slammed him in the face, knocking him down. Ghul was laughing when the interrogator helped him up and while he paid off his push-up debt.

Detainees were allowed to do almost anything that kept them occupied and out of trouble. Hassan Ghul and Hambali both liked doing martial arts alone in their cells. The guards were initially uncomfortable with it, but since neither detainee ever made an aggressive move, it was allowed. Ghul is the terrorist doing karate in the viral al-Qa'ida recruiting video that was shot before 9/11. In the video a masked Hassan Ghul does a head-high spinning kick. It wasn't unusual to glance at the closed circuit TV and see him stretching or practicing high kicks in his cell.

The detainees weren't staying in a five-star hotel, but it wasn't twenty-three hours a day in isolation in a federal supermax prison cell either.

The things the detainees would choose to talk about during our morale visits could be odd. One time Bruce and I were at one of the black sites together because we happened to have a day or two of overlap before the handoff. The morning I'm writing about, we were splitting up the morale visits. I finished one, stopped by the control room to see who was next on the list, and located Bruce on the closed circuit TV. I saw him with KSM. Bruce was comforting KSM, who was in his arms like a child, crying on his shoulder. I stopped by to see what was going on. KSM's wife had been pregnant when he was captured, and now KSM was despondent because he knew it was past time for the child to be born but no one would tell him whether the birth had been successful, whether the child was a girl or a boy, or the child's name.

KSM loved his family, and despite what a monster he was, it was heartbreaking to see him crying in Bruce's arms. After that, Bruce and I mentioned to Jose Rodriguez's chief of staff that we thought it was important to give KSM news about his new baby. We thought it was the humane thing to do and believed it would keep his mood up and help ensure his continued cooperation. She got permission and found out the information, and Bruce and I eventually told KSM he had a new baby boy. We also told him his son's name. KSM cried and thanked Bruce. He then looked at us and said, "A man's sons are all he leaves of himself in the world." Too bad he didn't feel that way about other people's children.

Not all visits to detainees by CIA personnel worked out so well. Once a clinical psychologist, a contractor, was evaluating KSM. During the visit he started telling KSM he would burn in hell for killing innocent people. He then launched into a religious harangue, cursing KSM, telling him Allah was not a real God, screaming at him. KSM started screaming back. The guards had to pull the psychologist out. One of the interrogators—I think it was Bruce—had to calm down KSM. That contract psychologist was never allowed to interact with KSM again, but I did see him at other black sites evaluating other detainees. If it had been up to me, he would not have had any contact with detainees after his blowup with KSM because he had let his feelings get in the way of his objectivity. But this incident occurred during that period, discussed earlier, when Bruce and I were transitioning out of performing duties as psychologists, and so the agency had to continue using this guy because so few people had been briefed on the program.

## Life on the Road

During our travels Bruce and I tried to maintain some sense of normality. Here are two stories that illustrate how we were often unsuccessful.

Whenever we got the chance, Bruce and I, either together or alone, would go running. Sometimes, because we were trying to keep our footprint in the area small, we would be restricted to running around the perimeter of the building at night and had to do it a hundred times or maybe more to get any mileage. Later, when the facilities improved, we could run inside on a treadmill. But that was a poor substitute because we both liked running outside. Occasionally, however, we would find ourselves somewhere where the probability of our being linked with the agency was remote and we could actually run out in the countryside.

In one relatively uninhabited place we were passing through, Bruce and I decided to go for a long run through nearby woods and over the hills on a narrow dirt path. We started off on a dirt road. About a hundred yards before the place where we needed to cut off into the woods we saw five or six buffalo calves. They were standing in the middle of the dirt road by themselves, looking off into heavy vegetation in the swampy areas that fell away on both sides. We slowed but kept advancing when we didn't see any adults. When we were forty or fifty feet from the calves, one of them made a noise that sounded like a blending of a mew, a bleat, and a bellow.

The tall weeds and vegetation on each side of the road erupted, and suddenly Bruce and I found ourselves surrounded by a large herd of buffalo that formed a protective circle around the calves. They were enormous, each about the size of a military Humvee. They flipped their ears and shook their enormous heads and chewed and stretched their necks out, sniffing the air.

Bruce and I had stopped and were contemplating what to do next when they started trotting toward us in a mass, bellowing. The whole herd, maybe forty-five or fifty buffalo. We turned on our heels. Bruce took off running back down the middle of the dirt road in the direction from which we had come. I sprinted away from the road for the trees.

It didn't matter; the buffalo caught both of us. I heard Bruce yelling, "Where are you? You're abandoning me, hiding in the trees?"

"No," I shouted back. "I'm trying to lure them away from you." Something that was completely untrue that I made up on the spot. Having grown up being chased by cows, I knew we were not going to outrun them and I was looking for a way up off the ground where they couldn't reach me. In my panicked thinking, running down the middle of the road didn't seem like such a great idea.

But neither strategy worked, and we found ourselves surrounded by slobbering buffalo. To my surprise they were pushy but not aggressive. They brushed against me. They smelled my arms and thighs with nostrils the size of dinner plates. They looked at me with eyeballs the size of softballs. They put their big knobby heads down and wanted me to scratch them between their horns. Their very menacing-looking horns. I walked back up to the road followed by about half the herd, bumping and shoving, pushing others away with their heads and horns. The other half had congregated around Bruce. I could just make out the black T-shirt and yellow running shorts he was wearing between the legs and backs and bellies and butts and flipping tails of the enormous beasts.

"I think they want us to milk them," I heard Bruce say from inside the buffalo scrum. I was trying to work my way through the herd, carefully threading my way to him, hoping not to get kicked or gored or stepped on as I elbowed my way through the monsters. They would look around at me as I flanked one of them and smell my arms as I walked by.

"It's just a hypothesis," Bruce said. "Reach down and grab a teat and see if I'm right. Grab two if you want to run the definitive field test."

The buffalo escorted us to where the narrow path broke away from the dirt road and headed off into the woods. Some buffalo mingled on the roadbed, and others disappeared back into the swampy areas.

Bruce and I were back to running. We made a mental note to come back by a different route and settled into an eight- or nine-mile cross-country run. We thought the excitement was behind us. Now it was just one foot in front of the other, sometimes making small talk but mostly lost in our own thoughts. I remember wondering if I had enough water. We dropped down over a steep hill and into a deeply wooded area. Brush and vegetation and bushes closed in on the trail and made it feel like we were running in a cave.

Suddenly behind me, right on my heels, was a loud, horrible screech, somewhere between an elk's rutting call and the noise an angry horse makes just before it hands you your ass. Both Bruce and I were startled, and I can say with certainty that I have never before nor since performed a vertical leap of such raw power, height, and distance. We moved, high stepping like something out of a Road Runner cartoon. Poof: all that remained was dust, swirling leaves, and maybe just a little bit of pee.

A hundred yards on we stopped. I was so scared that my running shoes ran on for another quarter mile without me. We looked back, alert and ready to fight for our lives, expecting the Abominable Snowman or a skunk-ape or a Tasmanian devil or something grizzly at least eight feet tall and made of claws and teeth.

But instead we saw a dwarf donkey stallion about two feet high at its withers. It brayed and showed its teeth and pawed the ground as if it were going to charge us. It wanted us out of its territory. Behind it, four or five equally tiny donkey mares and the cutest little donkey foal hardly bigger than a tiny dog came cautiously out of the bushes. The foal was curious and started toward us. The stallion put himself between us and the foal. The foal kept trying to get around the stallion and with each run got closer and closer to us. Bruce and I decided we better head on down the trail. It would be embarrassing to get our backsides kicked by something that was only a couple of feet tall and ate grass.

We wanted to avoid all that coming back, and so our eight-mile run became more like twelve because we had to drop over a ridgeline to cut over to a trail that wound back to the parking area a different way. After we were safely back at the car, I told Bruce that maybe there was something to be said for running inside on treadmills.

The second story illustrating the difficulty of maintaining normality was potentially much more serious. Bruce was in the passenger seat of an SUV, and it was well after dark. The only light was the cone of illumination from the black Range Rover's headlights. The streets were narrow and filled with debris from the shot-up buildings and mud walls on both sides of what seemed like more of an alley than a roadway.

Suddenly, Bruce and his companions were cut off by a vehicle that blocked the road in front of them. The CIA officer who was driving threw the SUV into reverse, stomped on the gas, and was immediately rammed on the passenger side by a second vehicle. The long gun, the MP4, slid off the front seat and became jammed in the seat brackets. The linguist riding in the backseat was initially thrown to the floor but then clambered over the backseat and began yelling what sounded like a prayer of supplication. Something shattered the window on Bruce's door. Broken glass flew everywhere.

Bruce was drawing his Glock from his holster but stopped when he noticed that their Range Rover was surrounded by dozens of screaming tribesmen brandishing AK-47s and gesturing for them to get out of the damaged SUV.

"We're Americans," the CIA officer shouted, "Americans."

The screaming stopped. The tribesmen still pointed their weapons in their general direction, but the atmosphere was not as charged with malice. The mob parted, and a man stepped out of the crowd and approached. "Americans?" he asked in English.

"Yes," the CIA officer replied in kind. "We got turned around on these narrow streets." He pointed to the photograph of a martyred warlord kept on the sun visor of the Land Rover. It was a gutsy move. Any warlord's tribe that was against Americans would have shot them instantly.

"Get out of here," the man said with a dismissive wave of his hand, "and never come back."

They disentangled the Range Rover, backing it out of the rubble and away from the truck that had rammed them. It was beat up, with broken windows and smashed door panels, but it ran.

I saw the Range Rover a few days later awaiting repair in a fenced-in vehicle lot. It was hard to believe that no one was seriously injured when it was rammed in the ambush. But providence or good judgment or just blind luck was in play, and other than an ass-chewing by the COS no one was worse for the experience. In fact, some could argue they were wiser by having the operational necessity of staying situationally aware, not overreacting in emergencies, securing firearms, and perfecting defensive driving indelibly ingrained without any scars to show for the lesson.

## The Terrorist Think Tank

When KSM started cooperating, useful information didn't just trickle out of him; it came in a flood. So much so that we set up a process that eventually was called the Terrorist Think Tank.

The idea was to use the high-value detainees in CIA custody as a brain trust made up of senior terrorists who would unknowingly work together to address our intelligence requirements and provide insight into the mindset and worldview of this elite group of people who were trying to kill us. Our intent was to use this information to undermine future terrorist operations.

Interrogators, debriefers, and subject matter experts could quickly query high-value detainees on a variety of intelligence-related subjects. For example, we could show the same surveillance photograph to multiple high-value detainees in short order, using what we learned from each to question the others in real time. Sometimes we circled back when detainees later provided information that suggested that those who had been questioned earlier had additional information that they were hiding or had forgotten or that we had not asked for in a way that would pull for what they knew. Here is an example of how something as simple as showing a photo might yield dividends beyond the identification of the main target of the surveillance.

For reasons of classification, I can't go into too many details, but imagine that we showed a photograph of a suspected terrorist to the detainees in the think tank. Several might know the main suspect, but one might recognize jihadi brothers in the background. Armed with that knowledge, interrogators, debriefers, or subject matter experts could go back to detainees who had been interviewed earlier and question them in more detail, all within a few minutes or hours of first receiving the photograph. This significantly cut down the turnaround time and often created a kind of synergy that resulted in more complete answers than did questioning detainees days apart. The same kind of thing happened with identifying voices, decoding encrypted messages, or identifying the significance of different locations where terrorists were thought to be hiding out and filling in details about them. It also allowed us to ask them one by one how they would go about locating a detainee in hiding or help us understand al-Qa'ida attack planning. When President Bush ordered that detainees in CIA custody be transferred to the military at Guantanamo Bay in 2006, the loss of this capability was in my opinion a major setback. Terrorists killed in Predator attacks can't provide insight into the intentions of the leaders of various groups that are our mortal enemies. Generally, neither can outsourcing interrogations to foreign services.

Let me tell you about an interesting characteristic of captured high-value detainees who were more or less compliant. Bruce and I noticed early on that when they first started cooperating, high-value detainees would answer questions exactly as asked, nothing more. Initially most would not volunteer any information or correct your question if you were off base. Some never got over this. But Abu Zubaydah and KSM both passed through this stage and eventually provided information beyond what was being sought.

For example, there were times after EITs had been discontinued for months when I would ask KSM something and he would provide an answer. Then he would say, "But that's not the question I would ask," and he would rephrase the question in a way that would call for information not in the original intelligence requirement. Then he would say, "Now ask me *that* question." I would, and he would provide a fuller and more complete answer to the issue I was asking about. It was his way of providing the information without volunteering it in the absence of a specific question.

I once asked KSM and Abu Zubaydah why detainees went through this phase of answering questions exactly as asked. Both told me that once a brother believed in his heart that he could be forced to provide information, there was no sin in answering questions precisely as they were put to him (this we knew already), but it was a sin to volunteer information your enemies weren't asking for and might not know you had. It was a betrayal of Allah and of the brothers still fighting. The result was that we sometimes had to play a form of the children's game Battleship. Interrogators would lob questions at the detainee, and the detainee wouldn't respond with the sought-after information until one of the questions struck the mark. This insight became important when I later began to provide consultation to foreign law enforcement and intelligence services on noncoercive interrogations and used the lessons learned from the Terrorist Think Tank.

The Terrorist Think Tank project also allowed us to interview the detainees to gain insight into their worldview and mindset.

One illuminating discussion I remember involved talking with Khallad Bin Attash about his March 2001 role in blowing up the two sixth-century Buddhas carved into the sandstone cliffs in the Bamiyan Valley northwest of Kabul, Afghanistan. It is a UNESCO World Heritage Site. Bin Attash told me that Mullah Omar, leader of the Taliban, wanted the Buddhas destroyed because they were idols. Allah condemns idol worship, he explained, and demands that all idols be destroyed. This is the primary reason ISIS is destroying the ancient carvings, statues, and artwork as it razes Iraq and Syria, stripping the gold out of churches as it destroys them and looting museums and smashing antiquities.

Bin Attash said that the Taliban wanted to destroy the idols but didn't know much about explosives, and so al-Qa'ida sent him to help them because he was an explosives expert. He said he showed the Taliban how to set the charges and then helped them destroy the idols. I asked him how he felt about destroying a World Heritage Site that people traveled from around the world to visit.

He seemed to take great pride in the key role he had played and suggested that the fact that it was a World Heritage Site made it that much more important to destroy the idols, not less, as we in the West might foolishly assume. He said that because the place was so famous, lots of idolaters went there to worship, resulting in much sinning. He said that his destruction of the Buddhas was the same thing as the Prophet Muhammad's destruction of the hundreds of idols in the Kaaba, an act of faith to rid the world of idolatry. The Kaaba is a cube-shaped structure in Mecca, Saudi Arabia, long thought by Muslims to have been built by the prophet Abraham and his son Ishmael in pre-Islamic antiquity and a destination for Muslims during their annual pilgrimage. In Muhammad's time it supposedly was filled with 360 idols of various pre-Islamic gods that he destroyed. Bin Attash said that Allah would see his participation in destroying the Buddhas as an act of love and devotion and reward him in paradise.

Though those of us in the West may see the uniqueness, the beauty, and the status of the Bamiyan Valley Buddhas at a UNESCO World Heritage Site as reasons to protect these antiquities, those subscribing to Bin Attash's brand of Islam view those qualities as reasons to destroy them.

When I discussed a religious topic with a high-value detainee, my goal was to understand his beliefs, not criticize them. Later, when I got the chance, I would read about the topic in English translations of original Islamic documents such as the Koran or the Sunnah (sayings and teachings of Prophet Muhammad) or the hadiths (stories about Muhammad's life and deeds) or a volume of Sharia law such as *Reliance of the Traveller*. After reading about the topic or discussing it with other detainees, I often would stop in to see the original detainee for clarification and to try to get a more nuanced understanding of his worldview, especially as it related to attacking America, and a better feel for how the religious principles we had discussed guided his cooperation or resistance when questioned.

Americans often assume that for the most part terrorists think the way we do, but those who subscribe to al-Qa'ida and ISIS's brand of Islam do not. The interviews that Bruce and I and others did as part of the Terrorist Think Tank highlighted several dangerous ideas that are part of the worldview of these violent jihadists, ideas that increase the likelihood of violent terror attacks against the West, especially America.

They believe that Muslims who subscribe to their brand of Islam are superior people chosen by Allah for a special destiny: true dominion over the world. They believe that Allah has commanded them to establish dominion by any means necessary, including violence. They believe that because the West, especially America, is so strong, the only hope for achieving this destiny and obtaining their God-given entitlement to rule the world is through violent jihad. They believe that the fact that we oppose their taking over the world and imposing their religious values on us proves that we harbor harmful intentions that make them vulnerable; therefore, we are a threat that must be destroyed.

People who harbor these dangerous ideas are not likely to adopt the live-and-let-live prospective of most Americans. They don't think the way we do, and they seek to use these differences, our tolerance, our values, and our freedoms as weapons to aid in our destruction.

"It is inevitable," Abu Zubaydah once said to me with a wry smile and a tone of absolute confidence. "It is Allah's will."

He was explaining to me that the imposition of Salafist Islam on all of humanity could not be stopped or defeated, only delayed. However, even such delays, he said, were part of Allah's larger plan: the alignment of events in preparation for the return of the Mahdi, the Prophet Muhammad's successor who will conquer the world for Islam and whose arrival portends the apocalyptic End of Days when the damned are judged and the blessed start to taste the pleasures of paradise.

I don't know how I expected him to act during the exchange, but I wouldn't have been surprised to hear veiled threats or sense a hostile urge to strike out. But there was none of that. No belligerence, no angry spewing of Koranic verses, no fanatical Islamic rants, just an amused twinkle in his eyes and the sense that as he was explaining his beliefs to me, he was experiencing the joy of giving his life over to something that was greater than he was.

We didn't start off talking about the apocalypse; we started off talking about how Abu Zubaydah had lost his way morally as a teenager and about how he returned to the true path of Islam by strictly relying on the words and deeds of the Prophet Muhammad for guidance in how to act in all things.

Allah had blessed him, he said, with discontentment—an ache to do more for his Palestinian people—and a hatred of the Jews, gifts that motivated him to seek fulfillment beyond a life of material possessions and the pleasures of women and Pepsi. Taking up the jihad allowed him to focus those gifts and gave his life renewed purpose. Abu Zubaydah said that by surrendering to Allah's will and accepting his obligation to wage jihad he became a mujahideen, a holy warrior, in a continuous line that stretched back unbroken to the Prophet Muhammad.

We drifted into discussing the apocalypse and the End of Days, and our conversation carried us into talking about why it was so important to impose his brand of Islam on the rest of the world. The spread of Islam and the imposition of strict Sharia law are important preparations for the end of the world, one of the things that must happen before the souls of good Muslims trapped in their graves can enter paradise on Judgment Day.

I got the impression that Abu Zubaydah viewed imposing his brand of Islam on all humanity as an act of devotion, not as a hostile act but rather as an invitation to join him in the bliss that comes from actively surrendering oneself to the one true god. You become Abu Zubaydah's enemy only when you reject that invitation and by doing so declare yourself an enemy of Allah and thus subject to being conquered or killed by any means consistent with Koranic revelation and the teaching of the Prophet Muhammad.

Abu Zubaydah told me that Allah imposed on him the obligation as a mujahideen to take the fight to his enemies wherever they were and to never quit, with the full knowledge that if he stalled or fell in battle, future generations of mujahideen would rise up and faithfully carry on the struggle until all of society was under Sharia law or the apocalyptic End of Days was at hand.

The thing that most impressed me about these discussions and similar discussions I had with other high-value detainees was the certainty of their beliefs. They were not using religion as an excuse for what they did. Instead, they acted as they did because their strict and literal reading of the Koran and the hadiths caused them to believe that they were steadfastly following the prescribed rules of war against infidels laid out by Allah in revelations to the Prophet Muhammad.

As others have pointed out, we see a similar nexus between belief and action with ISIS as they attempt to purify the land they conquer in their fight to reestablish the Islamic caliphate in Iraq and Syria. Slavery, crucifixion, beheading, burning, stoning, looting, hacking off limbs, blinding, throwing gays off tall places, raping captives as spoils of war—these are not modern innovations but a revival of medieval customs drawn from the exegesis of ancient holy texts and carried out by Islamists deliberately trying to breathe new life into dormant Islamic traditions. To them, the conquest and slaughter of Allah's enemies, especially those who are helpless to prevent it, is a blissful act of worship done for the love of their god, not out of hatred for their enemies.

To expect ardent subscribers to these beliefs to abandon them willingly is dangerously unrealistic.

## Helping Debriefers and Subject Matter Experts Question HVDs

"You're a liar, a son of a bitch, and you're always going to be a lying son of a bitch." The white-haired lady was leaning over the table, yelling in Ramzi bin al-Shibh's face. His eyes bugged out. He rolled them and looked over at me with a "see what I have to put up with?" expression.

I was there because bin al-Shibh was giving one of the CIA's best debriefers a hard time. He had been lying to her. Their relationship had been contentious because she was scary smart and very assertive and bin al-Shibh thought women were chattel to be possessed and do his bidding, with no right to question a man's decisions. It was a spicy mix, but she was generally good at getting information out of him and had been questioning him for several weeks. It wasn't the first time she had debriefed him, either. She knew about his attitude toward women. But this time they were getting on each other's nerves. She was really fed up with him.

Headquarters sent me there to see if I could sort it out and get bin al-Shibh to admit he had lied and get on with the debriefing. Thank goodness, I was going to be there only one night.

I don't even remember what the questioning was about. Something to do with one of KSM's terror plots, I think. Anyway, I spent a half hour or so with her going over what bin al-Shibh had told her and what she thought he was lying about. She told me she wanted to "cut his nuts off." Not an option, really, although the thought of him fathering children makes me shudder even today.

Later I talked alone with bin al-Shibh. "That woman does not know her place." Now it was his turn to tell me his side of events. "She talks down to me. . . . Me . . . bin al-Shibh!" as if he couldn't get his mind around it.

"What do you think she told me about you? I mean, what's her side of the story?"

"She says I'm a liar. That there has to be more than what I've told her. She called me an ugly name."

"Yeah, she's a scary lady," I said, hoping to disarm him with a little "we guys have got to stick together" empathy. "But are you lying to her?"

"Maybe," he said, and gave me a conspiratorial look that said he clearly was, and out of spite at that.

"So what's next? How do we get past this?"

"Bring me somebody else to talk to me—a man."

"Not going to happen. You're doing this out of spite. Headquarters is never going to let you pick and choose who you work with. You have to work with her. Here's a suggestion. Why don't you tell me what you lied to her about and the two of us will come up with some way to tell her."

He told me. As I said, I don't remember what it was, but I'm sure it had something to do with stuff other detainees had told us and that bin al-Shibh would not acknowledge as true. I told him, "She's too smart for you to try to claim you just now remembered something like that, something she's been asking you about for days. You're better off coming clean."

Bin al-Shibh agreed. I could tell he wasn't looking forward to it. He was acting like a kid who had been caught shoplifting and now was being forced to admit it to the store manager and apologize.

To smooth things, I got together with the white-haired lady before our meeting with bin al-Shibh and stressed that it was important for her not to punish him for coming clean about lying because it would make it less likely that he would admit to lying in the future. She said she understood.

Once the three of us were in the meeting room, I said, "Bin al-Shibh has something he wants to tell you." And then bin al-Shibh admitted he had lied to her out of spite because he didn't like her. I think it would have gone smoothly if he had not disparagingly addressed her as "woman" during his apology.

She was out of her seat and in his face before I could say anything, again calling him a son of a bitch and a liar. But unlike when the FBI called Abu Zubaydah a son of a bitch, I got the impression this wasn't the first time bin al-Shibh had been called that. He looked over at me and gave me a "see what this woman is like?" gesture. The look wasn't something that pleased the white-haired lady. It prompted her to aim another string of invectives at him and the stink eye at me.

I told bin al-Shibh, "Don't be looking to me to rescue you. You brought this on yourself. You know what she is like. You've been talking to her for weeks. This is what happens when you lie to her." To her I said, "He admitted he lied and is ready to answer your questions. Let's do that. Let's ask him your questions and see if he keeps his word." This earned me another glance, albeit with less stink eye this time. But she understood my point and calmed down. She admonished bin al-Shibh not to lie to her again and then debriefed him on the topic he had been lying to her about. The two of them seemed to have worked out their differences, at least temporarily. I left the black site and was never called in to help the white-haired woman again. Bin al-Shibh, however, continued to be difficult.

The debriefers and targeters and subject matter experts were amazing professionals, and most of the time nothing like that happened. But the vignette above is an example of the sorts of problems I was dispatched to resolve to make it possible for those professionals to debrief high-value detainees.

Here is another story. A young CIA officer, not a contractor, got into a dispute with al-Nashiri. As I mentioned in chapter 3, al-Nashiri could be very difficult to deal with, especially when he had a migraine headache. On this occasion, al-Nashiri pitched a fit and once again smeared snot and feces on the cameras and walls in his cell. The young CIA officer and several of the guards went into the cell with the intention of forcing him to clean it up. Things escalated, and the young CIA officer told the COB that he intended to physically force al-Nashiri to comply if necessary.

Bruce objected. I objected. We had both dealt successfully with al-Nashiri when he was in one of these moods, and we knew nothing good would come of trying to force him physically. We knew that if that happened, al-Nashiri would be out of sorts for weeks. Bruce voiced his objections to the COB. They got into a bit of an argument. The young CIA officer who wanted to force the issue was a blue badger, an agency employee. We were contractors: green badgers with no authority. The young CIA officer acted like Bruce was trying to order him around rather than just trying to save us all a lot of grief dealing with al-Nashiri later. The COB initially sided with the young CIA officer.

What they did not know was that al-Nashiri had a ritual he insisted on following when he had a headache. The ritual was simple: he wanted to take two aspirin with caffeine and an antacid tablet, put toilet paper in his ears, and then wrap his head in a towel. Allow him to follow it and he was no problem at all. Keep him from doing it and he would throw feces around his cell and fight you. Medical personnel had made the aspirin and antacid available to him, but al-Nashiri seldom directly asked for them. Instead, he would stand in front of the camera and indicate that he had a headache through a series of grunts and then pantomime a headache by placing his hands on his temples and rocking from side to side. If you didn't know what he was doing, it looked a little nuts. With the turnover at the site, the guards didn't know what they were looking at, and things quickly escalated. Finally Bruce got through to the COB, who let me go into al-Nashiri's cell alone and take care of the problem without further incident.

Other examples of detainee challenges were described in earlier chapters. KSM's office hours and vitamin disputes, the debriefer who alienated KSM by claiming to know more about KSM than he did himself, and subject matter experts looking for Perry Mason moments are all examples of the sorts of things Bruce and I dealt with to facilitate detainee debriefings.

## Consultation with Foreign Liaison Services

Starting in 2004, the chief of the CTC's Special Missions Department began sending me to consult with non-Western foreign intelligence and law enforcement services that were detaining terrorists who were thought to have information that the CIA needed to stop attacks against the United States and our allies.

My marching orders were clear. No physical coercion could be involved. If I saw any rough stuff, no matter how minor, I was to leave the scene immediately and report it. I was to have no direct contact with detainees held in foreign custody. I couldn't even be in the room when detainees were questioned. I was to observe through one-way mirrors or on closed circuit TV.

My job was to help liaison partners develop interrogation strategies and individualized interrogation plans tailored to the high-value detainees they had in custody. The aim was to better service CIA intelligence requirements.

This was a somewhat complicated process. I started by learning as much as I could about the specific person being detained by a foreign liaison. I then familiarized myself with the specific questions the CIA wanted to have answered. Fortunately for me, I was always accompanied by one or more brilliant subject matter experts, analysts, and targeters who knew far more about how the detained terrorist fit into the threat matrix than I ever could. I then met with the foreign interrogators to get to know them and find out about their interrogation approaches.

After that, I watched liaison interrogations in real time, accompanied by subject matter experts who could provide me and the liaison with immediate feedback about whether the CIA's questions were being answered. Usually, after covering each major section of the questions, the interrogator would take a short break and check in with us. That gave us a chance to provide feedback about how adequately our questions were being answered. If the interrogator was finding out what we needed to know, we quickly discussed the next set of questions; if the detainee was withholding, we came up with a game plan for what to do next in the interrogation session tailored to that terrorist in that time and place. After each session was over, we would meet with the liaison interrogators and their bosses and hot-wash the session. I spent a surprising amount of time teaching basic questioning skills.

Some liaison interrogators were brilliant; others, not so much. This was one reason analysts were often unhappy with the responses they got back from liaison services before the CIA established its own interrogation program. It was also the reason I was asked to get involved.

Previously, CIA officers would provide a list of questions several pages long with supporting facts and suggested ways of asking the questions. Then they would get back answers from the liaison that were only marginally useful if not completely worthless.

For some liaison services, interrogators learned their skills on the job as an apprentice to a senior investigator without formal training. A lot of my work consisted of watching what the interrogator was doing during interrogations and then providing training to address the shortfalls.

For example, I would teach interrogators to construct time lines around critical events and fill in key pieces of information, particularly about a detainee's actions. I also taught them how to recognize the importance of vague answers. Vagueness in an answer to a specific question is a clear indication that additional follow-up is needed that focuses specifically on the vague parts. It doesn't mean the detainee necessarily knows the answer, but it does mean additional questioning is required.

I would spend some time talking about how human memory works. Interrogators and debriefers often have to make real-time intuitive judgments about what is reasonable for a detainee to remember or forget. Some thought that memories were recalled and played back like a movie; they are instead reconstructed.

I taught them how to help detainees think back and reconstruct important events. I reviewed the impact of emotions on recall, pointing out how the emotions in play when events happen influence what can be remembered later. I also explained how the emotions they experience during recall influence how memories are re-created and thus the information available to the interrogator. I covered the things that can distort recall and plant false memories. And I reviewed questioning techniques that increase the risk of eliciting false confessions, inaccurate descriptions of real past events, or the recall of confabulated information and cautioned against their use.

I shared what we had learned about the tendency of detained jihadists who appeared to be cooperating to answer questions exactly as asked and not as was intended by the interrogator. And I passed along other observations about frequently observed resistance strategies employed by captured terrorists.

When questioning a detainee about a letter written or addressed to that detainee, liaison interrogators would often hand the letter to the detainee and ask, "Is this your letter?" The reply was almost always "No." Even if the answer wasn't "No," the interrogator usually took back the letter before the detainee could read it and then started asking questions about the letter's content. Detainees who were intent on withholding would often use the way the interrogator handled the letter and the way the interrogator's questions jumped around to delay responding and withhold information.

I recommended that first the detainee be asked to hold the document and read it completely through out loud. Then the detainee should be asked to read it out loud again, only this time, when the detainee got to a portion of the letter that we were interested in, the interrogator should stop him and say something like "What were you thinking of when you wrote those words you just read?" or "What does this word refer to?" or "How did you think [the letter's recipient] would interpret what you just read?" or some similar question related to what had just been read out loud.

From a psychological point of view the initial readthrough activated the areas of memory associated with the document, making it easier to recall why the document was originally created. The readthrough also had the added effect of triggering, for lack of a better term, "guilty knowledge" concerning the intent behind writing the letter. This guilty knowledge made it more likely that a detainee's body language and word choice would betray efforts to withhold information because he was mentally engaged with what was in the document. It was easier for him to be deceptive when he could deal with it at a distance, much harder when he had just read aloud incriminating content that was either written by or intended for him.

One challenge that was unique to working with Muslim interrogators was the impact of Islam on their interactions with a detainee during interrogation. Often the detainees I was sent to offer advice on interrogating were enrolled in an Islamic reeducation-rehabilitation process. In the course of rehabilitation, a detainee would review his life story and the choices he made from the perspective of following the true path of a Muslim man. The problem this created for interrogations was that once the religious teachers working with the detainee declared that he had returned to the true path (i.e., repented and abandoned his terrorist ideologies), the interrogators were bound by their religion and in some cases by government policy to accept his answers at face value.

At first this confused me. It seemed obvious that terrorists lie and that accepting anything one of them said at face value was risky. When I asked the foreign interrogators I worked with to explain the reasoning to me, I was told that it was based on a strict interpretation of Sharia law. It was in most cases a sin to lie blatantly to another Muslim; it was also a sin to accuse another Muslim of lying to you without proof. Interrogators who didn't appear to accept the word of a terrorist who had been declared by religious scholars to be back on the true path risked committing the sin of taking the word of an infidel over that of a True Muslim and of getting sideways with leaders who wanted the rehabilitation programs to succeed.

I encountered this a fair bit and worked with interrogators to help them brainstorm ways to readdress things that the detainee was clearly lying about without appearing to question his word. The detainee was in a bind, because if he admitted he was lying, he would be off the true path of a Muslim man and possibly committing religious crimes that in their minds had far worse consequences than trying to blow up a few Americans. Often my contribution was to help interrogators devise and orchestrate face-saving ways for the detainee to "suddenly recall" important details or to pray the *Istikharah* to receive guidance from Allah and tell the interrogator what was "revealed" in dreams. It was not the first time liaison interrogators had dealt with the problem. Some were much better than I was at devising work-arounds. My contribution often amounted to helping them psychologically tailor the face-saving device to the specific detainee's temperament and worldview.

My presence also served another critical function. Most of the

CIA subject matter experts I worked with were women—brilliant, attractive, competent, outspoken women—and some Muslim male interrogators had issues working with them. Hell, they scared me. It was helpful for me to be around. Since subject matter experts always accompanied me, these interrogators could save face and work with the knowledgeable females by including me in the conversation. They weren't supposed to be alone with women they weren't related to. I was a male escort, and some interrogators were more comfortable if I was there. In retrospect, I think it would be more accurate to say that the subject matter experts dragged me along as camouflage so that they could do their jobs protecting Americans while being immersed in a culture that didn't appreciate the capabilities of Western women. Although I've seen subordinates act like male chauvinists, I never saw this problem with the senior leadership of any liaison services with which I consulted. Those leaders tended to be bright, Western-educated, and not as prejudiced toward women.

"THERE IS A man on an airplane right now, headed to the United States, and we fear he may be a troublemaker."

It was late 2006, the middle of the night in a Middle Eastern country. The man who asked to see me urgently was sitting at a conference table with four or five cell phones fanned out in front of him like a hand of playing cards. We were drinking strong cardamom tea. I could smell it and the faint honey aroma that emanated off the pastries.

"Here are his details," he said, sliding a folded piece of paper across the table to me. "You might want to keep an eye on him when he gets to the United States."

I glanced at the contents and then slid the folded paper to the CIA officer sitting beside me.

"Any chance he will make mischief on the plane ride over?" I asked.

"No. His girlfriend says he is going to the States to take an engineering class, but he has said that he would like to do operations against the United States, and we're concerned that he might act out once he gets there. You should keep an eye on him."

Then the CIA officers and the subject matter expert who accompanied me from home on this trip joined the conversation, going over more precisely why the liaison was concerned enough that they would feel compelled to tell us about the suspect and providing more details about what the actual threat might be. It seemed the liaison had tried to stop this person from leaving for the United States, but the flight had left before they had had a chance to pull him off it.

This illustrates what for me was one of the most interesting aspects of my work with foreign liaison officers. After I had worked with their interrogators, the leadership of the liaison services often would ask for me by name to attend late-night meetings. They would pass bits of intelligence to me. They would tell me things, often alarming things, that would end up in intelligence reports and urgent cables sent back home. One of the COSs of a Middle Eastern country recognized this, took me under his wing, and had me attend meetings with him. Later we would split the report-writing chores.

In many ways these foreign liaison trips were some of the most productive times I spent working for the agency, as were working one-off problems, helping debriefers and subject matter experts obtain intelligence without using coercion, and furthering our understanding of terrorist beliefs, motives, and priorities. But the 5 percent of my time that I had spent that involved EITs always came back to haunt me.

# CHAPTER 10

# The Wheels Come Off

It was in late 2003 when KSM told me that eventually the United States would "present its neck for slaughter." Little did I know that his prediction would come true so soon.

On April 28, 2004, I was at home, just back from forty-one days out of the country, when the Abu Ghraib photographs slammed into the American consciousness and set in motion a cascading series of events that eventually would cause the wheels to come off the CIA's interrogation program.

The photos were awful. Naked prisoners piled on top of one another with grinning U.S. military police in the background making a thumbs-up gesture. A soldier sitting on a detainee pressed between two stretchers. Naked prisoners led around on leashes. Some poor prisoner standing on a box, hooded, draped in a black blanket, arms out as if he had been crucified, with electric wires attached to his fingers.

My heart sank as soon as I saw them. I understood what had happened. I had studied the psychological mechanisms that lead to that sort of abusive drift. Even so, I was surprised and dismayed to see it. I was also angry.

Not only was it morally wrong to treat detainees that way, I knew the CIA's interrogation program would take a hit because of the stupid and self-indulgent criminal activities of a few bored and poorly supervised military police officers.

Our nation and the world were outraged, and justifiably so. The awful photos accelerated a downward spiral for the CIA interrogation program that had started a year or so before.

Although the interrogation program in 2002 and 2003 was enormously productive, its success was its own worst enemy. The CIA gained tremendous insight into the organization, leadership, and plans of its terrorist enemies. As a result, al-Qa'ida leaders who were still at large spent much of their time staying out of our clutches and had a much harder time pulling off major attacks. But politicians and pundits started to assume and assert that the lack of terrorist strikes proved that the threat wasn't so bad after all.

As time went on, speculation about the existence of the black sites and what occurred at them started appearing in the press. The CIA was in no position to fight back. It had promised the nations hosting the black sites its silence, and any description of the interrogation techniques would only strengthen the hand of al-Qa'ida.

As rumors swirled, members of Congress who once had been supportive of the interrogation program started developing amnesia and the Department of Justice showed signs of moonwalking away from some of its previous pronouncements about the program's legality.

In the late 2003–2004 time frame, the CIA's inspector general, John Helgerson, began to question the legal foundation for using EITs and reported his thoughts to the oversight committees in Congress. Despite acknowledging that the attorney general had said repeatedly that the use of the EITs by the CIA was legal, Helgerson expressed concerns that their use could violate the United Nations Convention Against Torture.

Many people don't know that the CIA itself suspended the use of EITs several times between 2004 and 2007, insisting that the DOJ issue classified opinions revalidating that the use of the EITs by CIA was legal and did not violate the Constitution or, in later opinions, the torture conventions.

In late May 2004, the director of the CIA, George Tenet, sent an e-mail to the black sites suspending the use of EITs. In early June, Tenet formally directed CIA interrogators to use only question-and-answer techniques pending clarification from the DOJ of the constitutionality and legality of the EITs. He also requested reaffirmation of the policies and practices of the interrogation program from the National Security Council.

On July 22, 2004, the attorney general confirmed in writing that the use of all EITs except for waterboarding addressed in the August 1, 2002, opinion would not violate the U.S. Constitution or any statute or treaty obligation, including the Convention Against Torture. On August 6, 2004, the DOJ extended that opinion to include waterboarding on a specific detainee as long as it was done consistent with the CIA's proposed limitations, conditions, and safeguards. That detainee was never waterboarded, however.

When the DOJ reviewed the CIA's enhanced interrogation procedures in 2002 and concluded that their use was lawful, it issued two memos detailing its opinions. The first was an unclassified memo for the White House that outlined the commander in chief's broad constitutional powers to override the torture laws if necessary. The second was a classified August 2002 memo sent to the CIA saying that it was lawful to use the original set of EITs on Abu Zubaydah. Critics of the CIA's interrogation program make much of the DOJ's

June 2004 withdrawal of an unclassified memo on the president's constitutional powers regarding torture laws, as if that signaled to the CIA that the use of EITs lacked a legal foundation.

To the contrary, while withdrawing the unclassified opinion, which it said was too broad, the DOJ reaffirmed the classified August 1, 2002, opinion that was the legal basis for CIA use of EITs, in its words, "because that opinion was more narrow in scope." Thus, contrary to what has been said in the press, rather than a repudiation, that withdrawal of the broad unclassified opinion while leaving the narrow opinion that applied to the CIA in place was a reconfirmation of the legality of the program.

In May 2005, the DOJ issued three classified legal opinions analyzing the legality of specific EITs. All three concluded that CIA use of the approved EITs, including waterboarding, was constitutional, did not violate any U.S. statutes, and did not violate the Convention Against Torture.

In December 2005, in response to the passage of an amendment authored by Senator John McCain to the defense spending bill, the CIA again suspended the use of EITs. No new detainees were taken into CIA custody at the time, but since none of the existing detainees was still being interrogated with EITs, debriefing continued for them.

The wheels really started to come off the program after the 2004 Abu Ghraib prison scandal, which had absolutely nothing to do with the CIA's detention and interrogation program. Subsequent DOD investigations proved that the CIA was not involved in Abu Ghraib. But government reports are no match for powerful pictures.

Not inclined to let a good crisis go to waste, the critics of the CIA's interrogation program used the Abu Ghraib scandal like a club.

Media reports criticizing the CIA's enhanced interrogation program began to appear with greater regularity. A frequent source was an unnamed ex–FBI agent who turned out to be Ali Soufan. Leaks from the office of the CIA's inspector general made matters worse. Suddenly Bruce and I found our names showing up in media reports suggesting erroneously that we bore some responsibility for Abu Ghraib. We didn't. I had never been to Iraq, and neither had Bruce. Neither had we ever participated in anything even remotely like what happened at Abu Ghraib.

Throughout the remainder of 2004 and into 2005 and 2006, CIA headquarters repeatedly dialed back our authority to employ EITs.

On September 6, 2006, President Bush publicly acknowledged the existence of the CIA's detention and interrogation program, which for some time had been one of the world's worst-kept secrets. The president announced that all the existing CIA detainees had been moved into military custody at Guantanamo Bay Naval Base. As a result, the CIA lost the ability to tap into its al-Qa'ida knowledge base. KSM University and the Terrorist Think Tank were closed for good. I understood and appreciated that it was important that high-value detainees, especially KSM, eventually be tried for their crimes: Americans had a right to justice. But I knew the nation would miss being able to rely on their collective understanding of al-Qa'ida terror networks, their knowledge of key players moving into al-Qa'ida leadership roles, and their capacity to help us make sense of coded or obscure messages.

I've already mentioned that the CIA suspended its use of EITs several times. The last time the CIA stood down its interrogation program, we were waiting for Congress to act on legislation related to the program. During that wait, interrogators were asked to provide a bare-bones list of EITs pulled from the list of those already approved that the CIA could submit to the DOJ for yet another review. The idea was that the shortened list would be used to seek congressional support. All the interrogators converged on Langley and spent several days putting together recommendations. Almost unanimously we agreed that only two EITs were required for the conditioning process: walling and sleep deprivation. The others, though occasionally useful, were not critical, and some, such as nudity, slaps, facial holds, dietary manipulation, and cramped confinement, Bruce and I now believed were unnecessary.

We presented our recommendations to the midlevel CIA officers who were working the issue for the CIA's leadership. We told them we needed only walling and sleep deprivation. But the midlevel managers told us they already had told the senior leadership that the interrogators were going to recommend sleep deprivation, dietary manipulation, attention grasp, facial hold, facial slap, and abdominal slap but not walling. And they *were not* going back upstairs and telling the bosses that what they had told them earlier was wrong. They ordered the interrogators to sit down and write a recommendation for using the EITs they had told the bosses would be on the list.

Out of earshot of the others, Bruce and I told the midlevel managers that the use of the reduced set of EITs was likely to be ineffective if a detainee was skilled at resisting, accustomed to harsh conditions, and intent on protecting his secrets. We had learned over the preceding years that the EITs the midlevel managers intended to retain did not lend themselves to the conditioning process as reliably as walling did.

We told them press leaks had removed the fear of the unknown associated with the CIA's interrogation program by making it clear that the objections to the agency's methods by some in Congress had watered down the EITs. That had not always been the case. Abdul Hadi al Iraqi was captured before the program had been completely gutted in the media. Abdul Hadi was held first by a foreign intelligence service and then by the U.S. military before he was transferred to CIA custody. In each instance he had steadfastly insisted that he was not Abdul Hadi despite the fact that when he was caught he was carrying identification documents with his photograph on them identifying him as such. Nothing they did could get him to admit who he was.

When Abdul al Hadi was transferred to CIA custody, Bruce and another interrogator did the neutral assessment to see if he would talk without the use of EITs. When Bruce took the hood off him, Abdul al Hadi said, "I know who you are. I know what you can do. You don't have to do that to me. I will cooperate." And he did, without the use of EITs.

Thanks to the brouhaha in the press, that sort of capitulation from fear of the unknown was no longer likely. The terrorists knew that most of our harshest techniques had been removed from our kit bag and that many of the remaining ones were essentially bluffs.

Back at headquarters, the midlevel managers told Bruce and me that they were trying to save the program, and since they were not going to go back upstairs, it was either accept their list of EITs or nothing. Even though Bruce and I doubted that we could do the Pavlovian conditioning with the techniques that the midlevel managers had decided to keep, we reluctantly agreed to help them write up those recommendations.

It wasn't our call. It was a CIA policy decision. At that point, as consultants, our job was to help those who had hired us make the best case for the course of action they chose. I wouldn't have chosen that subset of EITs, but it wasn't my program. It was theirs.

The wheels on the program were now wobbling badly.

Even though we thought our job was to support the course of action the managers of the program decided to undertake, two CIA directors asked our opinions, and Bruce and I again voiced our concerns to them. At least once when Porter Goss was CIA director and then again later after General Michael Hayden took over, Bruce and I separately or together told the directors that walling and sleep deprivation were the only two EITs necessary and that the others were either completely unnecessary or likely to be far less effective. I remember General Hayden telling me that he heard me and understood and appreciated what I was telling him but that the CIA officers running the program had given him a list of what they said they needed and he was obliged to support them.

In June 2007, we were asked to provide a personal briefing to Secretary of State Condoleezza Rice outlining the reduced set of EITs. John Rizzo, the CIA's acting general counsel, accompanied us. The managers of the program made it clear to us that we were to be supportive of their pared-down list of EITs, and we did our best to be enthusiastic supporters. They told us what to cover: our backgrounds, the origins of the original set of EITs, the way the program had evolved, the safeguards, and so on. Secretary Rice was gracious and easy to talk to.

For our part we wanted to be sure that Secretary Rice had a clear mental picture of what the techniques actually looked like in use. Therefore, we illustrated a couple, much as I had for CIA Director Tenet in 2002. Rizzo and John Bellinger, the State Department's legal advisor, looked at us contemptuously, as if we were acting inappropriately or disrespectfully. They acted as if she were a hothouse rose. At one point they exchanged a glance that suggested that they thought Bruce and I were clumsy, unwashed street urchins who somehow had found their way into the royal castle's china closet with a hammer.

But we didn't care what they thought. We cared what Secretary Rice thought, and she seemed curious and interested. It wasn't Rizzo or Bellinger who would be asked to use the techniques and suffer any grief that came from that; it was us. We already had heard rumors that members of Congress who had been briefed from the beginning were starting to claim they had not been told about the program or had been misled. We wanted to be sure Secretary Rice knew un-equivocally what our country was asking us to do.

In January 2014 Rizzo published a book, called *Company Man*, that has an entirely different take on the meeting, suggesting that we had gone off script and risked offending the secretary of state by excessive candor and description. After Rizzo's book came out, Bruce reached out to Secretary Rice through a mutual friend. Rice assured him that she was not offended and was grateful for our insight into the program.

Although President Bush revealed the existence of the interrogation program in 2006 and the fourteen detainees then in CIA custody were moved to Guantanamo Bay, he left open the possibility that the agency would temporarily hold and interrogate additional detainees who might come into its custody in the years ahead. That is what happened in 2007 when the agency gained custody of a bin Ladin associate by the name of Muhammad Rahim al Afghani. In my mind that was when the wheels came completely off the program.

**IT WAS LATE** 2007. The person on the other end of the secure line back to headquarters was trying to be patient with me. "They said you used the word *tape* in your last cable to headquarters. Never do that again."

"Never use the word *tape*? Why?"

"The investigation into the destruction of the Abu Zubaydah interrogation tapes has everybody on edge back here, and they don't want anyone thinking we're taping Muhammad Rahim's interrogations." Rahim was a senior al-Qa'ida facilitator who was thought likely to have information on the location of senior al-Qa'ida leaders, including bin Ladin. He was the last detainee held by the CIA.

"We're not. Al-Nashiri was the last time we taped an interrogation . . . in 2002. Whoever has their hair on fire must not have read the cable. I was only suggesting, as a ploy, that we tell Muhammad Rahim that we are going to dummy up some tapes to make it look like he is cooperating with us if he doesn't start being more forthcoming. I never suggested that we really tape anything; it would have been a ruse. I suggested we threaten to fake a tape that would make him look bad to al-Qa'ida operatives still at large."

"So, you did use the word *tape*?"

I could hear an exasperated sigh on the other end of the line. I counted to ten and made another run at it.

"Yes," I said, feeling my voice go up an octave, something that happens when I get ruffled.

"They sent me to this godforsaken place, told me the reduced set of EITs weren't working on Rahim, and instructed me to think outside the box for something nonphysical that might have an effect on him. He really values what his family and the jihadi brothers still at large think about him. My suggestion was that we try to leverage that by convincing him that we can make it appear that he is cooperating with us."

I was agitated. I felt like I was being taken to the woodshed for doing exactly what I had been sent there to do. From the briefing I had been given and from my own review of the cable traffic coming out of the black site, it was clear that the newly revised set of EITs had not been effective on Muhammad Rahim. The analysts told me they weren't getting anything useful out of him. Not a single disseminated intelligence report had been generated. And no wonder: he was a hard man who was used to austere conditions, psychologically resilient, and willing to endure hardship to protect what he knew. Thwarting interrogation was his chief priority, and the EITs we had been left with were not sufficient to change that.

Bruce and I and the other interrogators had warned them this probably would happen, and now it felt like we were being blamed for being right. In our view, in the aftermath of the Abu Ghraib scandal, some officers at the CIA had become risk-averse. Understandably so. Congress was quickly distancing itself from the program, and some managers at the CIA could sense it. They were scrambling to limit the damage to their careers and suddenly were more interested in appearances than in effectiveness. Or maybe they were just practical enough to see that the program had been whittled away so much that it didn't even resemble the program Bruce and I had helped put together a few years before.

Now no EITs were authorized for use. My marching orders were: "See what you can do. Think outside the box for something that doesn't involve EITs that might get him talking."

I didn't like being put in that position. If the idea was to use an approach that did not involve any physical coercion, that approach should have been tried before EITs were employed. Half-assing the job by starting limited EITs and then stopping before conditioning was complete just pissed him off and left him that much more confident that he could take anything the CIA could dish out.

But it was actually worse than that in Muhammad Rahim's case. In the short time he had been in CIA custody, before I arrived at the site, CIA headquarters had ordered abrupt changes in approaches several times. They were floundering. Every few weeks a new interrogator with a different approach would show up at the black site with marching orders to try something different. The use of EITs was on again and off again. They were not adverse enough to shift Rahim's priorities and were applied inconsistently.

When I arrived, Bruce was already there. The initial interrogation with the reduced set of EITs had not gone well. He said that there was tremendous pressure from headquarters to get results. The midlevel managers had told the bosses that their pared-down set of

EITs would be effective, but they weren't. And now it seemed they were trying everything and anything to get results, short of settling on a plan and sticking with it.

The inconsistent orders coming out of headquarters produced morale problems and conflicts among the interrogators and debriefers at the site. The interrogators were piled up there, each with a different set of instructions and each thinking his approach had priority. The result was chaos. Depending on whom you talked to at headquarters and what time of day it was, you could get diametrically opposed instructions.

Amid all this chaos, I questioned Muhammad Rahim and watched others do the same. My assessment was that he was withholding information for at least two reasons: there were secrets he actually wanted to protect, and he was enjoying the contest. He saw himself as being engaged in a battle of wills with the interrogators, and he was continuing his jihad by jerking them around. My read was that keeping faith with al-Qa'ida operatives was a key motivator. That was why I suggested that we consider telling him that we could fake a tape that would undermine other terrorists' opinion of him. I sent back the suggestion to headquarters, and the midlevel and low-level CIA officers there went ballistic. The frenetic switching of approaches continued.

"Hear me. I need to be clear with you," the voice on the other end of the line said. "The only thing you are authorized to do is ask him questions and write down his answers. You can't lie to him, you can't deceive him, you can't threaten him, you can't bargain with him. You can't even raise your voice. You are only allowed to ask questions and write down his answers. That's it. No more."

"What about the Army Field Manual?"

"Off the table."

"So, that's it . . . we've given up?" I said, repeating what Bruce and some of the interrogators on-site had told me when I arrived. Some in headquarters were looking frantically for something that worked, and others were just going through the motions until the program died. That or waiting until another attack on the homeland caused another change of heart in Congress. Those providing oversight—the very people who had said, "Are you sure you're doing enough?"—had become our most vocal critics. We were taking friendly fire from the same people in Congress who had been briefed and had approved or hadn't objected to the program from the start. They were scrambling to hide their complicity behind newly minted outrage and posturing for the press.

Muhammad Rahim had us beat, and he knew it. He told me and Bruce as much. He said, "You're not going to get the best me. You're not going to get me to tell you anything. You feed me, you clothe me, you take care of me medically, you even check my teeth."

In March 2008, Rahim was transferred from CIA to military custody without revealing anything of value.

# CHAPTER 11

# Investigations and Witch Hunts

From the beginning of the CIA's interrogation and detention program in 2002 until 2014, Bruce and I were the subjects of five major investigations. None of the investigations found that Bruce or I had done anything illegal, but they did result in our names and association with the program (which the government considered classified information) being leaked. What's more, rather than clearing up matters, the investigations tended to inject and spread misinformation about what the CIA's interrogation program involved and our role in it.

This chapter is about my involvement in the first three of those investigations: the 2002–2004 CIA inspector general's investigation into detainee interrogations, the 2007–2010 Senate Armed Services Committee investigation into the treatment of detainees in U.S. custody, and the 2008–2010 Department of Justice investigation into the destruction of Abu Zubaydah's interrogation tapes from 2002.

I realize that for some readers the details of these initial investigations will seem like insider trivia. Readers who have no interest in the specifics of these three investigations can skip ahead to chapter 12, where the last two investigations—the 2009–2012 Justice Department investigation into the use of "torture" during detainee interrogations and the 2009–2014 Senate Select Committee on Intelligence investigation into the CIA detention and interrogation program—will be discussed. Understanding the handling and mishandling of those two investigations is critical to following this story. Those who are interested in what it was like to be caught up in the earlier investigations should keep reading.

## 2002–2004 CIA Inspector General's Investigation into Detainee Interrogations

The CIA inspector general, John Helgerson, asked me if I had punched Abu Yasir al-Jaza'iri in the mouth. We were in a cramped conference room, me and maybe three or four others from the CIA inspector general's office, seated at a table stacked with folders and documents. It was 2004.

"No," I said. "I did not. Where's that coming from?"

Helgerson told me that someone had reported that I had punched Abu Yasir in the face and knocked him down. "Not true," I told those at the table. "It didn't happen that way." I speculated that the person must have been confused, because Abu Yasir jumped and fell down when I slapped him. I suggested that they talk to the security guard who had been in the room when it happened and to those monitoring the incident on closed circuit TV. The guards had had great views of the action.

It turned out that the inspector general had opened an investigation of the program. Whether he was asked to do so by higher-ups or initiated it on his own, I never knew. It seemed to me from his tone and the questions he asked that Helgerson was starting out from a position of being skeptical about and perhaps hostile to the interrogation program. Maybe inspector generals always sound that way. I don't know.

I knew he had some valid reasons to be concerned about the program. During this interview, I told Helgerson and his staffers about what I observed the New Sheriff and his newly minted interrogators do to al-Nashiri. I also complained about being held incommunicado at the black site against my will. But from the tone and content of their follow-up questions, I got the impression they thought I was a disgruntled contractor making up false allegations or exaggerating to be vindictive.

Helgerson asked me a few questions about waterboarding. Later, his report raised troubling allegations about interrogators using too much water, but he didn't ask me to address that during the questioning.

They asked me about the time Abu Zubaydah threw up rice and beans as if it had been a major medical emergency involving a full-on emergency room crash-cart response by physicians. I explained that it was a passing incident in which there was no medical intervention other than me pushing on his stomach just below his breastbone to ensure that he cleared his airway. His airway wasn't blocked; I just did it as a precaution because we didn't want him to breathe in any thrown-up food he might have in his mouth.

Months later, a few days before Inspector General Helgerson released his final internal report, which was titled "Counterterrorism Detention and Interrogation Activities (September 2001–October 2003)," Bruce and I were shown a draft. Our boss at the time, the chief of special missions, asked us to provide comments and corrections for consideration. Bruce and I sat before a single computer terminal in a small cubicle writing our response to the many errors in the draft report. We tried to correct what we thought were significant misrepresentations. For example, the inspector general had conflated the number of times water was poured with the number of waterboard sessions. In addition, the report misrepresented the description of waterboarding as it appeared in the 2002 DOJ opinion.

The IG report also raised concerns that too much water was used when Abu Zubaydah and KSM were waterboarded but didn't seem to base that conclusion on anything other than the total number of separate pours without taking into consideration how short the individual pours were. As was explained earlier, shorter pours mean more applications but also less water and more chances to breathe.

I remember looking at Bruce when I read that section and thinking out loud, "They didn't do the math or they wouldn't have come to that conclusion." I had done the math for the way the DOJ approved waterboarding for use by the CIA; it's in chapter 2 of this book. We used nowhere near as much water as was allowed by the Department of Justice.

Bruce and I gave our rejoinder to the chief of the Special Missions Department, who passed our comments, along with his own thirty-two-page rebuttal pointing out inaccuracies and a list of suggested corrections and comments, to the CIA's IG. Not one of our comments or corrections made it into the final IG report, and as the chief of the Special Missions Department told me later, his did not either.

When Bruce and I read the final IG report in May 2004, we immediately voiced our concerns to the chief of special missions. I was especially concerned about the way waterboarding was incorrectly described and about the suggestion that we had used too much water and waterboarded KSM in too many sessions. I knew it would create problems for us later.

I was angry and felt betrayed. If the CIA thought I was doing it wrong, they had had plenty of opportunities to tell me to modify or stop what I was doing. At this point, the IG report was still highly classified and could be read by only a relatively small number of people, but I had been around long enough to know that reports like this don't stay secret long. The more inflammatory and wrong they are, the more quickly they seem to leak.

I was especially disappointed with comments in the report allegedly from the physicians and medical personnel who had been at the black sites. The medical personnel, who had been involved every step of the way, seemed to be implying that no one had consulted them. That surprised me. Not only had they been involved in developing safety procedures for waterboarding and in briefing interrogators and guards about potential medical emergencies, they had been present when the detainees were waterboarded and could have stopped it any time they chose to for any reason. But they didn't. Instead, the medical personnel made suggestions about what to feed detainees before they were waterboarded and how long to wait after they ate before starting a session. The doctors even required that for reasons of safety we switch from using water to using medical saline. They maintained crash carts nearby: medical tool chests on wheels stocked with the emergency room lifesaving gear. Physicians on-site examined the detainees after waterboarding sessions and gave us updates on potential problems a specific detainee might encounter during future waterboarding.

Not one physician, not one nurse, not one physician's assistant ever said anything to me or Bruce about overusing water or waterboarding incorrectly. Neither did one senior agency officer or CIA lawyer. If they had, I would have shown them the math. I would have explained that although shortening the length of time for a single pour resulted in more pours (applications), the detainee had more chances to breathe. If ordered to use the twenty-second minimum each time, Bruce and I would have refused because we thought it was too harsh. If they wanted us to use less water, we would have done that gladly.

I asked the chief of special missions why, if the CIA thought I was waterboarding incorrectly or using too much water, no one bothered to mention it to either Bruce or me. I told him they had had plenty of chances since videotapes of Abu Zubaydah's waterboarding were seen by senior CTC leadership and multiple attorneys during the videoconference in which we requested that they send their most skeptical targeter, and again later, when Abu Zubaydah's last waterboarding was watched in real time by senior CTC officers and a senior CTC attorney who were in the room while it happened.

The chief of special missions was a matter-of-fact former Marine. He was always direct with me and didn't sugarcoat anything. He told me in no uncertain terms that if he had thought I was waterboarding incorrectly or not following the DOJ guidelines, we wouldn't be having the conversation because I would be gone. He said he frequently discussed what Bruce and I were doing with senior CIA officers, some very senior, and no one had ever raised any concerns about us with him.

To confuse things further, Helgerson's report was filled with mixed messages. He questioned the legal basis of the program and the legality of the way we waterboarded Abu Zubaydah and KSM. But in the same report he said the attorney general was aware of how we waterboarded those two detainees and said it fell "well within the scope of the DOJ opinion and the authorities CIA derived from it."

I wasn't comforted by the assurances of the chief of special missions. The CIA IG report was out there, inaccurate and misleading, and so were those damn interrogation tapes.

Bruce and I fretted about the situation on the drive back to our hotel the afternoon we read the final version of the report. My temperament is to get energized and take action; Bruce's temperament is to get quiet and reflect on the role his actions might have played in unfolding events. Someone driving next to us would have seen me talking and gesturing incessantly and Bruce looking thoughtfully at the dashboard, occasionally glancing over at me as if he were expecting my head to explode.

I felt that we were being set up to be the fall guys. We had done what the CIA had asked us to do to save American lives, it had worked, and now bureaucrats were writing things in official reports that were inaccurate and misleading and were not giving us a chance to defend ourselves. We would see that pattern again with Senator Feinstein's 2014 SSCI report.

Not for the first time, Bruce and I were glad that unmasked senior CIA officers appeared on those interrogation tapes along with us. At the time we believed it was the only thing that might keep the tapes from eventually being released publicly. We had been vocal in our desire to see the tapes destroyed, but the CIA seemed to be dithering. In the aftermath of the Abu Ghraib prison scandal in Iraq, the public release of those tapes would have been horrific for the country. We didn't do what they did at Abu Ghraib. Our actions were cleared by the DOJ, approved by the president, and reported to senior members of Congress. But I had no confidence that some members of our government would keep their covenant with us. As it turned out, I was right.

Bruce and I decided that short of extraordinary circumstances (a nearly certain indication of a nuclear device in an American city, for example) and additional assurances from the CIA and the DOJ that we wouldn't be embroiled in legal difficulties later, we were not going to waterboard any more detainees. And we didn't. But I *did* waterboard two government attorneys, including a woman lawyer from CTC. Here is how that came about.

We were in the basement of a nearly abandoned military base. I glanced around for the physician, made sure the guards were ready to raise her up to clear her sinuses, and then looked down at the CTC attorney strapped to the waterboard.

"Are you sure you want to do this?" I asked. "It's an ugly experience."

She nodded. I lowered the black cloth over her face, and the senior CTC officer helping me started pouring water on the cloth. I could tell she didn't like it. She was snorting and trying to blow water out of her nose. When it was over, she was surprisingly composed, standing there beside the waterboard, drying her wet hair, her eyes red. "Well, that sucked," she said. "I can see why nobody would want to do that again."

Nope, I thought, still feeling a little creepy about waterboarding her. I did not think it was necessary. I had tried to talk her out of it, but she had been adamant. Later that day, we were scheduled to waterboard the head of the DOJ's Office of Legal Counsel (OLC), Assistant Attorney General Daniel Levin, the guy in charge of the office reworking the DOJ opinion on enhanced interrogation techniques. He wanted to know what it was like to be waterboarded, and the CTC lawyer insisted that we waterboard her before we waterboarded him.

Later, standing there watching Levin sit down on the waterboard and lie back, I realized I didn't feel as creeped out about waterboarding him. In fact, I welcomed it. I thought the DOJ needed to know what the CIA was asking me to potentially do. And I wanted to know for sure it was legal. I figured if it wasn't, he would immediately tell us to not do it anymore.

Levin took it well. He was stoic. I don't recall his exact words, but after it was over he said something like "It was terrifying. I felt like I was going to drown."

A mutation of an old joke about lawyers in a car accident intruded into my thoughts momentarily: "Two lawyers waterboarded in one day—it's a good start, but there's room for improvement."

Levin got off the waterboard and dried himself. That would have been an excellent time for him to tell me that waterboarding was torture and ban it, but he didn't. Instead, the DOJ once again said it was legal and in a later opinion approved it for use on a fourth detainee, although it was never done.

I was not involved in discussions or planning for use of the waterboard on the fourth detainee. But if I had known of the August 6, 2004, letter (which was subsequently publicly released) from Daniel Levin to John Rizzo, acting general counsel for the CIA, I would have recommended that the CIA use far less water than was authorized by the letter. Paragraph 4 of that letter says the "technique will be used in no more than two sessions, of two hours each, per day. On each day, the total time of the applications of the technique will not exceed 20 minutes. The period over which the technique is used will not extend longer than 30 days, and the technique will not be used on more than 15 days in this period."

When Bruce and I waterboarded for the CIA, the total time a detainee such as KSM spent strapped to the waterboard was twenty minutes per session, not two hours, and that included the amount of time the detainee could breathe unobstructed. If we did two waterboarding sessions a day, which we did at times with KSM, the total amount of time a detainee spent strapped to the board was forty minutes a day for both sessions combined. That means the greatest amount of time we had KSM strapped to the waterboard for both sessions was only one-third as long as a single session allowed under the August 6, 2004, letter from Levin. Not only that, Levin's letter authorized the use of the waterboard for fifteen out of thirty days. With two sessions a day authorized, that equals thirty waterboarding sessions.

Assistant Attorney General Levin's August 6, 2004, letter says that waterboarding following the procedure outlined in his letter "would not violate any United States statute . . . nor would it violate the United States Constitution or any treaty obligation of the United States." But more relevant to the point I'm trying to make here, the letter also says the guidance it provides is consistent with the August 1, 2002, letter from Jay Bybee, the assistant attorney general in charge of the Office of Legal Counsel, to John Rizzo and with previous uses of the technique.

In late 2003 the CIA's IG and his staff went nuts when they learned that KSM had been subjected to fifteen waterboarding sessions over two weeks. But the August 6, 2004, guidance the CIA received from the DOJ (over a year after KSM's waterboarding was complete) authorized thirty sessions in fifteen days, twice as many sessions as KSM actually was subjected to. Yet the CIA's IG ran around for years asserting as fact that we had "gone beyond what had been agreed to with the DOJ" by "excessively" waterboarding KSM. In 2003 and 2004, Helgerson accused us of using too much water on KSM and not following DOJ guidelines in multiple briefings to the leadership of both the Senate Select Committee on Intelligence (SSCI) and the House Permanent Select Committee on Intelligence.

This previous point is important, because it directly contradicts the false claim by some members of the Senate and House oversight committees who claim that they first heard of waterboarding years later. They not only had heard of it; they knew the CIA's IG had concerns because he reported those concerns to them.

I believed then and I believe now that Helgerson and his staff's objections were triggered primarily by their moral objections to EITs, especially waterboarding. My belief was buttressed when I later found out that one of the major sources of media leaks about the

CIA's enhanced interrogation program was a senior official in the CIA IG's office doing the investigation.

As was noted previously, my conversations after Levin was waterboarded were not the only opportunities the people in charge had to tell me and Bruce that waterboarding was wrong or that we were doing it inconsistently with DOJ guidance, nor would they be the last. During 2007, even the SSCI support staff and Senator Feinstein, then a senior member of the SSCI, had a chance.

In November 2007, Bruce and I briefed the SSCI staff on the enhanced interrogation program. There were a lot of people present. I don't know how many, but it seemed like more than a dozen, including the staff director. We sat around a long table in a secure conference room and meticulously described the program to them, including the EITs and how they had been used. My thought at the time (and I'm sure Bruce shared it) was that so much misinformation and controversy had been generated by the press and critics of the program that to cut through the crap we needed to be sure these folks knew both how the techniques had been used in the past and how they were being used at that time. We then took questions, which seemed to fall into two categories: What exactly did you do? and What was it like to interrogate the bad guys? They asked the lawyer with us a few questions about the legal underpinnings, but no one at that meeting raised any concerns about the legality or constitutionality of our actions or expressed any moral objections. That question-and-answer period would have been a good time for them to tell us they thought we were torturing people, but they didn't.

Neither did Senator Feinstein, who now calls us torturers, when Bruce briefed her personally in 2007. Bruce spent over an hour in the director's office with her and the director of the CIA, General Michael Hayden. Following General Hayden's lead, Bruce briefed the senator in detail on the EITs and answered any questions she had. That would have been an excellent time for her to tell him that what we were doing on behalf of the U.S. government was wrong, that it amounted to torture, that it was a stain on the moral fiber of America. Instead, Feinstein thanked him for the sacrifice he was making and the hard work he was doing to keep Americans safe.

## SASC Investigation into the Treatment of Detainees in U.S. Custody

In early 2007, the Senate Armed Services Committee (SASC), the Senate oversight committee for the Department of Defense, began investigating the treatment of detainees in U.S. custody. The SASC's jurisdiction and focus should have been the Pentagon's treatment of its detainees. But shortly after the investigation started, articles pointing fingers at the CIA and those involved in the agency's program (notably me and Bruce) started to appear in some media outlets and blogs.

In early May 2007, I received a document request from the SASC signed by its chairman, Senator Carl Levin. The committee wanted everything my company had in its possession relating to helping any agency of the United States elicit information from detainees in U.S. custody. They wanted all documents, communications, and records of communications from October 1, 2001, through April 1, 2007, and they were demanding that we get those documents to them in less than a month.

I immediately reported that I had received the document request to Jose Rodriguez's chief of staff and to attorneys in the CTC and the CIA's Office of General Counsel. We were told by the attorneys that we could deliver responsive documents we had relating to work eliciting information from detainees done by me or my company for the Department of Defense (there wasn't any), but we were not authorized to give the SASC any documents related to work we had done for the CIA. The reason for this was that the work we performed under contract for the CIA was classified and "compartmentalized" and members of the SASC, whose duties were to provide oversight for the military and not for the CIA, weren't authorized to receive it. The lawyers stressed that our program had been reported to the Senate Select Committee on Intelligence, which had the special clearances and whose job it was to provide for CIA oversight. The agency said that documents related to our work for the CIA were available to the SSCI if it wanted to review them. They stressed that we were prohibited from providing documents to anyone who had not been authorized to be briefed on specific programs. I didn't get the impression that the CIA was trying to avoid congressional oversight, only that it didn't want me and Bruce to pass classified documents to a committee that didn't provide agency oversight.

Bruce and I felt that we were in a bind. First off, I didn't know how Senator Levin got our names. I had heard rumbles that the SASC was looking into the treatment of detainees in DOD custody, but that didn't have anything to do with us. I was blindsided by the request for documents. Later, I found out that General Hayden, the director of the CIA, had mentioned our names in a classified meeting with SSCI committee members in which Senator Levin was sitting in as a guest. Shortly after that Senator Levin's request for documents arrived.

Bruce and I felt we were caught up in a game of push me–pull you, with the CIA and the SASC tugging us in opposite directions. Two weeks before the deadline, I began to get phone calls and e-mails from an SASC investigator prodding me to start handing over the documents.

Bruce and I recognized that we were in over our heads. We obtained legal representation from a former deputy attorney general of the United States and consummate Washington insider, Jamie Gorelick, and another highly skilled lawyer from her firm.

**OUR ATTORNEYS WORKED** with the CIA and the SASC and gave the committee the documents it requested. I had not done any of the things that the SASC was investigating for the DOD, but Bruce was in a slightly different position. He had not been involved in DOD interrogations. However, before he started working for the CIA, he had been a civilian employee of the Joint Personnel Recovery Agency (JPRA), the military agency that oversees survival training. As the senior SERE psychologist for the JPRA, he had worked on a few minor issues on the edges of the activities the SASC was investigating.

We didn't fight it. We made it clear to our attorneys that we had no desire to impede the SASC investigation, and, albeit reluctantly, we volunteered to be interviewed. But the interviews were delayed because of legal wrangling among all the lawyers. Eventually, we were allowed to meet with committee investigators and answer questions concerning what we knew about the use of EITs in military interrogations of detainees in DOD custody.

On July 10, 2007, Bruce and I were interviewed separately. One at a time, our attorneys ushered us into the Capitol Building, where we were questioned by the same SASC staffers and investigators.

I was shocked when SASC investigators first told me that the DOD had teams of survival instructors from JPRA assisting in harsh interrogations using SERE-derived enhanced interrogation techniques and then asked me what I knew about it. I was stunned, because the president had directed that enemy combatants in DOD custody be treated consistently with the principles of the Geneva Conventions. I assumed that Common Article 3 applied, which prohibited violence to life and person and outrages to personal dignity, in particular humiliating and degrading treatment. On the basis of what the SASC staffers told me that day, the DOD didn't appear to be following the president's instructions. In contrast, detainees in CIA custody were not subject to Common Article 3 until after the U.S. Supreme Court handed down a decision in 2006 in a case called *Hamdan v. Rumsfeld.*

SASC investigators showed me several documents. My recollection is that one of the documents said that SERE interrogation methods, including the waterboard, could be used on detainees with minimal risk of physical or mental harm. That floored me. I told the investigators that I couldn't imagine that anyone in the DOD would write a document like that in light of the president's directive regarding the Geneva Conventions. I couldn't imagine it originated with the JPRA. At the time I had no knowledge of who was behind the requests. Subsequently, I learned from the SASC report that the Office of General Counsel of the DOD requested that information.

The investigators asked other questions. Most addressed work I'd done for the DOD in the past. A few addressed issues I was completely unaware of, such as the alleged use of enhanced techniques by DOD interrogators and survival instructors in interrogating detainees. They didn't ask and I didn't answer any questions about the CIA's interrogation program.

When my SASC interview was over and I was leaving the room, I asked one of the staffers in passing where certain libelous news stories about me and Bruce that had started popping up recently were coming from. He said some Democratic SASC committee staffers had been telling their friends in the media what horrible people Bruce and I were.

I can't prove that Democratic staffers were leaking our names and spreading slanderous remarks. However, I believed they were because it was about the time when the SASC staffers started pressuring us for an interview that stories primarily attacking our character started to appear in the media.

The essence of some media reports was that the military was cruising along fine using the interrogation techniques in the Army Field Manual until Bruce and I reverse-engineered the basic survival school SERE interrogation techniques, road-tested them at the CIA's black sites, and in the process created the "myth" that those techniques actually worked to elicit actionable intelligence. The military heard about our supposed success with EITs, and their use then "whipped across continents and jumped from intelligence to military communities." The migration allegedly culminated with the military joining the intelligence community in using SERE-based interrogation techniques on detainees, resulting in abuses such as those seen in Iraq's Abu Ghraib prison.

But that scenario is completely false. On November 20, 2008, the SASC finally issued its investigative report, which was titled "Inquiry into the Treatment of Detainees in U.S. Custody." The report unequivocally shows that those journalists got the story wrong. The military was looking into using SERE-based EITs several months before the CIA first considered using them.

According to the SASC report, the military contacted the JPRA, the organization that oversees all military survival and resistance training, in December 2001 about the possibility of using SERE-derived EITs. That was four months before I was asked to deploy with the team that interrogated Abu Zubaydah, seven months before I suggested that the CIA consider using EITs, and nine months before the DOJ approved the use of EITs to interrogate Abu Zubaydah.

The military was asking about the use of EITs before the CIA had an interrogation program. The media stories that claimed that the CIA influenced the DOD to seek out SERE-based EITs can't be true, because the time line doesn't work. Something that happens in the future can't cause something to happen in the past, at least not on the planet where I live.

A careful reading of the SASC report indicates that this is what actually happened. Terrorists were not as easy to interrogate as were foreign military personnel. Maybe the terrorists were better at deliberately withholding information and more motivated to do so than were rank-and-file enemy soldiers from the militaries of foreign governments. E-mails submitted to the SASC revealed that interrogators were writing in from the war zone, complaining that the interrogation techniques in the Army Field Manual were not effective on captured Taliban and al-Qa'ida fighters and requesting permission to use interrogation techniques like the ones they encountered in SERE school.

In December 2001, the DOD Office of General Counsel sought the JPRA's input on the problem. Eventually, the JPRA responded to requests by various organizations by conducting interrogation training and then participating in the interrogations of detainees in DOD custody.

It was a similar impression that DOD detainees were successfully thwarting interrogations by military interrogators at Guantanamo Bay that prompted CIA officers to ask me and Bruce in December 2001 to write a paper based on the Manchester Manual, the al-Qa'ida manual for resisting interrogations created from stolen U.S. SERE training materials. They wanted us to describe what the behavior of detainees trained to resist interrogation using the techniques in the Manchester Manual would look like while they were being questioned. We read dozens of Guantanamo Bay interrogation reports describing the behavior of senior-level detainees, and it was clear they were successfully using sophisticated resistance techniques.

The military units seeking SERE-related interrogation techniques might have bumped up against the CIA in passing, but the initiative came from Department of Defense military interrogators and started before Abu Zubaydah was captured and long before the CIA was even thinking about using SERE techniques.

## The Destruction of CIA Interrogation Tapes

When I first heard in April 2002 that the interrogations of Abu Zubaydah were going to be videotaped, I was indifferent. I viewed it as a policy decision by the CTC's leadership. It had its pros and cons, but it didn't seem controversial to me because in advanced SERE training interrogations were taped routinely so that they could be reviewed afterward by instructors and students. We often garnered good information from those tapes.

Thus, it seemed reasonable that something useful might come of taping Abu Zubaydah. Also, I was aware that some U.S. law enforcement agencies routinely taped interrogations. Enhanced interrogations were not even a consideration at the time (they didn't begin until months later), and so they didn't enter into my thinking. I might have felt differently if the suggestion to tape had coincided with the first use of EITs, but I doubt it. I knew everything I had done had been deemed legal by the DOJ. Therefore, although I wouldn't want tapes of me released to the public for both national and personal security reasons, I had no objection to a review of those tapes by fair-minded fact finders, assuming they were knowledgeable about what was authorized at the time and took that into consideration when they viewed the tapes.

The management and protection of the tapes and the actual taping were done by security personnel at the black site where Abu Zubaydah was held. Just before CIA and FBI interrogators entered the room with Abu Zubaydah, one of the guards monitoring on closed circuit TV would push a VCR tape into the recorder and press "Record." The guards then would monitor the recording process and switch to a new tape when the old one was running out of room to record.

In the beginning, this was a pretty simple process: tape in, hit "Record," tape out, label, enter start/stop time in written log, and put on a shelf in a secure area for safekeeping.

But as days and weeks passed and the tapes started to pile up, minor human error began to creep in. Someone would mislabel a tape, someone would forget to hit the record button for a few minutes, or the tape would run out and the guard monitoring the recording process would miss a couple of minutes of ongoing action as he changed the tape. But overall the guards were highly conscientious, and errors that could be corrected were corrected on the spot.

The 2004 CIA IG's report lists the status of the Abu Zubaydah interrogation tapes when the CIA IG's office reviewed them. The report says that eleven tapes were blank. Yes, that would be the supply of unused blank tapes intended for future recordings but not used because headquarters changed recording practices. In late 2003, headquarters decided for security reasons that it didn't want to keep a stockpile of interrogation tapes. Therefore, in November 2003, starting with the interrogation of al-Nashiri, interrogations were taped, made available for report writing, and then taped over the next day. As a consequence, the site wasn't using as many VCR tapes as it had in the past. We had so many unused tapes because we also kept extra blanks on hand. We were at a black site and couldn't run down to the local video store and buy "just in time" supplies.

In addition, comparisons of the tape logs, cable traffic, and videotapes revealed that there was "a 21-hour period, involving two waterboard sessions, that was not captured on videotape." This must have been one of those times when the usually diligent guards forgot to hit the record button or thought they had and were wrong. What most people don't realize is that in the beginning the guards at the black site where Abu Zubaydah was held were police officers and brought their professionalism and objectivity to work with them. When instructed by headquarters to record something, they would do so. I'm sure it was simply human error.

The tapes did come in handy once, in the spring of 2002, while the FBI and CIA were still doing the interrogations jointly. At one point Abu Zubaydah started faking confusion when interrogators were in the room, but only then. Abu Zubaydah would be sitting in a chair, CIA and FBI interrogators would enter, and suddenly Abu Zubaydah would start rolling his good eye, rolling his head from side to side, acting sleepy, and talking nonsense. As soon as they left, he would go back to his normal activities. We had the interrogators enter and leave his cell several times over the course of a couple of hours to show how he experienced a sudden onset of his symptoms when interrogators entered the cell, followed by a miraculous recovery every time they left. The COB and medical personnel were able to view his deceptive malingering live by watching it unfold on closed circuit TV and then review it more carefully on tape to be sure he really was faking.

At the time, my job was to advise the interrogation team on the psychological aspects of Abu Zubaydah's interrogation. That meant coming up with a way to get him to stop this nonsense. Here is what the chief of base did on the basis of my advice.

He entered the cell, and again Abu Zubaydah started acting confused and delirious. The COB congratulated him on the fine quality of his acting. He picked out several things he liked about his performance and praised them. The COB then read aloud Abu Zubaydah's diary entry in which he painstakingly described how he had in the past used this technique of faking cognitive impairment successfully to thwart the Pakistani police's efforts to question him. Abu Zubaydah even got them to let him go. The COB told him that just between the two of them, it was a bad idea to have written about how good he was at faking confusion and then try to pull off the exact same act in front of people who had his diary. The COB then gave him a few bogus tips for switching up his symptoms so that it wouldn't be as obvious the next time.

Throughout the COB's comments, Abu Zubaydah continued murmuring nonsense and rolling his eye around, acting weak and disoriented. Every now and then the COB would say something like "Good job! I like the way you're drooling; it adds realism. I'm almost buying it. You wouldn't think a grown man would do that."

Finally, as the COB was leaving, he said to Abu Zubaydah, "We've had the doctors evaluate your symptoms, and they're sure you are faking. But they say that even if you are not, the sort of problem that would create the on-and-off symptoms you're displaying is short-lived. So the next time I come back in about an hour, you will have regained your senses. If that happens, we won't have to try to get to the bottom of whether you were faking. We can just go on as if nothing happened."

An hour later Abu Zubaydah was completely normal when the interrogators entered his cell. The on-again, off-again malingering never happened again in all the years he was with us. Years later I asked him about this episode. He told me that it was "worth a try" but that he felt silly acting impaired while the COB was critiquing his performance, and he was glad the COB gave him a face-saving way to drop the whole thing and move on without having to admit he was faking.

It was only when Bruce and I started using enhanced interrogation techniques that I started to worry about the tapes. I didn't object to being taped, but I did mind not knowing what was going to happen to the tapes. The interrogation program was one of the nation's most closely held secrets (the technical term for it is compartmentalized). But despite the stealth, there were already rumors of leaks. The COB and the law enforcement interrogation expert were the same two CIA officers who had been interrogating Abu Zubaydah before Bruce and I got involved. Therefore, they were on the early tapes and had as much interest as we did in those tapes not being leaked. The black site began to ask for permission to stop taping and destroy the tapes. We were told by headquarters that they would take it under advisement (a phrase I have subsequently learned means "not going to happen") and instructed them to keep videotaping. That was how it continued all through the enhanced interrogation of Abu Zubaydah. The site occasionally would ask for permission to destroy the tapes, but we would be told to keep taping. And we did.

With the capture of al-Nashiri, headquarters decided that we should tape a day's worth of interrogations, use them to supplement our notes for report writing that night, and then tape over them the next day. That way, if something went wrong during an interrogation, it would be on tape. We could review it and set it aside and send it to headquarters if necessary. But we wouldn't be adding to the large pile of tapes we had from taping Abu Zubaydah. That system worked fine.

In December 2002, as a result of leaks to the media about the existence and possible whereabouts of the black site, we heard that we were going to abandon our current location and move Abu Zubaydah and al-Nashiri to another country. That was another chance, I thought, to destroy the tapes. One of the last things I said to the base chief and anyone else who would listen as I left the site for the rendition aircraft with Abu Zubaydah and al-Nashiri in tow was "Don't forget to get rid of the tapes."

Years later I talked to one of the security officers who had been at the black site at the end, shutting it down. He said he had been told by the COB to burn everything that he could in preparation for sanitizing the black site. He had the tapes piled in a pit and was about to pour gasoline on them and light a match. Then he thought, I'd better check with the COB one more time. When he did, he was told to hold off until she could check with headquarters to see if the instruction to sanitize the site included getting rid of the tapes. Sadly, headquarters punted and told her to retain them. No one at the black site was happy. The chief of station of the country was on those tapes. He said he wanted to keep them in his office, where he could be certain access was tightly controlled, ensuring that they couldn't be easily taken or duplicated and guaranteeing that only those with a legitimate need would view them.

This back-and-forth about destroying the tapes while closing the black site was happening simultaneously with my dustup with the New Sheriff, who was using unauthorized techniques, as was described in chapter 4. When I finally was allowed to leave the second black site where I was held against my will and found out the tapes had not been destroyed, I was sick to my stomach—not because I was concerned about what a fair viewing of the tapes would reveal but because the New Sheriff had made it clear that he was going to try to damage my reputation and I didn't like the idea that twisted SOB might have access to the tapes someday.

I made it no secret that I wanted those tapes disposed of, but I was still surprised when Jose Rodriguez ordered them destroyed in November 2005. He checked with the lawyers to see if he had the legal authority to do it, and when he was told that he did, he ordered them destroyed. No dithering, no effort to cover his own ass. His integrity is amazing. The Internet trolls can say what they want, but Jose put the security of the country and the safety of the people who worked for him ahead of his self-interest. He had no personal reason for ordering the destruction of those tapes. Far from it; that decision subsequently brought him considerable grief. The easiest thing for him to do would have been to kick the can down the road and let the politicians who were running scared because of Abu Ghraib eventually throw his people under the bus. But he didn't, and I will always be grateful to him for that.

Neither Bruce nor I was involved in the decision to destroy the tapes. The tape destruction took place in the middle of an increasing number of leaks about the enhanced interrogation program and a growing effort by those in Congress who were briefed to distance themselves from the CIA's interrogation program. In late December 2007, the *New York Times* published a story revealing the existence and destruction of the tapes two years previously. A few weeks later, in January 2008, the Justice Department announced that federal prosecutor John Durham would conduct a preliminary investigation into the destruction of the tapes. That investigation dragged on for almost three years.

I was interviewed by the FBI in conjunction with that investigation. I didn't have much to say during the interview, because I wasn't involved in the final decision to get rid of the tapes. But I vaguely remember that they asked me if I had any personal copies of the tapes. That question stemmed, I'm sure, from the New Sheriff's false rumor that I had smuggled copies home from the black site.

Nicely done, I thought. That rascal was dead, and he was still making trouble for me.

In November 2010, it was announced that there would be no charges of criminal wrongdoing stemming from the destruction of the tapes, but some in the media speculated that some CIA employees might yet be criminally charged for making false statements to the grand jury during the lengthy investigation. No such charges were ever made.

As significant as the three investigations I have just recounted seemed at the time, they pale in comparison with the two that followed.

# CHAPTER 12

# KSM's Prophecy Comes True

Many times in recent years I have reflected on KSM's comment to me in his black site cell that our own government would turn on those of us who were trying to stop the next terrorist attack. With the swearing in of the Obama administration, KSM's prophecy quickly and chillingly came true.

Although the investigation into the destruction of the videotapes had resulted in no charges, it seemed that some in the government still held out hope for taking CIA scalps. The tape investigation was launched during the Bush administration by Attorney General Michael Mukasey. But before the federal prosecutor, John Durham, finished the job, the Obama administration was in office. The new attorney general, Eric Holder, expanded Durham's original mandate. It was no longer just about tapes. In August 2009, Holder announced that Durham had been ordered to "conduct a preliminary review into whether federal laws were violated in connection with the interrogation of specific detainees at overseas locations."

## The 2009–2012 Justice Department Investigation into the Use of "Torture" During CIA Detainee Interrogations

By the time this investigation kicked off, I was no longer working for the CIA. One of the first things that happened in the immediate aftermath of President Obama's taking office was that he shut down the CIA interrogation program. There was work we could have done for the CIA that didn't involve EITs, but our contract was canceled because of pressure from Senator Feinstein and other Democrats in Congress.

I found myself a "subject" but not a "target" of the DOJ's expanded investigation into detainee mistreatment. To me it was a distinction without a difference. Being a subject meant that although I wasn't being investigated per se, any wrongdoing on my part uncovered during the investigation or any false statements I made during the investigation could result in criminal charges. I was certain that I had not done anything illegal, but I was not certain that Attorney General Holder wouldn't try to trump up a phony obstruction of justice charge just to please political cronies demanding my hide.

After all, in June 2008, seven months before he became attorney general, during a speech he gave at the American Constitution Society, Holder claimed that President Bush had authorized torture and promised his cronies "a reckoning." He subsequently filled the third-highest position in the Justice Department with a lawyer who had represented terrorists before he came to work for Holder. But that wasn't all. On February 8, 2010, Holder sent a letter in response to questions from Senator Charles Grassley indicating that nine of his DOJ appointees had been involved in work on behalf of terror suspects: five of them had acted as lawyers for detainees, and the other four had either filed amicus briefs or acted as advocates. He brought in a lawyer who had served as senior counsel for Human Rights Watch and put her on the Detention Policy Task Force. His principal deputy solicitor general once had been the lawyer for one of Usama bin Ladin's drivers.

To me it felt like Holder was stacking the Justice Department with al-Qa'ida's lawyers and looking for any excuse to file criminal charges against the men and women of the CIA who had been keeping Americans safe, including me.

In the press and in the statements of political leaders speaking out about their newly contrived objections to the detention and interrogation program, the CIA received no credit for actions it had taken to punish wrongdoers who were part of it. The CIA received no credit for the numerous criminal referrals it had made to the DOJ, for the dismissals of CIA officers and contractors who were out of line, or for the August 17, 2006, conviction of a former CIA contractor, David Passaro, for assault in conjunction with the 2003 beating death of an Afghan detainee at a U.S. military base in Asadabad, Afghanistan. Passaro, by the way, was not part of the CIA's interrogation program. I don't know what section he worked for because I wasn't read into the case, but it wasn't part of the CIA's interrogation program.

By this time I had a new lawyer, Henry Schuelke, a former federal prosecutor. Gorelick had had to recuse herself some months before because of a conflict of interest. Schuelke tried to assure me that the special prosecutor, John Durham, was an honest and honorable man who would review the evidence meticulously and base his recommendations on fact, not political pressure.

That made me feel better, but I was still concerned that I'd forget a date, misremember some event, not remember some event at all, or say something that I thought was correct but that ultimately wasn't. I knew I had not broken any laws, but in a game of political scalp hunting with gotcha questions and tricky maneuvering, I wasn't sure the playing field was level. I had a great attorney, but I was not allowed to look at any of the records or documents to refresh my memory.

At one point my lawyer and I had a series of strange exchanges about a hard drive the CIA had installed and maintained in our company's offices. After Senator Feinstein had our contract canceled, CIA personnel pulled their equipment and took it back to Langley. Here is our conversation about the hard drive.

"Durham wants the hard drive," my lawyer said.

"What hard drive?"

"The one out of your old offices. John Durham wants you to send him that hard drive."

"I don't have that hard drive," I said for what felt like the hundredth time. "That hard drive and all the security hardware and software associated with it belonged to the agency. They sent a security crew. They removed it and took it back to DC. Durham will need to get it from them."

A few weeks later: "Durham wants the passwords to the hard drive."

Not again, I thought. I knew I'd gone over this before. "I don't have the passwords. I never did. It wasn't my hard drive. I didn't have administrator access. In fact, I was never allowed in the specially constructed room where that hard drive and encryption gear were kept. I would have given it to Durham if I had it and it was legal to do so, but he'll have to get that from the agency. I don't have it. Never did."

"He says the agency doesn't have the passwords and they are telling him that they can't break the encryption. He wants you to tell him how to access the hard drive so he can pass that information to the FBI."

"Let's see if I got this right. First the CIA said they didn't have the hard drive. Then they found it and gave it to him. Now the CIA can't break its own encryption on one of its own hard drives. The FBI can't break the encryption either, and somehow I'm supposed to magically unlock that thing for them."

"I know, I know," he said, "but they asked me to inquire. So I am."

There were several times when I asked my attorney, "Can't we just pick up the phone and let me answer his questions?" It would have been so much simpler.

But, of course, we couldn't. Durham wanted me to testify in front of the grand jury, and my attorney wanted to be cautious. I wanted to help Durham in his investigation, but I didn't want to get ensnared in some kind of trumped-up obstruction charge, so I waited.

Meanwhile some in the press were certain that Bruce and I were about to be perp-walked as war criminals and were making the case in the media with smoke and innuendo as evidence. They continued to link our names with every horrible thing, real or imagined, alleged to have happened as part of that program. Because of our nondisclosure agreement, we were unable to defend ourselves publicly.

Meanwhile, the people who actually had done the things that the DOJ's special prosecutor, John Durham, was investigating were getting a pass in the press. The focus should have been on the guys who used unauthorized techniques such as threatening a detainee with a drill and gun or putting a broomstick behind the knees of a kneeling detainee. But instead the press was focused on the authorized techniques that had been used against KSM.

Eventually my lawyer was satisfied with Durham's assurances.

He successfully negotiated immunity for Bruce and me, and in spring 2012 I testified in front of the grand jury. I'm not going to go into my testimony here, but it was actually a relief to get it over with. Durham was a professional, and the grand jury asked interesting questions. The only person who concerned me was one of Durham's investigators who seemed overly interested in clever verbal jousting during our pre– and post–grand jury meetings. But even he settled in and turned out to be a pretty decent guy.

But I still didn't trust Holder, and some in the press continued their ugly and inaccurate accusations. (They're still doing it as I write this.) Finally, sometime in August 2012, my attorney called and said he had received word that Holder was going to announce closure of the investigation. Once again, no charges were to be filed against anyone.

I thought that would be the end of the false accusations in the press about me torturing people. After all, one of the country's most highly respected criminal investigators, John Durham, had been tasked with, in the words of Attorney General Holder, examining "whether any unauthorized interrogation techniques were used by CIA interrogators, and if so, whether such techniques could con-stitute violations of the torture statute or any other applicable stat-ute." This prosecutor from the highest law enforcement agency in the land and a federal grand jury spent years examining all the evidence and returned no indictments. No charges were ever filed against me, Bruce, or any other CIA officer.

In my mind the conclusion of John Durham's investigation should put to rest once and for all the question of whether I tor-tured people. But apparently being cleared by the Justice Depart-ment wasn't enough; I was still subject to indictment by a kangaroo court.

## The 2009–2014 Senate Select Committee on Intelligence Investigation into the CIA Detention and Interrogation Program

It was mid-December 2014, over two years after Eric Holder's Justice Department completed its multiyear criminal investigation into whether any CIA interrogators used unauthorized interrogation techniques and broke the law.

It was clear and sunny and windy. I was off the coast of Bayport, Florida, fishing with my younger brother. My airboat was pinned to the bottom with two long black carbon fiber spikes driven into the sand and rocks underneath it. We held fast, unmoving in the current rushing out of the mouth of the crystal-clear Weeki Wachee River. Huge manatees came up to the boat, unafraid, curious. An armada of predatory fish swam with them, mostly cobia, darting out from the moving gloom of their shadows and ambushing bait fish spooked by the great beasts passing. White egrets and great blue herons waded in the shallows. Eagles and ospreys rode the thermals overhead, occasionally plunging into the water, snatching unsuspecting fish.

My cell phone rang.

"How does it feel to have Senator Feinstein call you a torturer?" blurted the reporter on the other end.

"What? Repeat that," I said. I could hardly hear him over the wind and the sound of head-high saw grass swaying along the riverbank. I motioned to my brother to stop walking around so that the boat didn't rock and I could concentrate on what the guy on the phone was saying without falling in.

"Senator Feinstein and the Senate Select Committee on Intelligence say you were paid $81 million by the CIA to torture people. Want to comment on that?"

"If that's what they said, they're wrong, but what makes you think it's me they're talking about?"

"One of the Senate staffers gave reporters your name on background."

Suddenly I was besieged with more calls from the media, most of them asking the same one or two stupid questions, trying to provoke a reaction, trying to get a sound bite or quote that put me in a bad light: "How does it feel to be called a torturer?" or "Feinstein says you aren't qualified to interrogate terrorists. What do you say to that?"

Such allegations had been made before. Always in the past, I had refused to confirm or deny my involvement with the CIA's enhanced interrogation program not because I was ashamed of it but because I had a nondisclosure agreement that prohibited me from doing so without risking going to jail. The result was that people could say or write anything they wanted, no matter how inaccurate, and I couldn't defend myself. As a consequence, the media got most of what they wrote about me wrong.

Feinstein left my name out of her report but not my identity. She would have named me if she could have. That was part of the food fight between the CIA and the Democrats in Congress. But the CIA dug in. I was told they thought naming us and any of the other CIA officers and contractors involved in the interrogation program would unnecessarily endanger our lives.

Apparently Feinstein's staff didn't feel that way or didn't care. In the media feeding frenzy immediately after the report's release I had two reporters from different media outlets tell me that Democratic staffers on the SSCI had acknowledged on deep background which pseudonyms referred to me and Bruce. Feinstein's office denied it. You know how Washington works. I know what I believe.

The only one who wasn't allowed to say that I was part of the CIA program was me. I contacted the CIA and asked them to allow me to identify myself; they reluctantly agreed but didn't fully release me from my nondisclosure agreement.

I was tired of being coy. For several days, I alternated between feeling betrayed and being angry. The one bright spot in the whole thing was the way people around me reacted. I discovered that the majority of people outside the Washington Beltway actually supported what the CIA had done to keep them safe. The few I met who didn't fully support what was done said they appreciated why we had done it.

One of the things that struck me when I saw Feinstein's report was how much it read like a prosecutorial brief. I remember standing in my kitchen with my wife, who was taking it in stride, discussing not the content of the report but rather the way the report was put together. It reminded me of some of the legal briefs from lawyers that I'd encountered in my past forensic work.

Then it struck me that that was exactly what it was. It was a prosecutorial brief. Realizing this cleared up something that had puzzled me: it explained why the Democratic SSCI staffers, the lawyers who put Feinstein's report together, refused to correct errors of fact when they were pointed out by the CIA in its response to a draft of the document, and why they never interviewed anyone from the CIA who had been directly involved in the interrogation program.

Feinstein's final report was never intended to be about all the facts; it was never intended to tell the whole truth. The intent was to win an adversarial contest with the CIA by telling a version of the truth that influenced what Americans thought about the program and the people involved with it. She wanted to use a lawyer's trick to rewrite history.

Let me explain. As you know, our judicial system is adversarial; attorneys for both sides of an issue approach a case with different, competing stories of what happened. The story that is most persuasive to those who decide the case wins the proceeding. It is not about establishing the truth; it's about establishing a winning version of the truth that supports what you are trying to accomplish.

Lawyers are trained to use something called narrative framing, a persuasive form of storytelling, to construct a concisely phrased statement that justifies the sought-after decision or verdict. Here is the narrative frame for Feinstein's report: The CIA's enhanced interrogation program tortured detainees. It was illegal, brutal, unnecessary, and completely ineffective. Nothing of value came out of it. It was administered by corrupt and incompetent CIA officials who lied to the president, Congress, and the American people. It was put together and run by two greedy contractors who lacked the necessary skills and experience. The program was a stain on the fabric of American morality, and as a result the United States is less safe and its standing in the world has been tarnished.

It is a nicely put together prosecutorial narrative frame, simple and easy to digest or put into talking points. But it is a false narrative designed specifically to hide the fingerprints of some politicians on the program by smearing the CIA and the people who worked hard to protect America.

SSCI staffers had cherry-picked the CIA's documents, choosing some and excluding others to present an inaccurate picture of what was going on. Friends of mine who were familiar with the true history of the program were stunned and appalled.

"This report was never about presenting a truly accurate picture of what was going on," I said. "It was about denigrating the program and destroying the reputations of the people involved."

To separate themselves from the program, the committee members needed a powerful, emotionally charged story to poison the minds of Americans against the CIA officers and contractors who had kept them safe after 9/11, and so they manufactured one. The key to getting away with that ruse was to create a story that had the appearance of being based on fact. In my opinion, this required the Democratic lawyers on the committee staff first to develop their theory and then to cherry-pick through CIA documents, selecting some and excluding others, to amass those which supported the story they wanted to tell.

From their perspective, it would have been counterproductive to include documents that didn't support what they wanted Americans to believe happened or to correct the many errors pointed out by the CIA before releasing the report. The same goes for interviewing CIA officials and contractors who undoubtedly would have tried to correct errors and present a story of what happened that conflicted with what Feinstein wanted Americans to believe. A winning case does not present evidence that supports the opposing counsel's position unless it means to set it up as a straw man to knock down later.

The difference between seeking the whole truth and fabricating a selective version of the truth highlights the difference between the culture of CIA officers and that of lawyers like those working as staff on Feinstein's committee. They both strive to collect and analyze information, but that's where the similarity stops. CIA officers do it to prepare intelligence briefs that reflect what is actually going on in the world so that our political and military leaders can make informed decisions. Lawyers, in contrast, do it so that they can construct a version of the truth that leads to an outcome they advocate. These are not at all the same things.

There is another interesting strategy the SSCI may have employed. They selected the data they wanted to include to support the conclusion they were looking for. They removed it from the original data set and put it in its own database to isolate it from those things in the original data set that might not have supported their findings. The cherry-picked data were the data they used. When there were inquiries or criticisms, they could present their own preselected data set and act as if conflicting data did not exist.

It is a little like someone going through your e-mails from the past eight years, picking out every one of them that puts you in a bad light while excluding those which don't, and then using those cherry-picked e-mails to tell people you are a bad guy. When someone asks about you, they can say, "No, come look at his e-mails. There's nothing in here that suggests he is a good guy. Everything I've got says he's a dirtbag."

**PLEASE DON'T ASSUME** that I'm saying the interrogation program was flawless. Far from it. You know from reading this book that in the early days, as the CIA scrambled to defend the nation, a number of major errors were made. Most were well intended; a few were not.

The CIA has acknowledged that mistakes were made early in the program and that some officers and contractors did things they weren't supposed to do. But the CIA brought the troubled detention sites under one office for closer supervision and referred personnel who had done questionable things to the Justice Department. According to the website ciasavedlives.com, there were twenty-nine CIA inspector general investigations plus two wide-ranging reviews and six accountability boards related to the detention and interrogation program. The CIA disciplined some of its officers and got rid of others. But it did not discipline me or Bruce and did not get rid of us. Instead, it gave us Agency Seal Medallions, the highest award a civilian can be given by the CIA.

The SSCI report said my behavior was excessive. I would have welcomed an opportunity to answer any questions or concerns about my behavior in a fair and bipartisan setting, and I would have welcomed the chance to answer any questions members of the SSCI had that were based on the documents they reviewed. I believe I should have had a chance to defend myself before the report was released and my family was endangered.

The terrorists who killed thousands of Americans have the chance during military commissions to address the charges against them, but I didn't, nor did any of the other men and women of the CIA. *The SSCI and its staff didn't interview anyone from the CIA who was actually involved in the program or give those people a chance to explain what happened on the ground.* Five years and $40 million later, they issued a one-sided, inaccurate report that stirred up the crazies and the jihadists, essentially putting a target on my back and the back of everyone past or present working to protect Americans from jihadi terrorist attacks.

The pretense is that the report represents the SSCI's bipartisan assessment of the CIA's interrogation program. It doesn't. It only represents what the Democrats wanted the report to say. The witch hunting was so egregious that the Republicans on the SSCI withdrew from the investigation in 2009 and issued a rebuttal in 2014 documenting the successes of the CIA detention and interrogation program.

Those in Congress investigating what happened could have provided a real service to the country by accurately describing the successes and failures of the program, but they did not.

Recently, the former acting director of the CIA Michael Morell articulated precisely what I've thought all along. He noted that from early on, Senator Feinstein made it clear to everyone she spoke with, including her staffers, that she wanted the SSCI "report to be the nail in the coffin of the country ever doing anything like this again." He speculates that her saying that day after day signaled the kind of report she was looking for and biased the report's final conclusions.

Morell also pointed out something else that sheds light on why

Senator Feinstein and the Democrats in Congress are acting as if they never heard of the program or as if the CIA lied to them. He said the leadership of both parties, Republicans and Democrats, in the House and Senate were briefed multiple times on the CIA's detention and interrogation program from its inception in 2002 and as long as it was operating. Not only did the leadership in Congress approve of the program and encourage going further, but when the program was shut down for reconfirmation of its legal status, some of these leaders accused the CIA of being too risk-averse. The only way that Democrats such as Senator Feinstein can distance themselves from a program they approved of and urged those working in to be aggressive is to claim they were lied to by corrupt CIA officers.

That's their position: the CIA officers working in the detention and interrogation program were corrupt and incompetent, they lied to Congress and the president, and not one piece of actionable intelligence came from the program that couldn't have been obtained from somewhere else. Not one.

One of the odd things about the Senate report is that although it was advertised as being intended to lift the veil on the CIA's long-secret program, the document actually succeeded in cloaking it in a number of myths. Some were quite colorful.

Within hours of Feinstein's report being released, a longtime friend of mine, a special operations warfighter who caught some of the breathless reporting about it, gleefully asked me, "Did you really stick a hose up KSM's butt?"

"What?" I said. "No! Don't be gross."

I had never heard of such a thing. But sure enough the media were reporting that as part of the detainee interrogation program, the CIA supposedly used "rectal hydration" and, even more bizarrely, "rectal feeding" as part of its interrogation efforts.

"So you weren't there wearing rubber gloves and waving a hose around, shouting, 'Talk, you hairy bastard, or I'll—'" my friend continued.

"No!" I cut him off, not liking where this was going. Another couple of minutes and he would have been acting it out in exaggerated pantomime, hair wild, eyes gleaming.

"No? You didn't wear rubber gloves or—?" He wouldn't let it drop.

"The idea is nuts," I interrupted. "I'm just now hearing about it. So if it happened at all—and I'm *not* saying it did—it had to be some sort of medical procedure, something doctors did for a hunger strike or some other health reason. The rest is spin. I can't imagine anyone used it as part of an interrogation plan, and I *certainly* had nothing to do with it."

"Well, you wouldn't think that from some of the stories in the media," he said. "They leave the distinct impression that it was an interrogation technique. If that's not true, why do they say that crap?"

Good question, I thought.

When I finally was able to read a copy of the report's executive summary—not just journalists' accounts of what was in it—I found that the report alleges that five detainees were subjected to rectal rehydration or rectal feeding without "documented medical necessity." The report implies that in a couple of instances it was done as part of the interrogation process by the chief interrogator (my nemesis) but doesn't make that claim in clear language.

The CIA's response to the SSCI report says that *medical personnel* at CIA black sites administered those procedures because detainees were either dangerously dehydrated or on a hunger strike and at risk of harming themselves by ripping the IVs and nasogastric tubes out during attempts to feed them.

I never participated in anything remotely like rectal hydration. I believe the allegation was included in the report simply because it was titillating and would arouse public outrage. The fact that they had to use the awkward phrasing "no documented medical necessity" should tell readers something shifty is afoot. Here is yet another example of where it would have benefited the investigators to talk to the medical personnel who were on-site, but finding out the true story wasn't part of their agenda.

There were several other myths promulgated by the Senate report and by the media that I need to deal with briefly here.

One frequently repeated piece of misinformation is that two detainees in the CIA detention and interrogation program died. The allegation is that one froze to death and the other died from injuries sustained after he was assaulted by a contract CIA interrogator. It is true that two detainees died. However, it is not true that they were part of the CIA detention and interrogation program. Neither death occurred at one of the interrogation program's black sites.

In November 2002, Gul Rahman died in CIA custody. The cause of death according to autopsy reports was probably exposure. But Rahman was *not* a detainee in the high-value CIA detention and interrogation program that I was involved in, and the CIA officer responsible for questioning him was not an interrogator from that program. Rahman's death spurred the CIA's leadership to move the responsibility for managing that facility to the CIA detention and interrogation program a few days later to improve the management and supervision of what was happening there. To imply that his death was part of the program I was involved with is simply false.

A second detainee, Abdul Wali, died of injuries sustained during an alleged assault by former CIA contractor David Passaro on June 21, 2003. It is alleged that Passaro assaulted Wali with his hands, his feet, and a flashlight. Passaro was a CIA contractor but was never an interrogator for the CIA detention and interrogation program. Contrary to what has been reported in the media, he was not following rough interrogation guidelines established by the CIA to question Wali. At trial, even his lawyer didn't make that claim. Wali died at a U.S. military firebase in Afghanistan, not at one of the CIA detention and interrogation program black sites. In August 2006, Passaro was convicted of assault and sentenced to approximately eight years in prison.

It is regrettable that these two detainees died, and undoubtedly the CIA writ large bears some of the responsibility. However, the blame cannot be placed on the CIA's detention and interrogation program or any of the CIA officers or contractors working for that program.

The report also alleges that the CIA interrogation program subjected detainees to brutal, unauthorized techniques as part of its interrogation strategy. In its response, the CIA acknowledged that some of its officers and contractors used techniques that were not authorized. I mentioned some examples earlier in this book. But those incidents were reported, investigated, examined in administrative review boards, and referred to the Justice Department to determine whether crimes had been committed. Allegations about detainees being forced to stand on broken bones and chained for weeks in total darkness in what amounted to a freezing dungeon were made. If such things happened (and I cannot confirm that they did), most of the problems did not involve program interrogators and happened in places that were not under the program's operational control.

The truth is messy, more so than people on either side of the EIT issue would have you believe. It is not the case that no abuses occurred, nor is it the case that the CIA's interrogation program was rife with the illegal abuse of detainees. I've been told by some journalists that allegations are more important than facts, but that is patently ridiculous. Facts do matter, and allegations alone can never warrant lynching the accused, except perhaps in the minds of some advocacy journalists and Democratic senators who view the cause as so important that it is worth winning at the expense of honesty.

In that regard, I am repeatedly surprised at the number of different physically coercive acts some journalists claim were part of the CIA's interrogation tool kit.

Loud music is an example. If you read some media reports, you would conclude that loud music was played incessantly at earsplitting volume at all CIA black sites where high-value detainees were held for as long as they were in CIA custody. But like much of what has been written about the CIA's use of coercive measures, that is not accurate.

Loud music *was* played for the first three or four months after Abu Zubaydah's capture. And yes, it was used early on to soften him up by being an irritant, but it was also for security reasons: to mask sounds outside his cell where the guards were stationed. What has not been routinely reported is that Occupational Safety and Health Administration (OSHA) noise exposure standards were used to determine how loud the music could be and how long the detainee could be exposed.

The determination of what music or audio to play was left up to the guards. I recall there were a few audio loops from the SERE schools. A tape of a teething baby crying and a loop of a little girl screaming, "Daddy! Daddy! The bad man is hurting Mommy!" over and over was played occasionally. But the use of these SERE tapes didn't last long. We were all exposed to the same noise as Abu Zubaydah and couldn't get any work done. After that, the guards played their own music CDs, which consisted of everything: metal, country, hard rock, hip-hop. We tried to keep away from anything with explicit lyrics, but occasionally I'd hear "I'm from Wisconsin, I got a big Johnson" wailing out from the speakers by the guard station.

Sometime before August 2002 we switched from music to white

noise generators and then used them exclusively for security masking. Noise no longer was used as an irritant to soften up detainees. The generators were situated well outside the cells and away from the detainees to keep them from overhearing discussions in other cells or rooms. In fact, in most locations in a detainee cell you could barely make out the hiss from the generators when the cell doors were closed.

Keeping the cells cold was another physical pressure I saw mentioned in the media as having been used at the first black site. I saw it mentioned even in official documents. But I don't recall the temperature of the cell being used as an interrogation technique. I do recall there were a couple of times when it was uncomfortably cool, but usually that was because the guard staff was dressed head to toe in heavy black clothing with gloves, balaclavas, and goggles. The guards were the only people other than the COB who were authorized to change conditions in Abu Zubaydah's cell. Sometimes they couldn't accurately judge the temperature in the cell, and when they had to spend long periods in it, a few of them would keep cranking up the air conditioner until someone at the site not dressed as they were would complain and call their attention to it. I can't speak for other interrogators except for Bruce, but I can say that neither of us advocated using cold cells as an interrogation technique.

As I write this, I'm tempted to generate a list of physically coercive techniques that have been mistakenly conflated with the authorized EITs that were employed as part of the CIA's enhanced interrogation program. I could compile that list from those which were used without authorization by rogue CIA officers and contractors, from the multitude of abuses perpetrated by DOD personnel in places like Abu Ghraib, and from the list of harsh techniques employed with DOD authorization in places where the military was holding detainees. The list of things we did *not* do goes on and on and on. We didn't use dogs, or leashes, or sexual threats, or rectal feeding, or rectal hydration, or standing on broken bones, or drills, or guns, or stacking detainees up in naked piles, or attaching wires to their genitals, or . . . Well, I could list more, but you can see that it would get unwieldy, so I'm not going to do that. There is a much simpler way to address this issue.

The CIA's enhanced interrogation program that Bruce and I were part of used only the EITs that were cleared by the Department of Justice, approved by the president, briefed to congressional leadership, and authorized by CIA headquarters.

Another myth that I want to debunk is that Bruce and I made $81 million running the program. That is one story I wish were true. Here are the facts. When I first got involved in advising the agency regarding al-Qa'ida detainees in spring 2002, I was a single independent subcontractor. I asked that Bruce be brought in to help. He came on board as an independent subcontractor. In 2005, the agency decided it was going to combine most of the support required to help it run a very large program in numerous places around the world under one commercial contract.

Through our company, we bid on it and ended up providing interrogators, debriefers, operational psychologists (not me or Bruce), and security personnel for all black sites with high-value detainees. We also were tasked with conducting ongoing conversations with detainees to learn about the terrorist mindset (as part of the Terrorist Think Tank that was discussed in chapter 9), consulting with foreign liaison intelligence and law enforcement services on noncoercive interrogation of detainees of interest to CIA held in foreign custody, and sometimes serving as intermediaries.

I'm not allowed to give an exact number, but at times we had around a hundred people on our payroll, most of whom were serving in places of extreme hardship and in some cases combat zones. The money we were paid was used not just for their salaries but also for things such as insurance. Take a guess how much it costs to insure the lives and provide health insurance for scores of civilians in places the State Department designates as "high-risk" areas 365 days a year. Think millions and I'll bet your guess is still too low.

Ours was a multiyear commercial contract that deployed scores of people twenty-four hours a day year-round to dangerous places, embedded with the CIA and under the command and control of CIA officers. It was a commercial contract, and it was let under government contracting law.

The government awarded the contract, conducted multiple audits, and renewed it annually until it was canceled in January 2009 for the convenience of the government because of pressure from Senator Feinstein.

The percentage of profit I earned from the contract was in the small single digits. No one in the company took salaries as corporate officers or for sitting on its advisory board. Everyone in the company was paid by the hour in amounts approved and vetted by CIA contracting—everyone, including Bruce and I. I should add that our hourly rate was one-fourth the amount later paid to the lawyers hired to defend us.

There is something about the detention and interrogation program that brings out the worst in people. Not the people running it but the people reporting on it. Here I am not talking only about congressional investigators. Reporters too seem to lose all reason when they get the torture bug. Here is one more example. There are several reporters obsessed with the three Guantanamo prisoners who died on the night of June 9, 2006. The Pentagon announced at the time that the three had coordinated a suicide as an act of "asymmetrical warfare." I have no idea what happened to those detainees. But the press accounts luridly suggest that they were murdered and that on the night of the deaths "ear-piercing shrieks and wailings were heard coming out of this facility and one *James Elmer Mitchell* was seen entering it." No matter that I was in the United States at the time. It seems that to some my name is all you need to evoke fears of dastardly deeds and sell stories to the media.

I've been asked as a psychologist why some journalists reporting on controversial stories often go to the "darkest corner of the room." That is, why do they take an ambiguous story detail and spin it as if the worst and most nefarious interpretation of events were true?

The media coverage of the reports of rectal rehydration and rectal feeding in the SSCI majority report is an excellent example. Some journalists almost immediately published salacious stories spinning these activities as interrogation techniques with a hint of sexual sadism condoned by the agency, rather than medical procedures performed by physicians.

These stories follow a pattern. They start with one or two solid facts, then shift to facts that are partially true and partially matters of interpretation, and end with full-on fabrications framed as plausible truth. The content is believable because it starts off anchored in fact and there is buy-in by the reader before the story veers off into conjecture and innuendo.

There is also a first-strike intentionality to these stories by those who want to control what Americans think. Critics of the program want to be first in to frame the narrative so that when the stories are pushed back against, as will inevitably happen, the pushback repeats and reinforces the original narrative frame. If you say that interrogators put a hose up KSM's butt and imply there was a hint of sexual sadism involved, it is impossible to discuss and debunk the allegation directly without evoking the original idea. You end up trying to explain that it didn't happen the way it was reported, but meanwhile the people you are talking to have the image of KSM with a hose hanging out of his butt floating around in their minds.

Also, there is the blinding effect of emotions. Generate enough outrage at the authorities, and a monster who killed over three thousand people becomes a pitiable victim of sexual sadism. If your goal is to smear the agency's interrogation program and the people involved, you must attribute salacious and damaging motives to them.

My assessment is that most journalists take sides. I don't know if there was ever a time when more journalists were fair and impartial, but if there was, it is gone. We are now faced with the blending of advocacy journalism and the mentality and manners of Internet trolls. It is not enough for some journalists to slant their stories to advocate a point of view; it is now necessary for them to destroy the reputations of those in their crosshairs with innuendo, speculation that has not been fact-checked, and pernicious lies.

It reminds me of a conversation I had with a female journalist who ran some line of bullshit by me that she intended to publish. When I told her that what she was saying was not even remotely true, she told me, "Even if it's not, what I'm going to write about you speaks to a larger truth that may not come across if I stick to the facts of the situation."

Reporting untrue things about me somehow sheds light on a larger truth? That's the kind of crap self-serving reporters tell themselves to justify distorting facts to fit whatever narrative they happen to be pushing. Some journalists seem to think they are our betters. They believe their job is to shape American opinion so that it lines up with their personal ideologies because after all, when they think a thought, it must be correct.

There are other reasons, of course. It feels good. There is the excitement, the crack-like addiction to the adulation of those with similar opinions, the junkie fix from the feelings of schadenfreude (pleasure from another's suffering) that come from destroying the livelihood and reputation of someone who deserves to be brought down, and the rush of pride that comes from the reporter feeling that he or she is a significant part of something larger and more noble.

Hunter S. Thompson encouraged journalists to "use [their] art like a hammer to destroy the right people." He said he used reporting as a weapon: inventing quotes, fabricating facts, and outright flat-out lying for a cause. At least he was honest about it.

# Final Thoughts

We are not safe.

In fact, I believe we are less safe than we were before 9/11. Here is why.

As I write this, al-Qa'ida is still plotting catastrophic terror attacks against the United States and trying to acquire unfathomably destructive nuclear, chemical, and biological weapons. The Middle East is on fire. ISIS—al-Qa'ida 2.0—is ravaging Iraq and Syria, pillaging cities, looting churches, destroying antiquities, and slaughtering or enslaving everyone who doesn't follow its version of Islam or refuses to convert. Places such as Libya and Yemen have become hothouses for growing more terrorists.

We have largely stood by with our hands in our pockets while ISIS terrorists who have vowed to kill us and destroy our way of life rob hospitals of radiological material and dig up discarded chemical weapons in the desert. How long will it be before those lethal items are incorporated into improvised explosive devices and used to attack us?

At home, lone wolf terror attacks are becoming common, and our political leaders seem hell-bent on dismantling the protections that prevented the second wave of terror attacks after 9/11.

We are not safe. But the problem isn't with the men and women of the U.S. military and intelligence communities. Properly led, equipped, and resourced, they can protect us from our enemies. But they cannot protect us from ourselves.

Americans have hard decisions to make.

As a nation we need to decide which is more important, bestowing the rights of American citizens on foreign terrorists who have voluntarily taken up arms to kill our people and destroy our way of life or gathering intelligence to save American lives by stopping upcoming terror attacks. To those who would say, "We can do both," I ask, "How many intelligence reports have we gotten out of KSM since he lawyered up at Gitmo in 2006?" Answer: not one.

This illustrates one of the fundamental differences between a law enforcement approach to dealing with terrorists and a war-focused, intelligence-gathering approach.

Simply put, law enforcement's primary focus is taking a perpetrator off the streets and convicting that person in a court of law. That means a crime has already been committed. Americans have already died, and the lawbreaker is being questioned to obtain a confession that will hold up in court. Part of that process is to advise terrorists of their right not to answer questions and provide them with legal representation that serves as a buffer between them and incriminating inquiries by authorities.

In contrast, the initial priority of a war-focused, intelligence-gathering approach is to obtain actionable intelligence to prevent upcoming terror attacks before building a case for prosecution—that comes later. Advocates for this approach argue that terrorists who are not U.S. citizens, especially senior leaders and knowledgeable terror facilitators, captured outside the United States should be held as illegal combatants. While in custody, they should be interrogated for intelligence to prevent future terror attacks before they are given lawyers provided by the American taxpayer who will tell them they don't have to answer questions and shield them from the authorities.

**AMERICANS HAVE TO** decide how they want to defend themselves against terror attacks or risk having that decision made for them. Do they want to wait for something to happen and treat it like a crime? Or do they want to be proactive and capture or kill the terrorists before they have a chance to act?

There are those among us who say the threat has been blown out of proportion. I attended a conference at which one of the speakers, a college professor, said that terror attacks were rare and that the actual probability of a specific person being killed or injured in one was so remote that as a nation we can absorb the carnage as we do deaths and injuries from other random events, such as floods and tornadoes and lightning strikes and house fires and plane crashes and crimes of violence. It's just an ordinary part of being alive in America these days. A sporting event is bombed. Law enforcement officers treat it like a crime. They hunt down the bad guys, arrest them, tell them they don't have to talk, give them lawyers, and then try to build a criminal case. And we're just supposed to move on because relatively few of us are affected.

An alternative is to treat the fight against violent terrorists killing Americans to establish Islamic supremacy as an illegal act of war rather than a violation of U.S. civilian law. That is what the Bush administration and Congress did in the aftermath of 9/11. Until the process was abandoned by the Obama administration, instead of criminal conviction, the focus was on finding where the terrorists were hiding, destroying their capacity to harm us, and preemptively capturing or killing them to prevent future attacks. CIA interrogators were deployed as warfighters, not law enforcement officers, a fact that often gets lost in the press coverage.

I've been asked what I think we should do to protect ourselves in the future. I'm not a legal scholar and don't pretend to be, but it seems to me that we need an aggressive combination of both law enforcement and intelligence-gathering approaches. For lone wolf attacks and in dealing with U.S. citizens, law enforcement approaches make sense. But in my view, dangerous terrorists from groups such as al-Qa'ida and ISIS who are not citizens of the United States and are by their own declaration at war with us should not be afforded the constitutional rights of American citizens—the very rights they are willing to kill us to destroy.

We need an intelligence-oriented detention and interrogation program for obtaining actionable intelligence from the handful of high-value terrorists with knowledge that could prevent an impending catastrophic terror attack. It would be nice if those terrorists, the ones hiding the most actionable information, would voluntarily tell us what we need to know to stop future attacks, but that's not likely. Instead, it is probably going to take some legal form of coercion to get them to tell us what they know.

I wouldn't blame readers who have been following the EIT controversy for thinking there are only three options when it comes to gathering intelligence from captured high-level terrorists intent on protecting secrets: rapport-based techniques (the tea and sympathy approach), the Army Field Manual (an eclectic set of techniques, some psychologically coercive, that evolved over the years to question POWs from the standing armies of nation-states while adhering to the Geneva Conventions), and EITs. These approaches are the only ones that get tossed around in the media and subjected to sometimes heated debate among pundits and lawmakers and political leaders.

But these are not the only choices for gathering actionable intelligence from detained terrorists. In my opinion, a comprehensive approach would include things other than interrogation. It would include means of covertly collecting intelligence from detainees, such as deception, elicitation without revealing interest or intent, and technical collection.

I think the United States should establish a detention facility where detainees are interrogated using the full spectrum of human influence strategies, minus EITs. It would also be a place where deceptive events are individually staged for specific detainees to pull for reactions that reveal intelligence, where seemingly safe places to talk and share secrets among captives are subject to eavesdropping through technical collection, and where like-minded brothers whom detainees encounter elicit seemingly unrelated details that fit into an information matrix that yields actionable intelligence.

Some people ask me whether the next president should consider going back to using EITs. After all, they say, despite the negative spin, the EITs were actually safe and effective. They say that perhaps with more transparency and buy-in from the oversight committees in Congress and closer supervision by the managers in the intelligence communities, EITs could be used again.

To which I say good luck with that! Some form of coercion is apt to be necessary because rapport building and techniques from the Army Field Manual (which are all that is currently permitted) will prove ineffective against terrorists trained to resist interrogation and motivated to protect secrets. But I have a hard time imagining responsible individuals in the intelligence community queuing up to employ EITs after seeing how those of us who did so after 9/11 were treated.

The last time they were used, EITs were judged legal by the highest law enforcement agency in the land not once but multiple times. They were approved by the president of the United States and the national security advisor. They were reported early and often to the members of the House and Senate oversight committees, some of whom thought we should get rougher. Still, when it was politically expedient, some of the same people in our government faithlessly savaged the CIA officers and contractors they had asked to take on this mission on their behalf.

**I HAVE LOOKED** into the eyes of the worst people on the planet. I have sat with them and felt their passion as they described what they see as their holy duty to destroy our way of life. I have heard their eagerness to convert or kill millions of people in the process. Bruce Jessen and I and a handful of CIA officers and contractors did what we could to stop them. People who don't understand what we did, how we did it, or why will loudly tell you that our actions were contrary to American principles. It will come as no surprise that I disagree.

We were at war. Our actions were necessary, effective, legal, authorized, and helped save lives in America and in other countries where terror plots were disrupted. We pitched in when our homeland was in a street battle with cowards who blindsided us, trying to decapitate our way of life by simultaneously attacking our most important financial district, our center of military power, and our seat of government. The actions the CIA and intelligence community took helped keep our homeland safe for years after the 9/11 attacks.

Others among us are now in the process of dismantling the safeguards that prevented terror attacks. We no longer capture and interrogate terrorist leaders. Instead we kill them and those around them with missiles and bombs, destroying the opportunity to gather the kind of intelligence about their intentions and priorities that comes from questioning terrorists or from examining terror planning materials seized at capture—intelligence you can't tell from satellite photographs no matter how fine the camera's resolution. The intelligence community is being asked to dial back electronic surveillance. Our military is being decimated by budget cuts and personnel reductions.

Apologists in our midst blame America for the unimaginable acts of horror perpetrated by Islamists who, driven by Iron Age religious beliefs, seek to convert, enslave, or slaughter everyone on the planet who does not believe as they do. These apologists even refuse to honestly name those who are trying to destroy our way of life. They seem to worry more about the political correctness of potentially offending moderate Muslims than they do the real death and suffering of the victims of Islamist terror attacks. We are not safe now. And unless difficult steps are taken to protect our way of life, we will be less safe in the future.

We are shoving the problem down the road, forcing our children to deal with it. To pay for our political correctness and dithering, our grandchildren and great-grandchildren will have to be harsher, more violent, and more ruthless because we didn't take care of the problem when it was difficult but more doable than it will be for future generations. The cost of appeasement now is the blood of our children in the future.

KSM told me that he thinks that future generations of Americans will be too weak to defend themselves, that they will convert to worship his god or capitulate to subjugation or stand by while jihadists slaughter those around them.

But KSM underestimates us. I have great faith in the American people. My ancestors came to this country before it was founded. They fought in the wars that established our freedoms and protected them and made this country the great nation that it is. I have no doubt that ordinary Americans will not tolerate for long the reckless squandering of our freedoms to put ointment on some political leader's conscience or the reworking of our way of life to make religious barbarism and deadly terror attacks on our soil a normal part of our daily routine. Ordinary Americans of all races and religions will do what they have always done: they will fight and die and clean up the mess left by our political leaders.

# Acknowledgments

I would like to thank the men and women of the CIA who sacrificed much to successfully prevent another catastrophic terror attack on American soil in the immediate aftermath of 9/11. I would also like to acknowledge Dr. Joseph D. Matarazzo. He knew nothing of my involvement or the involvement of my company in the CIA's Enhanced Interrogation Program. He did nothing to support it. Joe has been treated unfairly in the press, and I regret any misery and grief that merely knowing me has brought him. I mention this here because clearing his name is too important to be obscured in the interior of a book.

My thanks go to Andrew Wylie of the Wylie Agency, who believed that I had a story to tell and who helped put me together with Tina Constable, publisher at Crown Forum, who kindly agreed to help me tell it. My editor there, Mary Reynics, was of tremendous help throughout the process and displayed great patience in dealing with both a new author and the CIA's labyrinthine clearance process.

Thanks also to Campbell Wharton, associate publisher; Megan Perritt; Ayelet Gruensprecht; and Julia Elliott.

I would like to thank the CIA's Publications Review Board, which has a very difficult job and, in my experience, performs it very well.

My coauthor, Bill Harlow, has been with me through every step of this project. I know of no one who combines his knowledge of the CIA and publishing worlds.

I am grateful to Dr. John Bruce Jessen for being my friend, business partner, and mountaineering and ice-climbing buddy. And to Sharon for giving Bruce a kitchen pass for all our adventures.

Finally, I would like to thank my wife, Kathy, for being there and believing in me all these years.

# Index

# About the Author

JAMES E. MITCHELL served as an interrogator for the CIA from August 2002 through January 2009. He was involved in the development of the CIA's enhanced interrogation program and was one of their interrogators from its inception until President Barack Obama shut it down by executive order on January 22, 2009. He interrogated fourteen of the most senior so-called high-value detainees in U.S. custody, including Abu Zubaydah; Abd al-Rahim al-Nashiri, the amir, or "commander," of the USS *Cole* bombing; Khalid Sheikh Mohammed (KSM), the mastermind behind the September 11, 2001, terror attacks; Hambali, the Bali bomber; and Abu Faraj al-Libbi, the man who took over for KSM as the leader of terrorist attacks against the United States for al-Qa'ida, to name a few.

Dr. Mitchell served twenty-two years in the U.S. Air Force, including seven years at the USAF Survival School in Spokane, Washington, and retired as a lieutenant colonel.

In addition to his experiences as an interrogator, Dr. Mitchell is a law enforcement trained hostage negotiator and served on a hostage negotiation team. He has also consulted with military counterterrorist units and the FBI, NSA, and CIA on divergent topics, including psychologically profiling war criminals, predicting violence, psychologically profiling and influencing foreign assets, surviving hostage situations, selecting individuals for high-risk missions, and handling hostages wired into improvised explosive devices during rescue.

Dr. Mitchell has a PhD in clinical psychology from the University of South Florida. He received his BS and master's in psychology from the University of Alaska, Anchorage.